Ars poetriae
Rhetorical and Grammatical Invention at the Margin of Literacy

Studies in Rhetoric/Communication

Thomas W. Benson, General Editor

Ars poetriae
Rhetorical and Grammatical Invention at the Margin of Literacy

William M. Purcell

University of South Carolina Press

Published in Columbia, South Carolina by the
University of South Carolina Press

Manufactured in the United States of America

00 99 98 97 96 5 4 3 2 1

Library of Congress Cataloging-in-Publication Data

Purcell, William Michael, 1955–
Ars poetriae : rhetorical and grammatical invention at the margin of literacy / William M. Purcell.
p. cm. — (Studies in rhetoric/communication)
Includes bibliographical references and index.
ISBN 1–57003–059–6
1. Poetics. 2. Rhetoric. I. Title II. Series
PN1042.P87 1996
808—dc20 95–4401

Contents

Acknowledgments

Research for this project was supported, in part, by Grants from the University of Washington Graduate School Research Support Fund in 1989 and 1991. Portions of this work have appeared elsewhere in slightly different form: "*Transsumptio:* A Rhetorical Doctrine of the Thirteenth Century," *Rhetorica* 5 (1987): 369–410, The International Society for the History of Rhetoric; "*Identitas, Similitudo,* and *Contrarietas* in Gervasius of Melkley's *Ars poetica:* A Stasis of Style," *Rhetorica* 9 (1991): 63–86, The International Society for the History of Rhetoric; and "Eberhard the German and the Labyrinth of Learning: Grammar, Poesy, Rhetoric, and Pedagogy in *Laborintus,*" *Rhetorica* 11 (1993): 95–118, The International Society for the History of Rhetoric. I am grateful to the International Society for the History of Rhetoric and the University of California Press for permission to reuse these essays here.

The efforts of any scholar are a product of teachers, students, and colleagues. I would especially like to thank three of my teachers: Professor Beth S. Bennett of the University of Alabama, and Professors Ian Thompson and William E. Wiethoff of Indiana University. Students in my seminars in Medieval Rhetorical Theory at the University of Washington read and heard many of the ideas expressed here in earlier forms. I am particularly thankful to Jon Bouknight, Judith McDaniel, and Robert Reid for their constructive and enthusiastic engagement with my ideas. My colleagues at the University of Washington, Professor John Angus Campbell and Professor Barbara P. Warnick have been helpful in reading and critiquing some of my work. My former chair at Washington, Professor Ann Q. Staton encouraged me to undertake this project. Finally, I would like to thank my reviewers at the University of South Carolina Press: Professors James J. Murphy, Paul Prill, and Marjorie C. Wood. My work would be far better were it the sum of their collective efforts; the limitations of this contribution are solely my own.

Ars poetriae
Rhetorical and Grammatical Invention at the Margin of Literacy

Part 1

Rhetoric and Grammar

Introduction

Histories of speaking, writing, and their pedagogies are histories of communicative technology. Marshall McLuhan identified four stages in the evolution of communicative technology: the oral stage; the manuscript stage; the printing stage (or Gutenberg galaxy); and the electronic stage.[1] Each stage overlaps the other, and each defines its practice by its previous stages. Indeed, in the current electronic age, orality and electronic media merge in television. An earlier interaction, still in use, is the overlap of orality and literacy. These two phases were at the height of their interactive tension, on the edge of the Gutenberg galaxy, in the thirteenth-century arts of poetry and prose, *artes poetriae.*

The six *artes poetriae,* which are the subject of this study (Matthew of Vendôme's *Ars versificatoria,* Geoffrey of Vinsauf's *Poetria nova* and *Documentum de modo et arte dictandi et versificandi,* John of Garland's *De arte prosayca, metrica, et rithmica* or *Parisiana poetria,* Gervasius of Melkley's *Ars poetica,* and Eberhard the German's *Laborintus*) were written on the eve of the printing press and flourished via the manuscript tradition well beyond the advent of moveable type. These works lay on the cusp of a shift from orality toward literacy. They are the progeny of the self-conscious marriage of rhetoric and grammar and, by extension, orality and literacy. Understood in this sense, they have much to tell us about orality and literacy, and the nature of rhetoric and grammar.

Oral discourse, in and of itself, is evanescent, ethereal, and powerful. The word spoken and unreproduced can move one's mind and soul—and the audience of such utterances is relatively defenseless. Uttered words are stored only in the minds of people and therefore, they are stored imperfectly. As a way of heightening the possibilities that could be wrought by speech, the ancient Greeks developed methods—technologies—that allowed the systematic generation of speech. Recognizing the powerful impact of speech, the Greeks also sought to constrain it. This systemization developed into a means of analysis, description, and preservation of speech that could ultimately be objectified into texts. As Walter Ong wrote, "Though words are grounded in oral speech, writing locks them into a visual field forever."[2] When speech was locked into texts it was controlled, made static. Power shifted from the one who generated speech to the one who could capture it in a text and thereby interpret and control it.

Among the phenomena surrounding speech and writing were the technologies developed to facilitate their use. Rhetoric was a technology with which one generated speech, primarily oral speech; grammar was a technology by which one identified correct speech and, more particularly, texts. Eventually, oral and written utterances were regarded as synonymous; speech (oratory) came to be frozen in texts; and rhetorical virtuosity shifted from the art of reacting to a situation with appropriate speech to one of displaying eloquence by the ability to rework a text.

These two ancient technologies, rhetoric and grammar, are involved in a necessary relationship with one another because neither one exists in a pure state. The idea of a text is always constrained by the idea of an utterance, and the idea of an utterance is always constrained by the idea of a text. Rhetoric was a method (a tool) by which a speaker created discourse (speech) in response to a particular situation. The rhetorical method consisted of a series of heuristics that addressed the varying nature of audiences and their responses to oral phenomena. The phenomena to which the audience responded were elusive. In their purest state, these phenomena existed only for the moment in which they were heard. In a secondary state, they existed in the minds of their audience.

Grammar, on the other hand, was a method by which language and, especially, texts were regulated. Grammar dissected discourse into its constituent components. It too consisted of a series of heuristics; but, rather than being used to respond to a situation, grammar was used to respond to utterances, texts. It regulated those texts by prescribing consistent forms analogous to similar utterances and usages. Grammar, then, was the inverse of rhetoric. Rhetoric was unstable. Its very method sought irregularity—effective discourse for varied audiences. Grammar was stable. The nature of its method sought regularity—controlled discourse for consistent texts.

Communication, then, was bound by two divergent, but interdependent, technological impulses. One sought to explore and exploit the power of language, and the other sought to control and regulate such language. These two impulses have coexisted for much of the history of human communication, moving relentlessly on a continuum framed by absolute orality on one end, and absolute literacy on the other. In many ways each extreme is reflexive of the other. Literature began as oralature and eventually became literature—that is texts. Thus, the oralature of Homer became fixed with the development of language and became a text. The same thing happened to the speeches of Demosthenes, Cicero,[3] and Jesus of Nazareth. The devices of literature, regulated by the science of grammar, nonetheless retained oral conventions that, in many ways, were changed by a textual emphasis. Indeed, much of the literature of Western history was conceived with a listening audience in mind, but constrained by the limitations of textuality.

As a time of primary orality moved toward a time of primary textuality, texts evolved. At first texts were technology with devices to regulate, control, contain, and perfect oral speech. Up to the time of the printing press, authors often spoke of their audiences as listeners rather than readers. Thus, even when texts became more valued than speech, they were seen as transcripts of speech, and perhaps viewed as the same thing as speech itself. Ultimately, with the advent of the printing press, the text became a thing in and of itself, moving away from the oral end of the spectrum and toward the literate end. At the same time, rhetoric—a more orally focused technology—moved toward the literate, and grammar—more literally focused technology—moved toward the oral. The tension created by the rhetorical / grammatical movement is reflected in the theoretical treatises in the *artes poetriae* themselves.

The oral/literal tension that marked the development of the two ancient communicative technologies (rhetoric and grammar) is likewise present in the histories that describe them. In the case of *ars poetriae,* two particular historiographical perspectives—grounded in the oral / literal split—have obscured appreciation of their theoretical contributions. The first involves the practice of classical rhetorical historiography and the second concerns the examination of treatises according to arbitrary identification with particular academic disciplines.

Scholarship on the history of rhetorical theory has emphasized classical doctrine, in particular its adaptation to the time period being studied.[4] This historiographical method, while useful, has often obscured the significance and unique characteristics of rhetorics of later time periods. Emphasis on classical doctrine by historians of rhetoric is particularly prevalent in accounts of the Middle Ages. Brian Vickers has gone so far as to portray medieval rhetoric as the fragmentation of rhetoric, which was ultimately restored in the Renaissance.[5] Contrary to Vickers' fragmentation belief, Marjorie Curry Woods has argued that the Middle

Ages have been marginalized by a hierarchical system that privileges the principles for oral persuasion developed by the ancient Greeks and Romans.[6] This system is exemplified in George Kennedy's *Classical Rhetoric in its Christian and Secular Tradition from Ancient to Modern Times.*[7] Kennedy's work essentially defines primary rhetoric as the classical system for developing speeches. Secondary rhetoric, on the other hand, generally pertains to the variant rhetorical approaches of later times, particularly those focusing on writing instruction in the Middle Ages—a phenomenon Kennedy identifies as *letteraturizzazione.* Kennedy thus privileges the oral tradition over the literal.

Ultimately, Woods turns Kennedy's assumptions about rhetoric upside down suggesting a historiography that deemphasizes rhetoric's association with adult civic discourse and the accomplishments of those with social, political, and financial power. Rather, she suggests that "the basis of rhetoric has always been the pedagogical tradition, a realm of experience where expressive as well as persuasive communication is recognized."[8] When viewed from Kennedy's classical rhetorical historiographer's perspective, the *artes poetriae* appear marginal because they do not produce oratory. Using Woods' approach, their particular function is highlighted. The *artes poetriae* are intended to instruct students in the composition of prose and poetry, not oratory. Their techniques center on the reworking of existing themes and stories rather than creating original orations that respond to particular circumstances. Many of the techniques used to rework those themes, however, did originate in classical rhetorical theory. Classical rhetoric may therefore be aptly utilized in understanding the doctrine found in *ars poetriae,* but only if the differences that this theory brings to this type of written composition are recognized.

Classical historiography's marginalization of secondary rhetoric has obscured the relative significance of the *artes poetriae,* particularly in regard to the figures of speech, which play a major role in the genre. Unfortunately, scholars of *ars poetriae,* beginning with Edmond Faral, have studied the genre's figurative accounts according to the seemingly exhaustive list of figures presented in the first-century, B.C., treatise, *Rhetorica ad Herennium.* As a result, treatises with figurative accounts differing from *Rhetorica ad Herennium* are often found to be wrong-minded or substandard. Faral, for instance, provided a detailed analysis of the figurative accounts in the *ars poetriae* by comparing them to *Rhetorica ad Herennium* and listing those figures in the margins of his edition of *Poetria nova.* His analysis was subsequently perpetuated in the works of J. W.

H. Atkins and James J. Murphy.[9] Moreover, Margaret Nims included Faral's marginalia in her translation of *Poetria nova.* This method of comparison and explication by means of the classical figures has caused previous studies of Geoffrey of Vinsauf's *Poetria nova* to ignore the doctrine of *transsumptio*—an important concept that combines argument and style. Similarly, previous attempts to equate the figurative vocabulary found in Gervasius of Melkley's *Ars poetica* with the list from *Rhetorica ad Herennium* have obscured—indeed, concealed—a unique system of compositional invention. This method of analysis, which insists on defining the figures, ignores the contributions of grammar: there is a different tradition of the figures found in ancient grammatical treatises that inform *ars poetriae.* The relative ignorance of the grammatical figures in previous studies points to the second historiographical perspective—disciplinary categorization.

Disciplinary categorizations are equally confounding to the understanding of *ars poetriae.*[10] Classification of particular treatises as rhetorics, grammars, or poetics often prevents an understanding of what these treatises may have represented to the people who wrote and read them. Such is the case with *ars poetriae,* which has been categorized variously as rhetoric, poetic, and grammar.[11] Rhetoric is perhaps the most common classification, as the figures are a predominant feature of each of the six treatises that comprise the genre. None of the treatises features rhetoric in its title, however, and *poetica* or *poetria* appears only in half. Further, the tradition of grammatical figures is also featured in parts of *ars poetriae.*

Scholars of the last half century have observed that medieval rhetoric and poetic were inextricably intertwined.[12] Nonetheless, O. B. Hardison noted that rhetoric and poetic were two different disciplines in the Middle Ages.[13] Though Hardison believed that Charles Sears Baldwin was correct in asserting that rhetorical doctrine was incorporated into many poetical treatises, Hardison thought it was wrong to view the *ars poetriae* as a "variant of medieval rhetoric."[14] Viewing medieval poetic through the eyes of rhetorical theory acknowledges its debt to rhetoric, but ignores its adaptation to artistic purposes. Rather than a confusion of rhetoric for poetic, Hardison found in *ars poetriae* "a lively consciousness of the differences between them."[15] Suffice it to say that medieval rhetoric may be different from classical rhetoric and that medieval poetic is different from, though influenced by, medieval rhetoric.

Essential to the appreciation of *ars poetriae* is grammar. Though none of the treatises feature grammar in their titles, there are obvious grammatical components in several of the treatises. Versification is still another central theme that is identified in at least half of the titles. Labels and titles notwithstanding, the particular disciplinary heritage of *ars poetriae* does not necessarily account for the doctrine found therein. That is to say, a grammarian whose doctrine is gleaned from rhetorical theory may be something other than a grammarian, but not necessarily a rhetorician. Aldo Scaglione discarded presupposed disciplinary distinctions between grammar, poetics, and rhetoric in his examination of the development of ancient and medieval compositional theory. For Scaglione, classical and medieval composition focused primarily on word order and sentence structure.[16] Curiously, however, Scaglione saw *ars poetriae* as having little importance to compositional theory and focused his analysis on *ars dictaminis.*[17] Nonetheless, word order and sentence structure are important concerns in *ars poetriae.* Matthew of Vendôme and Eberhard the German base their treatises on composing individual lines of verse by means of a metrical framework determined by sentence structure, word order, and verb placement. The compositional focus, therefore, may be an enlightened way in which to view the genre; moreover, this focus highlights the rhetorical and grammatical heritage of *ars poetriae* with regard to orality and literacy.

Over fifty years ago, Richard McKeon argued that histories of rhetoric have treated the art as a fixed doctrine, ignoring the contexts in which rhetoric was applied and developed.[18] McKeon suggested that rhetoric should be conceived of as being in process—in transition—"for in the course of discussion all the terms are altered in meaning, and the contents and methods of each of the arts are transformed when grammar, rhetoric, poetic, dialectic, and logic change places or are identified one with another."[19] McKeon reminded his readers that most theories regard rhetoric as the province of no particular subject. Rhetoric, therefore, is a complicated matter:

> applied to many incommensurate subject matters; it has borrowed devices from other arts, and its technical terms and methods have become, with trace of their origin, parts of other arts and sciences; its own devices have been bent back upon themselves in such a way that any part of rhetoric or any matter incidentally involved in it—words and style, character and passion, reason and imagination, the kinds of orations, civil philosophy, practical action—have been made basic to the definitions of all technical terms and distinctions.[20]

In following this perspective McKeon focused his own analysis on medieval rhetoric's relationships with classical rhetoric, philosophy / theology, and logic.

To complicate medieval rhetoric one must first simplify it and chart it out in some coherent form. That was done by Murphy in his *Rhetoric in the Middle Ages: A History of Rhetorical Theory from St. Augustine to the Renaissance.* Murphy's work went beyond McKeon's, collating the results of hundreds of earlier studies and editions of rhetorical texts into a broad survey that identified discrete rhetorical developments. Murphy's survey performed the important task of condensing one thousand years of theory into specific time periods, movements, and genres.

In particular, Murphy outlined the development of three unique rhetorical genres: *ars praedicandi, ars dictaminis,* and *ars poetriae.* Each addressed a specific concern of the era; each applied rhetorical precepts to a situational need. *Ars praedicandi* provided a method for developing sermons. *Ars dictaminis* developed precepts for letter writing. *Ars poetriae* suggested guidelines for composing prose and poetry. Murphy's important work provided the context for smaller, more focused studies of medieval rhetoric. Accordingly, the study presented here focuses on one genre, *ars poetriae,* and on one time, a one-hundred-year period spanning the twelfth and thirteenth centuries.

A complete study of *ars poetriae* has yet to be written. A preliminary study of the genre, Faral's *Les artes poétiques du XIIe et du XIIIe siècles* was published in 1924. Faral introduced the genre and its principal features and provided brief outlines of some of the treatises as well as critical Latin texts of four of the six works.[21] Critical editions of the remaining texts have since been produced.[22] Each of the six treatises has been translated into English at least once.[23] A medieval commentary on the *Poetria nova* has also been edited and translated into English.[24] Additional scholarly attention has been paid to a few of the works, particularly Geoffrey of Vinsauf's *Poetria nova* and Matthew of Vendôme's *Ars versificatoria.*[25] The remaining treatises, however, have been relatively unstudied. In 1991, Douglas Kelly published a work entitled *The Art of Poetry and Prose.* The work features a bibliographic review of scholarship on the *ars poetriae* since Faral, some description and summary of doctrine, and, most importantly, a consideration of the cultural and intellectual milieu in which the genre appeared. Kelly's work is limited, however, in that he offers little discussion and analysis of individual treatises.[26] Instead, he discusses the contribution of the genre in a general fashion.

On the whole, previous scholarship on *ars poetriae* has often failed to grasp the significance of the various theoretical doctrines found in the treatises. Though grouped into a genre, each of the *artes poetriae* is unique; each adds a different dimension to the genre: some treatises are written in verse, while others are written in prose. Geoffrey of Vinsauf's *Poetria nova* and Eberhard the German's *Laborintus* exemplify the very principles they recommend as they explain them. Other treatises, Gervasius of Melkley's *Ars poetica* and John of Garland's *De arte prosayca, metrica, et rithmica* are quite pedantic. Eberhard the German's *Laborintus* offers its doctrine in the form of a riddle. Emphasis on the treatises' similarities has often tended to ignore their differences. No study has examined the treatises individually and commented on the significance of both the individual treatises and the genre as a whole. And no study has adequately tapped the grammatical tradition as a way of understanding *ars poetriae.*

This study is concerned with orality and literacy; rhetoric and poetic; grammar and versification; and *artes dictaminis, poetriae et praedicandi.* Indeed, it regards the *artes poetriae* as influenced by all the various disciplines and genres identified. *Ars poetriae* is viewed as a unique genre of discourse that should be understood primarily on its own merits rather than on its relationship with classical genres. By discarding the notion that all rhetorical doctrine is defined by classical sources—and that *ars poetriae* must be categorized as rhetoric, grammar, or poetic—one is better able to judge each work on its own terms. Thus, the ultimate aim of this study is to understand *ars poetriae* as a pertinent and significant development in history, rather than as a building block or impediment in the evolution of rhetorical theory. The oral/literal split complicates the analysis—as rhetoric's move from oral to written discourse essentially caused an inversion in the roles of rhetoric and grammar. In McKeon's words, rhetoric and grammar have "been bent back upon themselves" by their reverse movements on the oral to literate continuum. Rhetoric moved toward the literal and grammar moved back toward the oral.

Since *ars poetriae* is a preceptive genre, one may best understand it by first considering the pedagogical traditions—rhetorical and grammatical—by which it was influenced. The discussion will then continue with a careful analysis of each of the Latin *artes poetriae.* Finally, the contributions of *ars poetriae* will be considered in light of contemporary rhetorical concerns.

Chapter One

Ancient Rhetoric and Grammar
Orality versus Literacy

Rhetoric and grammar both stem from oral phenomena but were developed literally—that is organized and written in texts. Initially, each one addressed spoken language phenomena; ironically, however, both rhetoric and grammar moved toward the literal as soon as they were self-consciously identified. Though each art became literal, each retained a focus on its oral origin. Each one did so, however, in markedly different ways. Grammarians sought to classify language by its basic constituent parts: sounds, alphabet, syllables, words, and, ultimately, grammatical units. Those constituent parts were explained in conjunction with one another, so that larger language phenomena, indeed texts, could be explained according to a series of interdependent rules. Grammar was thus used to analyze and explain texts as exemplars of language use. Grammar was not concerned with composition per se, but with analysis. Its role was to explain and correct. Rhetoricians were not particularly concerned with explanations or correctness; and any regard they might have had for correctness was based on the situational appropriateness in regard to a particular subject, speaker, or audience. Rhetoric developed not so much as rules, as heuristics—techniques to facilitate oral composition. Oral discourse was concerned with the situational context and was therefore not as accountable to interdependence across situations. Its correctness was judged, or reacted to, instantly. The difficulty between the correct and the effective underscores the tension between the two arts. That tension can be seen more clearly by examining the early systems of rhetoric and grammar. Ultimately, the means by which rhetoricians composed became used as a means of analysis, and the means by which grammarians analyzed became a means of generating texts.

Rhetoric

Ironically, the initial articulation in the theoretical sense based rhetoric in the oral/literal tension. We are told that Corax and Tisias (ca. 467 B.C.) developed a *techne* for the composition of speeches in the law courts, consisting of an organizational scheme and a system of probabilities. Subsequently, Gorgias of Leontini (ca. 480–380 B.C.) is said to have advocated a system consisting of what we now call figures (*homoeoteleuton, isocolon, antithesis,* and *parison*) in conjunction with a sensitivity to timing (*kairos*), and appropriateness (*to prepon*). The figures were devices that pertained to the arrangement of utterances in particular patterns—quantification and balance of syllables, antitheses, parallelisms. Gorgias' figures were particularly oral ones. They did not address meaning as much as they facilitate the aural sensation of speech experienced by a listener. The figures created experience rather than conveyed meaning.

Along with the figures, Gorgias is known for the treatise, "On the Nonexistent or on Nature,"—a work that underscores the independence of the oral utterance and the difficulty one has in controlling it. Gorgias argued: "First and foremost, . . . nothing exists; second, that even if it exists it is inapprehensible to man; third, that even if it is apprehensible, still it is without a doubt incapable of being expressed or explained to the next man."[1] Gorgias existed in a primarily oral society and was a master of oral technology (he is said to have introduced rhetoric to Athens). His treatise points out the unrestrained, uncontrolled power of orality. When one is communicating ideas to another via the medium of speech—a medium that may be objectified only in the minds of the sender and receiver—it is nonexistent in an empirical sense. One who pretends to understand an idea can relay it to another. The idea, however, exists only in the minds of those relating the idea. There is no text, no objective thing to be scrutinized. As Gorgias said, *logos* is not tangible: "For that by which we reveal is *logos,* but *logos* is not substance and existing things. Therefore we do not reveal existing things to our neighbors, but *logos,* which is something other than substances."[2] The Gorgianic figures thus are the means of speaking in a memorable fashion that Jacqueline de Romilly compared to a magical incantation: "Gorgias' magic rests on the notion that all truth is out of reach. Sacred magic was mysterious; Gorgias' magic is technical. He wants to emulate the power of the magician by a scientific analysis of language and of its influence. He is the theoretician of the magic spell of words."[3] The words and the magic crafted into them by the Gorgianic figures are the elements of *logos* that allow a speaker to express thought in a striking, sonorous, almost hypnotic way. The ultimate point is that words are words, but not the things they purport to represent.

An additional early example of the oral/literal tension is seen in Plato's *Phaedrus,* when Socrates argues against the written word: "Anyone who leaves behind him a written manual, and likewise anyone who takes it over from him, on the supposition that such writing will provide something reliable and permanent, must be exceedingly simple-minded . . . if he imagines that written words can do anything more than remind one who knows that which the writing is concerned with."[4] Socrates then compares writing to painting; they both have the appearances of living things, but neither is able to respond to questions. Thus, written discourse presents some of the same problems inherent in spoken discourse, though from a different angle. Both Gorgias and Plato speak to a concern with the objectification of words.

Socrates' reservations about oral discourse (expressed in his earlier treatise *Gorgias*) were concerned with the fact that uninterrupted discourse did not allow for challenge, questions, and clarifications. In that scenario, it was quite clear that a speech, to its detriment, could not be examined. The problem Socrates saw with writing, however, was that it is easier to objectify. Writing allows speech to be regarded as a thing—and therein lies the problem Socrates expressed in the *Phaedrus:*

> Once a thing is put in writing, the composition . . . drifts all over the place, getting into the hands not only of those who understand it, but equally of those who have no business with it; it doesn't know how to address the right people, and not address the wrong. And when it is ill-treated and unfairly abused it always needs its parent to come to its help, being unable to defend or help itself.[5]

Socrates, though certainly concerned with the effect of unbridled orality, nonetheless was equally concerned with the effect of written discourse. The objectification of speech into a thing, a text, preserves the basic flaws in the uninterrupted speech, but this text also freezes the speech. The unrecorded utterance is always subject to discussion, correction, revision, and argumentation. The objective text, however, is a thing, a fact. And its "parent" cannot always be summoned. The power is no longer with the speaker and speech, but within the text.

By the time Plato's student, Aristotle, composed his *Rhetoric,* writing no longer seemed to have been regarded as a problem. Aristotle contributed significantly to the objectification and, ultimately, textualization of rhetorical phenomena in his *Rhetoric.* Aristotle shifted the focus of rhetoric from the utilization of the power of *logos* and to a categorization of that power.

Aristotle's definition of rhetoric as "the power of discovering the available means of persuasion in any given case"[6] focused rhetoric squarely on the process of investigating fixed, objective categories. The given cases for Aristotle and his Latin successors were those cases that required advocacy before judges in a court of law (forensic) and before decision makers in a legislative body (deliberative), and those instances of speaking before the public on ceremonial occasions (epideictic). In addition to identifying the particular types of situations requiring public decision making, Aristotle divided his system of discovery into considerations of how speakers could use their own character (*ethos*), the psychological characteristics of their audience (*pathos*), and the words of the speech itself (*logos*) to persuade an audience. Each of the various dimensions identified in Aristotle's rhetorical system was further broken down into a series of topics and patterns that a rhetor could use in discovering material pertinent to a particular audience.

The objectification of the elements of persuasion provided the rhetor with powerful heuristic tools that could assist in the composition of discourse for a variety of situations and audiences, and thus it represents considerable development in theoretical rhetoric. This objectification of the elements, and their subsequent canonization, allowed rhetoric to focus on certain components of the speech exercise—though possibly to the exclusion of other important things. John Poulakos writes that Aristotle presented a rhetoric grounded in actuality that placed humans in the present. Conversely, the Sophists grounded their rhetoric in the possibility of the future. Sophistic rhetoric "shies away from a stock vocabulary and conventional phraseology. Because it strives to present what is absent, it is necessarily metaphorical, mainly suggestive, pointing to open regions and unknown verities."[7] The careful elaboration of rhetorical concepts defined rhetoric more clearly, but in the process of conceptualization, rhetoric became less oral—less open. The definition and categorization was useful, but it may also have limited the potential of the phenomenon being identified. In essence, naming closes options.[8] Aristotle's heuristics were applied to an open, oral system that moved toward an indeterminate end. The indeterminacy was reduced by Aristotle's categorization. Nonetheless, the rhetor had to engage in some adaptation to people and to information outside the system to achieve his or her goal. Therefore, while moving toward the literal in categorizing rhetoric, Aristotle's *Rhetoric* also provided an open means of composition. Rhetoric as a theory or *techne* thus presents a paradox. When rhetoric becomes a method and is recorded, it is frozen—objectified; on the other hand, its categorization and control allows others to use the *techne* to compose. Rhetoric is therefore a double-edged sword featuring the advantages and disadvantages of both orality and literacy.

Aristotle's system of discovery, and other Greek developments, were codified even more by the Romans. The highly pragmatic Roman rhetorical tradition divided rhetoric into an inventory of five parts, or canons, which considered progressively the elements needed to produce an oration: invention, the discovery of the materials on which the speech was to be based; arrangement, the distribution of the material in an appropriate order; style, the selection of the appropriate language for the discovered material; memory, retention of the material and language of the speech; and delivery, the management of voice and body in a way suitable to the material and language of the speech. The further identification of the materials of rhetoric objectified the phenomena even more. The final two canons, memory and delivery, received brief treatments in the classical treatises and, as *ars poetriae* was a written genre, are of little concern to this study. The first three canons are central concerns because they were inverted, changed, and reappropriated in *ars poetriae.* Moreover, the figures of speech—essential elements of style—appeared in both the arts of rhetoric and grammar—and later in *ars poetriae* in different forms.

Invention became a highly technical operation in the Roman period. Its mainstays, the generative system of the topics and the analytical system of *stasis,* were introspective, but their application was outward toward a variety of audiences and situations. These mainstays became increasingly literal, though they were also applied to oral composition. The initial stage of invention concerns the isolation of the issue or controversy around which the speech should center. The isolation of the issue was facilitated by a system of *stasis* (status)—the legacy of Hermagoras of Temnos, a second-century B.C. Greek rhetorician. *Stasis* is a method by which a rhetor analyzes the issues involved in a particular rhetorical situation to determine the point of "clash" or controversy. In practice *stasis* consisted of a series of questions that determine the nature of the case and thus the required strategy. The system allowed the rhetor to winnow through the material of the case and decide upon the area of clash. Though most Roman rhetoricians indicated that the *stasis* system could be applied in each of the three rhetorical genres (forensic, deliberative, and epideictic) explanations of the system were generally applied to forensic cases. The impulse of *stasis* placed further emphasis on how one treated facts, perhaps to the exclusion of other relevant concerns. On the other hand, *stasis* was a generative doctrine of inquiry that provided a means for resolving conflict faced by an orator within situational constraints.[9] It was a progressive system by which a rhetor considered the various dimensions of a case to find the area most controversial and thus most susceptible to persuasion. In essence, a system of *stasis* served to focus the rhetor on the key strategy and was consequently at the very heart of rhetorical invention.

Associated with *stasis*, and often incorporated with it,[10] was the notion of rhetorical topics. According to Michael Leff, "a topic is a resource for an argument, or a seat of an argument, or a region in which an argument resides."[11] Topics are a system for generating the substance to be used in a speech. Aristotle's formulation of the topics identified the various sources of persuasion found in the three essential components of the speaking situation: *ethos, pathos,* and *logos.* His *Rhetoric* consisted chiefly of a systematic analysis of the topics specific to each category and common to all. Later topical systems, such as Cicero's and Quintilian's, isolated the topics by means of a series of questions. Donald Lemen Clark likened the questions asked by Quintilian to those of a reporter:[12] "In regard to everything that is done the question arises, Why? or Where? or When? or How? or By what means?" (5.10.32). In either case, the system provided places where a rhetor could look for the means of composing an argument.

Rhetorical invention, then, was a systematic inventory of the various angles from which a speaking situation might be approached. The student of rhetoric memorized the various *stases* and *topoi* in preparation of the speaking task at hand. Though they served to facilitate the composition of an oration, the development of inventional systems increasingly constrained and objectified the process of speech-making. As rhetoric became more systematized and user-friendly it moved further from orality and closer to literacy.

The inventional concern and the topical impulse were carried into the second canon of rhetoric—arrangement. Arrangement is a systematic inventory of the options an orator has in organizing a speech. The successful orator used the system in conjunction with his or her abilities; the nature of the speech; and the nature of the audience. The extensive structure—with its multiple divisions and options—further objectified the speech. A speech was clearly something that could be shaped by the rhetor. The object that the rhetor crafted, however, was produced in part through a consideration of the audience and its potential relationship to the diverse subjects that could be discussed in the speech.

Though the recommended structure of a speech varies according to the theorist, the options usually consisted of four to six parts, including: *exordium,* narration, partition (comprising the introduction), confirmation, refutation (the body), and peroration (the conclusion). Arrangement of orations was not as important to *ars poetriae* as was the system of topical invention included under the category of confirmation in Cicero's *De inventione.*

The sources of confirmation are found through a system of topical invention which considers attributes of persons or attributes of actions. The topics serve as a mental checklist with which the orator considers the various compositional elements available to the particular case.

A person may be considered by means of name, nature, manner of life, fortune, habits, feelings, interest, purpose, achievements, accidents, and speeches. Each of these categories is further divided into subcategories. For example, the nature of a person may be determined according to whether the person is male or female; according to nationality; according to kinship; or whether he or she is smart, dull, or mannerly. Similarly, the fortune of a person may be determined by asking whether he or she is rich, poor, a free person, a slave, a private citizen, or a public official. Attributes of action are found in the action itself, in the performance of that action, things adjacent to the action, and things resulting from the action. Performance concerns address such aspects as place, time, occasion, manner, and facilities. Adjacent concerns address the qualities of greater or lesser, equals, contraries, and genus to species (1.24–28). The devices that allow the rhetor to enliven the speech with the specific concerns of the audience and circumstances are reappropriated in *ars poetriae* to different purposes.

The most frequently appropriated and adapted rhetorical canon in the development of *ars poetriae,* however, was the canon of style. Style consisted of yet another set of categories—even larger than invention. Its function was to depict the oration in such language as to strategically reinforce the orator's purpose. The means of that depiction were the figures of speech. The figures, so important in *ars poetriae,* are the cornerstone of rhetoric. Moreover, their presence is a constant reminder of rhetoric's oral roots. These figures allow the orator to use language as an open, flexible entity that resists the closure of literacy. They enable the rhetor to use language not as a community code, but as a personal code. In particular, the tropes allow fixed words to be reexamined for new, more creative, meanings.

The most influential account of rhetorical style in the Middle Ages was that originally outlined in *Rhetorica ad Herennium.*[13] *Auctor ad Herennium* identified three kinds of style: grand (*gravis*), "smooth and ornate arrangement of impressive words"; middle (*mediocris*), "words of a lower, yet not of the lowest and most colloquial, class of words"; and simple (*adtenuata*), "the most current idiom of standard speech." Each style was depicted by means of some sixty-four rhetorical figures (4.8–10).

Auctor ad Herennium identified two types of figures that distinguish speech: *exornationes verborum* (adornments of words) and *exornationes sententiarum* (adornments of thought). *Exornationes verborum* are achieved through a certain polish of language. *Exornationes sententiarum* achieve their distinction through the ideas that they express rather than the words themselves. The *auctor* identified forty-five *exornationes verborum* and nineteen *exornationes sententiarum* (see appendix A). Of the *exornationes verborum,* the author identified ten special figures in which "the language departs from the ordinary meaning of the words and is, with a certain grace, applied in another sense" (4.31). Quintilian later referred to these figures as tropes.[14] With few changes, Quintilian's account of figures followed the account in *Ad Herennium.* One notable difference between the two treatments is that Quintilian used the Greek words for the various figures that are named in Latin in the *Ad Herennium.*[15] Another discrepancy between the two works is that Quintilian's account includes a trope called *metalepsis* or *transsumptio,* which is not in *Ad Herennium.* Though not completely developed in *Institutio oratoria, transsumptio* was later developed as a concept central to *ars poetriae.* The concept will be discussed in detail in chapter 4.

To a literate audience, *auctor ad Herennium*'s list of figures may appear exhaustive, but not very instructive. Indeed, even such a champion of oral rhetoric as George Kennedy has written that "such a list of figures was not very helpful in training an orator to speak persuasively, though it suggested ways that declamations could be artificially elaborated and decorated."[16] The *auctor*'s account of *exornationes* appears somewhat random, with little evident organizational scheme. The lack of systemization, however, is simply evidence of the *auctor*'s oral orientation. Coherence of order is something that only makes a great deal of difference when one has the option of seeing a text more than once. The most coherent literal order can be so bland orally as to put the listener to sleep.

From a literal viewpoint, the figures may seem haphazard. But when grouped in common categories—a decidedly literal method—these figures seem less arbitrary and quite persuasive. The first thirty-five *exornationes verborum* (see appendix A) are devices by which a rhetor arranges, warps, and manipulates language for persuasive effect. In particular, the figures were a means of achieving repetition (*repetitio, conversio, conplexio, traductio, conduplicatio, interpretatio*); opposition (*contentio, contrarium, commutatio*); strategic advantage (*interrogatio, ratiocinatio, subiectio, expeditio, correctio, praecisio, occulatio, permissio, dubitatio*); structure (*definitio, transitio, gradatio, conclusio*); and rhythm (*membrum, articulus, continuatio, conpar, similiter cadens, similiter desinens, disiunctio, coniunctio, adiunctio, dissolutum, adnominatio*). The repetitive devices (appendix A.1) involve the reiteration of words for emphasis. The devices of opposition (appendix A.2) allow for the comparison, contrast, and interaction of words. The strategic devices (appendix A.3) feature the use of an expression aimed at shaping thought to the rhetor's advantage, and range from patterns of questioning to ploys and forms of innuendo. Several of these are overtly argumentative, orienting the audience toward the orator's position. Structural devices (appendix A.4) allow the rhetor to arrange ideas and focus more on general organizational features, such as transitions and summaries. Finally, a significant number of devices deal with the manipulation of clauses, sentences, phrases, cases, and word endings for rhythmical and metrical effect (appendix A.5). The *exornationes verborum* provide the rhetor with the strategies that make language persuasive (rhetorical) rather than didactic. Significantly, it is the strategic figures—along with the *exornationes sententiarum*—that become known as the colors of rhetoric (*colores rhetorici*) in the Middle Ages and are excluded in large measure from the grammatical tradition.

The primary function of the ten special *exornationes verborum* (tropes) (see appendix A.7), is to provide a variation in the act of naming or identifying phenomena. Conventional meanings of words are vacated and replaced with tangential phenomena connected to the original meaning by means of substitution (*translatio, abusio, permutatio, pronominatio*); exaggeration (*superlatio*); part to whole and whole to part relationships (*intellectio*); representation (*denominatio*); circumlocution (*circumitio*); and change in word order (*transgressio*). In addition the tropes provided a means of creating words (*onomatopoeia*). The tropes give the rhetor varying approaches in order to reassign and create meaning. As will be seen in the forthcoming discussion of grammar, the very openness of the tropes makes them a problematic element in grammar.

The nineteen *exornationes sententiarum* (see appendix A) are distributed in a tighter fashion than the figures of words, but understanding for a literal audience may still be heightened by a reorganization. The *exornationes sententiarum* may be viewed as devices that perform four particular functions: organization, expression, comparison, and description.

The organizational figures (*distributio, divisio, descriptio, frequentatio, commoratio, contentio, similitudo;* appendix A.8) deal with the way thought is arranged to emphasize and demonstrate a point. Various devices arrange thought to consider the consequences of an action; assign functions or roles to people or things; use a variety of analogical relationships; and use certain organizational patterns for emphasis. The expressive figures (*licentia, deminutio, expolitio, conformatio, significatio, brevitas;* appendix A.9) include a variety of ruses used to facilitate persuasion: giving the appearance of humility while outlining one's accomplishments, recasting thought in different words, and using personification. The comparative figures (*exemplum* and *imago;* appendix A.10) involve models and examples used to support a particular point. Finally, descriptive figures (*effictio, notatio, sermocinatio, demonstratio;* appendix A.11) use a variety of means to describe: physical traits, character traits, patterns of speech used by particular people, and vivid description to depict an event. A final figure, *commoratio,* is one that pertains to the theme of an entire oration.

Again, many of these figures were discarded by the grammarians. For the most part, the *exornationes sententiarum* are means of composing arguments. They were discarded, therefore, because the grammarian's focus was on the explication of literature and not on argumentation.

Ad Herennium is a written work, but not self-consciously so. It is worth observing that *auctor ad Herennium* makes a special point of noting that each of the examples he used in explaining the figures is original. He spends several pages arguing against the practice of borrowing examples. The crux of his argument is that borrowed examples are forms of authoritative testimony. Thus, their use undermines the authority of the rhetorician because rhetoricians can have no authority if they are unable to demonstrate the principles they propound (4.1–6). The mastery of a rhetorician is demonstrated by displaying the art in his or her words. The *auctor*'s dislike of testimony underscores the tension between literal words as objective things divorced from the author, and the oral identification of words with the author. The issue of borrowed examples will be revisited when the ancient art of grammar is discussed.

Though theoretical rhetorics increasingly rendered the materials of rhetoric in static lists and categories, the actual use of the principles of rhetoric is quite dynamic. *Auctor ad Herennium*'s presentation of the figures ultimately underscores Gorgias' delineation of rhetoric as style. There is a difference between substance and style, fact and form, object and word. For the rhetorician crafting a speech extemporaneously, there are no facts. Utterances originate in the mind of the rhetor and are experienced through words that have a fleeting existence as substance, and survive only in the minds of speaker and audience. Both the speaker and the audience may regard the words as substance, but from different perspectives. The point is that rhetorical theory, in practice, facilitates a habit of mind that suggests a response to situational stimuli. A rhetorician responds to substantive things (facts) but insofar as those facts are filtered through the mind of the rhetor and the various techniques used, the figures do not ornament or decorate. Instead, the figures allow an orator to appropriate substances and recreate the information to the orator's advantage. Thus the figures are the substance of rhetoric. They depict ideas, feelings, and substance. In the absence of texts, they are substance. The figures also play a central role in early grammars, but in a different way.

Grammar

The history of grammar has neither the abundance of extant primary nor secondary sources as have been found in the history of rhetoric. Nonetheless, its roots lie in an ancient controversy—one that has also remained with us—the debate over *physis* and *nomos* (nature and convention). The controversy questioned whether language was a natural result of the relationship between words and phenomena, or whether it was an arbitrary system based on convention. Naturalists believed that language was a result of a necessary relationship between words and phenomena. Conventionalists, on the other hand, examined language and categorized it according to regularities or analogies found in the language. Naturalists, particularly the Stoics, denied that there was—

and maintained that there should not be—a regularity in language. Language, they felt, was an anomaly and its connection to nature lay in the etymologies of language that were obscured in actual usage. Conventionalists, Alexandrian grammarians in particular, took the categories they found in language's actual usage and created regulative grammars that featured the standard categories of verb, noun, gender, number, and so on. The Alexandrians, faced with the problem of deciphering ancient texts, felt that usage suggested patterns that could be standardized and imposed on language. The Stoics sought to purify language of its corrupted forms. Both of these groups contributed much to the origins of what we now know as grammar. The more philosophical Stoic approach, however, was not as influential as the more perceptive Alexandrian tradition passed on by Dionysius Thrax and others.[17] Jeffrey Huntsman writes that it was the Alexandrian tradition that was ultimately transmitted via Donatus and Priscian to the Middle Ages.[18] Scaglione and Louis Holtz, however, view the Stoics as having had a significant impact on the development of grammatical theory, particularly in regard to the figures of speech and composition in general.[19] Though many grammars, particularly Donatus' *Ars grammatica,* featured an account of the figures, the system in which the grammatical figures were presented was entirely different from the rhetorical system.

Few complete grammars survived from antiquity; the earliest grammar was Dionysius Thrax' *Tekhné Grammatiké.*[20] Dionysius' work was a brief outline of grammar that defined the art as "the practical study of the normal usages of poets and prose writers." Dionysius previewed the contents of his work as comprising six divisions:

1. Skill in reading (aloud) with due attention to prosodic features.
2. Interpretation, taking note of the tropes of literary composition found in the text.
3. The ready explanation of obscure words and historical references.
4. Discovery of the origins of words.
5. A detailed account of regular patterns.
6. A critical assessment of poems; of all that the art includes this is the noblest part.[21]

Though the first four elements and the last element of Dionysius' divisions are acknowledged as parts of grammar, his treatise is basically a detailed account of regular patterns. After brief sections on reading, accent, punctuation, and rhapsody, the bulk of the treatise focuses on *stoikheion* (the alphabet, vowels, diphthongs, consonants, and semivowels), syllables, words, nouns, verbs, conjugations, participles, articles, pronouns, prepositions, adverbs, and conjunctions.[22] Much of the doctrine remains with us to this day.

Latin grammatical theory experienced few of the controversies that marked the development of Greek theory. The Romans inherited a considerable body of knowledge from the Greeks and were more inclined to apply Greek grammar to the Latin language. As R. H. Robins wrote, "only Varro exhibits considerable rethinking of grammatical terms and concepts specifically to fit the Latin language."[23] However, Varro did not set out to write a systematic grammar and only a fourth of his *De lingua Latina* survives.[24] Substantive developments in Latin grammar did not come until the fifth and sixth centuries with the work of Donatus and Priscian. Donatus' *Ars grammatica* is a careful, incremental analysis that begins with a consideration of the basic units of utterance identified in Dionysius' *stoikheion*. Donatus then used those basic units as the foundation on which to base and generate progressively larger units, such as clauses, phrases, and sentences. The final products of this system are the figures.

There is a marked difference between the rhetorical and grammatical figures, however. Where *Rhetorica ad Herennium* appears haphazard, Donatus' account unfolds logically from a set of basic principles. The grammatical figures are literal; they explain language as a fixed entity that can be constrained. Indeed, all of the examples of the figures come from texts—texts of other people's words. Those people just happen to be the greatest names in Latin literature. Both factors are the opposite of what takes place in *Rhetorica ad Herennium. Rhetorica ad Herennium* was a rhetorical demonstration; Donatus' treatise was a grammatical analysis. Only the tropes escape the rule-bound systemization of grammar. Though the tropes escape the textual system, they are constrained by their exemplification in the words of Virgil.

Donatus' *Ars grammatica,*[25] in its various forms of transmission, is perhaps the most influential grammar in Western history. Indeed, Donat or Donet became synonymous with an elementary system of grammar that was taught in English, as well as Latin, as late as the eighteenth century.[26] Donatus' *Ars* consisted of three basic parts: the *Ars minor,* the *Ars major,* and book 3 of the *Ars major*—a part generally known as the

Barbarismus. The *Ars minor* is essentially a brief version of book 2 of the *Ars major.* Both the *Ars minor* and the *Barbarismus* circulated as separate works.

The *Ars minor* is written with a didactic purpose, having been rendered in a question and answer format for younger students.[27] It begins with a drill on the parts of speech: "How many parts of speech are there? Eight. What? Noun, pronoun, verb, adverb, participle, conjunction, preposition, interjection" (*Partes orationis quot sunt? Octo. Quae? Nomen pronomen verbum adverbium participium coniunctio praepositio interiectio*).[28] Each of these parts is subsequently analyzed in great detail, including various conjugations and declensions. For example, the section on the verb reads as follows:

> What is a verb? A part of speech with tense and person, without case, signifying "to perform some action," or "to suffer," or neither. How many attributes has the verb? Seven. What? Quality, conjugation, gender, number, inflection, tense, person. . . . How many conjugations of verbs are there? Three. What? First, second, third. What is the first? It has the indicative mode, present time, singular number, second person in the active and neuter verb, long "a" before the last letter; in the passive, common, and deponent, before the last syllable, as amo, amas, amor, amaris; and the future tense of the same mode, ends the syllable in "bo" and "bor," as amo amabo, amor amabor.[29]

This tedious catechism, spanning some eleven pages in the Latin text, was memorized by school children whose ages were somewhere between five and eight years.[30] It is no wonder that Eberhard the German referred to the pages of Donatus as "a flowing fount of tears for students" (*Donatos vertit, lacrimarum fonte fluentes, qui dantur pueris post elementa novis*).[31]

Though its actual transmission was fragmented, *Ars major* is a careful and systematic account of language and composition that begins in book 1 with the basic units of articulation: voice (*vox*), the basic sound utterance (367); letters (*littera*), the distinctions between basic sound utterances (367–68); syllables (*syllaba*), the combination of letters (368–69); foot (*pes*), a particular relationship between syllables and time (369–70); accent (*tonis*), stress on particular syllables (371–72); and punctuation (*positura* or *distinctio*), syntactical units—*comma, colon,* and *sententia* (372). These basic units, in essence, are the building blocks of language; they play a role in all subsequent composition, particularly figurative language. *Ars major* then moves to the *partes orationis,* treated in much the same fashion as in *ars minor,* but without the catechistic format (372–92). The *partes orationis* are also the foundation on which the grammatical figures are based.

Book 3 of *Ars major*—the *Barbarismus*—is essentially an account of figures (see appendix B).[32] It begins with a consideration of faults in language (*barbarismo et solecismo*). A *barbarism* is defined as a fault of a single part of speech, generally a word form (392); while a *solecism* is a fault of a part of speech used in connection with other linguistic units (393). That is, a *barbarism* is a fault derived from misspellings, mispronunciations, or similar mistakes; a *solecism* is a fault derived from improper grammatical usage. When a *barbarism* is used intentionally in poetry, it is called a *metaplasm;* while when a *solecism* is used purposefully in poetry it is called a scheme. *Barbarisms* and *solecisms,* then, become allowable faults when used knowingly in poetry.[33]

Barbarisms occur in two general modes: written and enunciated. Both of these modes are produced through four operations: addition (*adjectio*), subtraction (*detractio*), adaptation (*inmutatio*), and transposition (*transmutatio*). Each of the operations may occur in any of five language units: letters, syllables, tempo or quantity (*temporis*), accent (*tonis*), and aspiration (*adspirationis*). Donatus provides specific examples of *barbarisms* involving letters, syllables, and tempo, but he is less detailed in regard to accent and aspiration (392–93).

A *solecism* is a fault of connected parts of speech, contrary to the rules of grammar. It differs from a *barbarism* in that it deals with more than single words. *Solecisms* occur in two ways: through the parts of speech and through the attributes (*accidentia*) of the parts of speech: inflexions (*qualitas*), comparison (*conparatio*), gender (*genus*), number (*numerus*), form (*figura*), and case (*casus*). Donatus identifies some ten *barbarisms* and *solecisms* produced through the misuses of grammar: *acyrologia, cacenphaton, pleonasmos, perissologia, macrologia, tautologia, eclipsis, tapinosis, cacosyntheton,* and *amphibolia. Pleonasmos,* for example, involves the addition of words to an expression that is already sufficiently clear; and *tautologia* occurs when an expression features the repetition of words or phrases. Neither device is usually desirable in prose, but when a particular meter or rhyme is needed these devices can be quite helpful. Thus, Donatus notes that what is called a solecism in prose is called a scheme in poetry (393–94).

Metaplasms are also permitted in poetry for the sake of meter. Donatus identifies fourteen forms of *metaplasms*: *prothesis, epenthesis, paragoge, aphaeresis, syncope, apocope, ectasis, systole, diaresis, episynaliphe, synaliphe, ecthlipsis, antithesis,* and *metathesis.* Each involves addition, subtraction, adaptation, or transposition of the five basic language units. For example, *prothesis* allows one to add a letter or syllable to a word (*tetulit* instead of *tulit*); and *metathesis* permits one to transpose the letters of a word (Evandre instead of Evander).

The schemes are what had previously been called figures or *exornationes.* Donatus notes the traditional distinction between figures of thought and figures of words (*schemata lexeos sunt et dianoeas*), but he declares that only the figures of words apply to grammarians—as figures of thought are the province of the orator. Moreover, only some seventeen figures of words are deemed necessary for his discussion: *prolepsis, zeugma, hypozeuxis, syllepsis, anadiplosis, anaphora, epanalepsis, epizeuxis, paronomasia, schesis onamaton, parhomoeon, homoeoptoton, homoeoteleuton, polyptoton, hirmos, polysyndeton,* and *dialyton* or *asyndeton* (397). Many of Donatus' *schemata* directly correspond to the *exornationes verborum* of *auctor ad Herennium: zeugma / adiunctio, hypozeuxis / disiunctio, syllepsis / coniunctio, anaphora / epanaphora, paronomasia, homoeoptoton / similiter cadens, homoeoteleuton / similiter desinens,* and *asyndeton.* The figures are offered with a different emphasis than in the rhetorical traditions. For example, *prolepsis* (a figure not found in *Ad Herennium*) is a form of anticipation with which a scene or situation is set up before being related. Donatus exemplifies *prolepsis* with the following passage from *Aeneid* 12.161–65: "Meanwhile the kings ride forth, Latinus in mighty pomp drawn in four-horse car, twelve golden rays circuling his gleaming brows, emblem of his ancestral sun; while Turnus comes behind a snow-white pair, his hand brandishing two spears with broad heads of steel."[34] Not only is the example borrowed, but the device itself is one that facilitates poetic literary expression. *Prolepsis* is not a device that would be particularly helpful in argument.

Both *auctor ad Herennium* and Donatus feature repetitive devices—*anaphora* or *epanaphora, conversio, conplexio, traductio, anadiplosis, epizeuxis;* devices involving the use and placement of verbs—*zeugma / adiunctio, hypozeuxis / disiunctio, syllepsis / coniunctio;* and devices that utilize similar word endings—*homoeoteleuton / similiter desinens, homoeoptoton / similiter cadens.* All these devices involve some sort of distinction in form. Missing from Donatus' account, however, are the more overtly rhetorical devices that consist of a strategy or ploy: *contentio, exclamatio, interrogatio, ratiocinatio, sententia, contrarium, subiectio, definitio, transitio, correctio, occulatio, commutatio, permissio, dubitatio, expeditio, praecisio,* and *conclusio*. Also absent from his work are the basic linguistic figures: *membrum, articulum, continuatio,* and *isocolon*. The first three linguistic figures, of course, were identified as basic components of grammar. Clearly, Murphy was correct when he wrote that "in the realm of figures, there is a Roman grammatical tradition different in some ways from that represented by the Ciceronian rhetorical school."[35] The grammatical figures are truly grammatical. They are permitted exceptions to the rules of grammar and are allowed for the sake of diverse and striking expression. The figures excluded from Donatus' grammar feature more than exceptions to form. They are ploys and strategies that allow the rhetor to shape expression toward a particular end. Donatus' figures also display a literary, textual perspective. They focus on the kinds of linguistic distinctions that require reflection and analysis. They require that an utterance be removed from the ether and made into an object, which is subject to correction and revision. The excluded figures, on the other hand, belong to spoken language and will never look appropriate on paper (literally). Indeed, their duplicity is antithetical to textuality.

The tropes are the only part of Donatus' grammatical system that do not follow as variations of his basic grammatical foundation. Instead, they are additions to the grammatical system necessitated by their existence in Latin Literature. Donatus' failure to account for the tropes in his interrelated grammatical system is no doubt due to the open, amorphous nature of tropes. Nonetheless, he uses them as a means of analyzing texts. His grammatical focus is further demonstrated by a number of subtropes he adds to the corpus.

Donatus defines tropes as expressions converted from their proper signification to an improper likeness of that signification because of the necessity of ornamentation (399). He identifies thirteen tropes: the ten listed by *auctor ad Herennium,* two from Quintilian, and a new trope—*homoeosis*. In addition, *homoeosis* consists of three subtropes—*icon, parabole,* and *paradigma; hyperbaton* consists of five—*hysterologia, anastrophe, parenthesis, tmesis,* and *synchesis;* and allegory of seven—irony, *antiphrasis, aenigma, charientismos, paroemia, sarcasmos,* and *astismos*. As Murphy observes, the total number of tropes in Donatus is actually twenty-eight.[36] The new tropes and subtropes also reflect Donatus' grammatical focus. The subtropes are necessary because they explain particular forms of language used by Virgil. For example, the subdivisions of *hyperbaton* (the transposition of word order for expressive purposes) feature *tmesis* and *synchesis*. *Tmesis* is the insertion of a word into another word: *'septem subiecta trioni' pro septemtrioni.' Septemtrioni* has *subiecta* inserted between its syllables. Similar to *tmesis* is *synchesis* or the total jumbling of word order in an expression. Both *tmesis* and *synchesis* are necessary in poetry because they facilitate the poet's composition of particular rhythms and meters. Each device is found in Virgil. Thus, the subdivision of *hyperbaton* becomes necessary for the analysis of one of the classics of Latin literature. The additional subtropes are motivated by the need to analyze texts. Though the devices are oral, the emphasis is textual—literal.

Donatus' examples come from Roman literature, and his section on tropes is comprised of examples from Virgil exclusively. Another indication of his literary focus is that Donatus' account of tropes is less systematic than other literary devices such as, *barbarisms, solecisms, metaplasms,* and schemes. While the earlier devices generally adhered to the four operations and basic linguistic units, the tropes appear as ornamental options (a necessary evil). Donatus only included them in his system because they were used by Virgil. The addition of the subtropes of *hyperbaton,* however, displays the grammarian's linguistic focus on tropes. Each of the subtropes represents a specific violation of ordinary grammar and thus, this focus transcends the interests of the orator. The particular devices—described more as violations than options—are overwhelmingly oral. One must only listen to contemporary conversation to recognize its variations. Such grammatically correct expressions as "attorneys general" are almost always uttered "attorney generals." *Parenthesis* is the normal mode rather than the exceptional form of conversation. *Tmesis* is heard frequently when expressions are punctuated by the insertion of one of the more objectionable Anglo-Saxon obscenities. *Synchesis* is yet another frequently heard type of utterance that is filtered out in written expression. Donatus' textual orientation is anomalous when it is necessary to explain the oral composition of Virgil. Thus, Donatus had to describe the phenomena by means of oral devices outside his system. Interestingly, the figures are not included in the other landmark work of Latin grammar—Priscian's *Institutiones grammaticae.*[37] With these mostly oral options excluded, Priscian comes close to formulating a pure grammar.

Priscian's work spans some eighteen books in tedious detail. Similar to Donatus' treatise, Priscian's account begins with a consideration of the basic units of language: sounds, letters (1), syllables, words, nouns, verbs, phrases (2). He then progressively moves to the more complex concepts of language: comparatives, superlatives (3), denominatives (4), gender, number, form, and case (5). These units all come together in his account of the declensions—which are explained in laborious detail (6–7). Likewise, Priscian's consideration of the verb begins with basic notions of genus, tense, mood, form, conjugations, person, and number (8). These classifications come together in a detailed discussion of conjugations (9–10). In a similarly detailed and systematic fashion, *Institutiones grammaticae* closes with accounts of participles (11), pronouns (12–13), prepositions (14), adverbs, interjections (15), conjunctions (16), and constructions (17–18).

Though the figures are excluded, Priscian does incorporate a doctrine important to rhetorical theory into his grammatical corpus. His *praeexercitamina*[38] are a Latin version of the *progymnasmata,* a system of compositional exercises developed by Theon, Hermogenes, and Apthonius. Priscian's *praeexercitamina* differ from *progymnasmata* in vocabulary only—even having the same set of exercises. Clark argues that the *praeexercitamina* were important aids for the composition of literature during the English Middle Ages.[39] Englehardt has argued that the *progymnasmata* may have provided the structure for *Beowulf.*[40] Though Priscian expanded, fine-tuned, and further systematized grammar, his inclusion of *praeexercitamina* showed a generative, compositional turn for grammar. The exercises gave grammar a nudge back toward the oral and away from the literal.

Progymnasmata or *praeexercitamina* featured twelve exercises which students used to compose and practice speeches for each of the three rhetorical genres: epideictic, deliberative, and forensic. The scheme included exercises in fables, tales, *chreia,* proverbs, theses, confirmation, refutation, commonplaces, encomium, impersonation, comparison, and description.[41] The exercises on fables and tales involved the students retelling classic fables (those of *Aesop,* for example) or retelling a standard type of story through a different form—tragic, mythical, fictional, historical. As Clark wrote, "they were imitative exercises in paraphrase."[42] Exercises on *Chreia* and proverbs involved the amplification of a theme expressed in a proverb or striking saying. Refutation and confirmation were exercises in argumentation. The exercise in commonplaces allowed students to practice generating angles from which they could confirm or disconfirm a particular proposition. Encomium, similar to commonplace, allowed the student to generate various topics from which to speak in praise or blame. Impersonation (*prosopopoeia*) was an exercise in which students composed discourse in order to reflect the character of another person. Comparison was another form of amplification that generated various points of comparison that could be used in an argument. Description was an exercise by which students practiced developing graphic, detailed descriptions. And, thesis—one of the more advanced of the exercises—required students to prepare a complete composition on a particular subject. Even more advanced were exercises in which students composed forensic and deliberative speeches.[43]

The *progymnasmata* or *praeexercitamina* were compositional exercises that facilitated a student's understanding of the various means, angles, and types of writing and speaking. The student trained successfully in the *progymnasmata* or *praeexercitamina* had a compositional repertoire that allowed for a variety of circumstances. Like the figures, the *progymnasmata* or *praeexercitamina* were important aspects of both grammar and rhetoric.

Early rhetorical and grammatical systems moved steadily from the oral toward the literate, though in different ways. Grammar made language literal in a microscopic fashion by classifying, dividing, and analyzing it, and ultimately viewing it as text. Rhetoric was still used primarily to produce oral utterances, but its development was similar to grammar in that it objectified and classified the elements involved in producing speech. Grammar turned inward focusing on the text as an exemplar of its rules. Though always complicated by situation, rhetoric underwent a similar turn when it became rule-bound. Both grammar and rhetoric would require considerable innovation when faced with a world of language different from the one in which they were developed.

Robert Kaster has written that by late antiquity grammar and rhetoric had been separated into two related, but distinctly different, operations in the educational system. Grammar focused on the understanding and correct usage of language, while rhetoric focused on the strategic use of language to persuade. As a result, figures and the *progymnasmata* occupied an ambiguous role in both arts. In Kaster's words, "*Figurae* occupied a no-man's-land between the schools of the *grammaticus* and the *rhetor.*" Thus, when the figures came to be used in commentaries on Latin literature, they performed a dual role:

> The ambiguous place of *figura* in the structure of formal education conditions the ambiguous functions of *figurae* in the commentary, where they commonly mark the boundary between two opposing ideas (e.g., exegesis vs. prescription, the ancient vs. "us," the language of Vergil vs. correct language) but at the same time leave it porous or

> vague. So, for example, in the economy of Servius's commentary, *figurae* mediate between the two main purposes, exegesis and prescription: *figurae* make intelligible what the author is saying (and often defend his way of saying it) while segregating the author's usage from the grammarian's central lesson of correct speech.[44]

Thus, Servius' commentary (ca. 400) on Virgil is often torn between its role of teaching proper language use and its role in understanding and appreciating Virgil. This tension is alleviated by identifying certain uses of language as archaic:

> The basic relationship between the function of *figurae* and the function of archaism in the commentary can be stated fairly simply: as the demarcation of *figurae* is an attempt to deal with deviant usage synchronically, by applying the standards of correct usage to the author as though he were a contemporary, so the identification of archaism is an attempt to isolate such deviations diachronically, by constructing a temporal barrier between the author and student.[45]

Just as Donatus resolved Virgil's artistic use of language by identifying grammatically unaccountable variations as tropes and subtropes, so too did Servius account for inexplicable variation of language by identifying it as archaic. The necessity of having to identify archaisms demonstrates something of an intellectual shift in grammar that restricted it to look toward the past and eventually toward texts. Political changes and the gradual disappearance of the Roman Empire required that rhetoric adapt its rules toward different kinds of discourse. Likewise, grammar, having turned as inward as it could, needed to move outward—toward the rhetorical.

Chapter Two

Grammar and Rhetoric
Absorption and Inversion

By the time rhetoric and grammar had achieved statuses as separate but interdependent entities, the societal contexts in which they were developed had changed. The eventual transition of the Roman Empire into multiple kingdoms of Europe brought about changes in the way both rhetoric and grammar functioned in society. While rhetoric had been an open system concerned with adapting discourse to situations, the situations around which it had been developed had disappeared. The venues for deliberative and forensic discourse—on which so much of the Greek and Roman rhetoric had been based—were seldom available in the decaying Roman Empire. Rhetoric thus turned inward and was discussed as a theoretical, but not a practical, enterprise. Grammar, which had focused on the use of correct language and the interpretation of literature, moved outward and sought a means of generating and composing discourse. Each art diverged from its previous role and appropriated doctrine from its counterpart. Rita Copeland argues that, eventually, grammar and rhetoric fused in the western Middle Ages to form an art of textual hermeneutics.[1] Beyond the hermeneutical function, they fused to form an art of composition in *ars poetriae.* In order to see this evolution it is helpful first to discuss rhetorical and grammatical developments in late antiquity.

Rhetorics of late antiquity focused increasingly on invention[2] and became more technical. This technical move was somewhat introspective in that the increasingly abstract analysis of rhetoric was less oriented toward the composition of discourse. The extant treatises from the fourth century, Leff writes, feature invention almost exclusively. Julius Victor's *Ars rhetorica* spends eighteen of its twenty-seven chapters on an analysis of invention (mainly on *stasis*), whereas style receives only three chapters, and the remaining canons (and a chapter on letter writing) receive only one chapter each.[3] Fortunatianus' *Ars rhetorica* treats invention (again with an emphasis on *stasis*) in the first two of its three books, while the third book features the remaining canons. The pseudo-Augustinian *De rhetorica* examines civil questions and *stasis*, and Sulpitius Victor's *Institutiones oratoriae* spends 90 percent of its text on *stasis* and issue analysis.[4] Leff concludes that fourth-century treatises carry increased emphasis on forensic analyses and therefore the system of *stasis*. Their focus, he writes, reflects an "overwhelming concern for invention. Style still maintains a position of relative importance in the handbooks, but memory and delivery receive only perfunctory notice."[5]

The focus on invention may also be seen in the encyclopedic tradition of the early Middle Ages. Martianus Capella (fl. 410–27) devoted twice as much information in the rhetorical section of his *De nuptiis Philologiae et Mercurii* to invention as he did to style[6] and included a lengthy exposition on Cicero's theory of *stasis*.[7] Cassiodorus Senator (480–575) offered a "meager summary" of rhetorical doctrine[8] in his *Institutiones divinarum et saeculorium litterarum* that focused on *stasis* and rhetorical arguments.[9] Isidore of Seville's (ca. 570–636) *Origines* or *Etymologia* are based on Cassiodorus and again emphasized *stasis*—with the addition of an account of style drawn from *Rhetorica ad Herennium* and Donatus' *Ars grammatica*.[10] Boethius' (ca. 480–524) *De topicis differentiis* likewise emphasized *stasis* and, to a lesser degree, arrangement. Boethius' intention was to offer a close analysis of the topics and therefore his work features no consideration of style, memory, or delivery.[11] This detailed focus on the topical and *stasis* systems moves rhetoric toward the analytical, the textual, and the grammatical. It is an introspective turn that ignores both application and context.

Meanwhile, commentaries on poetry began to look toward rhetorical doctrine as a means of interpretation and explication. Paul Prill has written: "Those who stood on the cusp between the classical and medieval periods likewise understood that poetry was best understood from the precepts of rhetoric rather than those of grammar."[12] Prill cites three commentaries by Tiberius Claudius Donatus, Macrobius, and Fabius Planciades Fulgentius that all interpret Virgil as exemplifying the precepts of rhetoric. Moreover, asserts Prill, Fulgentius saw the *Aeneid* as a model of demonstrative rhetoric which sought to teach moral behavior to an audience by example.[13] A Carolingian commentor on Horace's *Ars poetica* analyzes the treatise rhetorically, using notions on invention, arrangement, and style gleaned from Fortunatianus, Sulpitius Victor, Martianus Capella, Donatus, and Macrobius.[14] Equally attractive to the poets of late antiquity were the *progymnasmata* or *praeexercitamina.*[15] Prill provides several examples of how the *progymnasmata* were used in Carolingian poetry.[16]

As the two arts shifted in focus and application, rhetoric became used as a means of interpreting texts and, conversely, grammar became used as a means of textual generation. Copeland compares the application of each art, showing the utility of rhetoric as an interpretive tool:

> Grammar positions the reader (student) in a pre-critical surrender to the text; rhetoric gives the reader the preceptive and critical tools with which to understand the terms of such surrender and hence to master them. Rhetoric, as an exercise in practical wisdom, also supplies a model of hermeneutics: the reader is engaged in a dialectical relationship with the text, as interpretation is fused with application.[17]

Ultimately, as grammar and rhetoric merged, invention became a hermeneutical tool,[18] divorced (as was rhetoric) from performance. Accordingly, Copeland writes: "This dissociation between invention and other parts of rhetoric . . . seems to have led to a kind of grammatization of *elocutio,* along with *dispositio, memoria,* and *pronunciatio.*" The result was that rhetoric was applied to problems of textual analysis—previously the province of the grammarian and the parts of rhetoric "atrophied in terms of their original rhetorical purpose and have very much taken on the pedagogical function of *progymnasmata.*"[19] The classical canons of rhetoric, applied to written discourse, became a means of grammatical analysis; however, Copeland argues that rhetoric also became imbued with a new system of invention. The rhetorical commentator "uses the plot, matter, and stylistic procedure of the text in the way that an orator uses rhetorical topics like the attributes of the person and the act, that is, to supply information out of which the exegetical narrative is constructed." Rhetoric, then, became involved in the grammarian's textual analysis, leaving "the practical problems of negotiating linguistic usage to the grammarians."[20] Rhetoric and grammar have, in effect, exchanged roles: "The rules by which orators compose have here become the rules by which grammarians-exegetes read."[21] Ultimately, asserts Copeland: "The generative force of rhetoric finds itself here in the interpretive direction of the grammarian-exegete: here rhetoric becomes a discursively productive 'grammar' of reading."[22] Eventually, however, rhetorical doctrine returns to its outward orientation, focusing once again on its cultural context.

By the tenth and eleventh centuries, medieval authors had begun to use classical rhetorical doctrine in their own creative ways. In his *Nova rhetorica*, the tenth-century author, Notker, adapted the inventional categories into monastic activities.[23] Notker viewed rhetorical doctrine as both a source of material and a source of artistic development. Moreover, he expanded rhetorical invention to include all controversial material.[24] Beth Bennett summarizes Notker's impact as follows: "Truly representative of medieval rhetoric, Notker's *Rhetorica* was neither strictly traditional, nor completely adaptive, but rather a consciously designed balance between tradition and adaptation in response to the needs of its age."[25] The rhetorical impulse was outward, dictated by situational concerns.

A similar development took place in the *Rhetorimachia* by Anselm de Besate, written in the eleventh century. Bennett writes that the *Rhetorimachia* was not so much a presentation of rhetorical doctrine as it was a forensic case—a *controversia* similar to those composed in the declamatory movement of late antiquity. While defending himself from legal charges leveled by his cousin Rotiland, Anselm uses the six-part-Ciceronian structure in his argument and generates his material by means of *stasis*. Moreover, he provides his own marginalia to demonstrate how rhetorical precepts can be used to produce discourse.[26] Bennett has also argued that *Rhetorimachia* and its predecessor, Martianus Capella's *De nuptiis Philologiae et Mercurii*, follow in the classical tradition of Menippean satire (a discursive genre that employs humor and fantasy to present the political, moral, or pedagogical views of its author).[27] Thus, we see rhetoric take an outward turn. There is no longer analysis for the sake of analysis. Analysis, then, becomes used more as a means of demonstrating the precepts of rhetoric for situational purposes than as a means of inventing new discourses. The author is displaying his knowledge about rhetorical theory to an audience of theorists. The generative utilization of rhetorical and grammatical doctrine will become evident in the *artes poetriae*.

Nearly contemporaneous with that development, however, were two other late-medieval genres, *ars praedicandi* and *ars dictaminis*. Each genre addressed a specific concern of the era. *Ars praedicandi* answered the need for a method of composing sermons. *Ars dictaminis* answered a need for precepts on letter writing. Both genres were concerned with literacy, though from different angles. *Ars praedicandi* focused on the analysis and interpretation of texts for the purpose of producing oral discourses (sermons); while *ars dictaminis* focused on the production of texts (letters). Each genre achieved its end through the considerable appropriation of rhetorical theory.

Ars praedicandi

Given the overwhelming impact of Christianity on medieval civilization, one would expect preaching (sermonizing) to have been the first of the medieval genres to have developed, but such was not the case. In fact, rhetoric's close association with pagan cultures and the age-old charges of sophistry probably retarded the development of Christian rhetoric. Rhetorical scholars cite only five treatises on preaching written in the period spanning 400 to 1200 that show a connection to traditional rhetoric: Augustine's *De doctrina Christiana* (426), Gregory the Great's *Cura pastoralis* (591), Rabanus Maurus' *De institutione clericorum* (819), Guibert of Nogent's *Liber de ordine sermo fieri debeat* (1084), and Alain de Lille's *De arte praedicandi* (1199).[28] None of the works is exceptionally rhetorical, but each treatise offers elements that were later included in most *artes praedicandi.* However, the most significant of these works, in regard to *ars poetriae,* are the works of Augustine and Guibert because both treatises feature methods of interpreting texts.

Augustine, educated in Roman rhetorical theory, trained as an orator, and employed as a teacher of rhetoric in Carthage, Rome, and Milan, was an ideal conduit for the transmission of classical rhetorical theory. His subsequent conversion to Christianity, however, transformed a perfect Roman rhetor into a Christian theologian. His theology, moreover, was based on a means of scriptural interpretation that made the Christian rhetor more a transmitter of scriptural truth than a creator of new knowledge.

Augustine's *De doctrina Christiana* manifests both the grammatical and rhetorical dimensions, as the first three books focus on the discovery of what is to be understood from scripture, the fourth and final book focuses on the instruction and transmission of what has been discovered.

Augustine notes that understanding the scriptures is problematic because of the cultural and linguistic ambiguities of language; moreover, language may be literal or figurative (2.9–3.10). Thus, the Christian rhetor is in need of a method for discovering the truth in scripture by distinguishing literal utterances from figurative ones. The method is relatively simple, for the Ten Commandments may be condensed into two basic rules: to love God and to love one's neighbors.[29] Therefore, scriptural utterances that do not endorse virtuous behavior and the truth of faith must be taken as figurative. Virtuous behavior, of course, pertains to the "love of God and one's neighbor; the truth of faith pertains to a knowledge of God and one's neighbor" (3.20.14). Virtuous and nonvirtuous behavior are determined according to the notions of charity and cupidity. Charity is defined as "the motion of the soul toward the enjoyment of God for His own sake, and the enjoyment of one's self and one's neighbor for the sake of God; but 'cupidity' is a motion of the soul toward the enjoyment of one's self, one's neighbor, or any corporeal thing for the sake of something other than God" (3.10.16). The scriptures recommend nothing but charity; therefore, passages that endorse charity are to be taken literally. Those passages, however, which seem to endorse cupidity, are figurative and must be examined closely in order to determine their true meaning. Figurative obfuscation needs to be stripped away from truth "as kernals from the husk" (3.12.18). A knowledge of the rhetorical figures, therefore, may be helpful, though not necessary to a literal interpretation of scripture (3.29). The connection of Augustine's system of scriptural interpretation to classical rhetoric is in regard to the figures. In this case Augustine's figures are tools of analysis or invention, not composition and transmission. They perform the role of figures found in Donatus' *Ars grammatica.* Copeland sees the figurative role as an early example of rhetoric in its hermeneutical mode.[30]

Augustine makes yet another move when it comes to the transmission of scriptural doctrine. That function is equally dependent on the figures, but this time in their generative, rhetorical mode. Augustine makes it quite clear, however, that book 4 will not be an account of traditional rhetoric, though he sees nothing inherently wrong with the doctrine (4.1.2).[31] The rules of eloquence, he notes, are not necessarily productive of eloquence and that eloquence itself may be produced independently of those rules; moreover, wisdom and eloquence do not necessarily go hand in hand. In support, Augustine quotes Cicero's *De inventione:* "Wisdom without eloquence is of small benefit to states; but eloquence without wisdom is often extremely injurious and profits no one" (4.5.7).[32] It is Cicero's view of eloquence that Augustine adopts for the Christian rhetor, but not the rule driven rhetoric of *De inventione* written in Cicero's youth; rather, the perspective Augustine adopts is that written by the mature Cicero in *Orator:*

> Therefore a certain eloquent man said, and said truly, that he who is eloquent should speak in such a way that he teaches, delights, and moves. Then he added, "To teach is a necessity, to please is a sweetness, to persuade is a victory." Of the three, that which is given first place, that is the necessity of teaching, resides in the things which we have to say, the other two in the manner in which we say it. (4.12.27)[33]

Although Augustine stresses teaching more than Cicero, he follows Cicero's analysis in *Orator:* "He is therefore eloquent who in order to teach, can speak of small things in a subdued manner, and in order to please, can speak of moderate things in a temperate manner, and in order to persuade, can speak of great things in a grand manner" (4.17.34).[34] The manner in which to accomplish these three duties is by the use of the three levels of style found in classical rhetoric since the time of *auctor ad Herennium:* plain, middle, and grand (4.22). The means of executing the various styles, of course, are the rhetorical figures.

Ĉelica Milovanović-Barham has demonstrated convincingly, however, that Augustine's use of the styles and the figures differs markedly from Cicero's. She asserts that Augustine's view of the styles reflects more the theoretical developments of the Second Sophistic and the practice of the fourth-century church fathers. More particularly, she observes, Augustine cannot restrict each duty of the orator exclusively to a mode of style. Indeed, the Christian rhetor is always charged with moving the audience spiritually and intellectually. The means to that end are balanced *kommata,* periods and clauses. By analyzing Augustine's own style and the examples he uses in book 4, Milovanović-Barham shows that Augustine's concept of style is focused much more toward the experiential and oral dimension of language.[35] In essence, then, Augustine uses the *exornationes verborum,* particularly the rhythmic devices, as a means of rhetorical expression and he uses the *exornationes sententiarum* and tropes as a means of grammatical exegesis. Milovanović-Barham regards the emphasis on the *exornationes verborum* as sophistic.

Baldwin, however, wrote that *De doctrina Christiana* marks a "clean break" from the sophistic rhetorical tradition of late antiquity and "begins rhetoric anew."[36] Ultimately, Augustine did begin a new rhetoric by rejecting the great bulk of traditional rhetorical lore and considering how it could be employed in the transmission of Christian doctrine. Murphy argued that the doctrine embodied in *De doctrina Christiana* placed a new focus on rhetoric and education: "It states flatly that rhetors do not persuade, but that hearers move themselves; that teachers do not teach, but instead that learners learn. Ultimately, this is a denial of the preceptive theories of Roman education."[37] Equally important, however, is Augustine's emphasis on style. As Kennedy observed, in *De doctrina Christiana* style is a key element in both scriptural interpretation and exposition.[38] Milovanović-Barham's analysis further underscores Kennedy's interpretation and provides the basis for a refutation of Murphy's analysis. Augustine did not abandon the preceptive tradition; rather, he modified that tradition by utilizing both the grammatical and rhetorical impulses. *De doctrina Christiana* used the same levels of style and figures that were used in both classical rhetorical theory and ancient grammatical theory; their substantive foundation was based on the interpretation of a text and a response to a situation. Both the closed and opened dimensions of rhetoric, grammar, and style were used by Augustine. Thus, the hallmark of the first medieval rhetorical work is its view of rhetoric as a living entity that must be adapted to its purpose and time rather than as a collection of rules that must be memorized and imposed on any rhetorical situation. Such is the eventual legacy of medieval theory—to assimilate the knowledge of the past into the creation of new rhetoric. Significant to the grammatical / rhetorical inversion, Augustine blends the grammatical tendency of textual interpretation and the rhetorical mode of composition and audience adaptation via the figures.

Guibert of Nogent came closer to offering precepts on how the scriptures should be used in preaching in his *Liber quo ordine sermo fieri debeat* (Book on the way a sermon ought to be given). Though of promising title, the work is chiefly a preface to a commentary on the Book of Genesis. Nonetheless, Guibert offers four ways of interpreting scripture that prove to be instrumental to *ars praedicandi:*

> The first is history, which speaks of actual events as they occurred; the second is allegory, in which one thing stands for something else; the third is tropology, or moral instruction, which treats of the ordering and arranging of one's life; and the last is ascetics, or spiritual enlightenment, through which we who are about to treat of lofty and heavenly topics are led to a higher way of life. For example, the word Jerusalem: historically, it represents a specific city; in allegory, it represents the holy Church; tropologically, or morally, it is the soul of every faithful man who longs for the vision of eternal peace; and anagogically it refers to the life of the heavenly citizens, who already see the God of Gods, revealed in all His glory to Sion.[39]

Guibert goes on to endorse the moral approach as the most appropriate in dealing with the lives of men. As limited as it is, Guibert's treatise represents one of the first explanations of how material should be used in a sermon.[40] What is more important are the four levels of scriptural interpretation that display the grammatical/exegetical function and offer methods of probing a text for meaning in the grammatical/inventional form. Guibert's scriptural interpretations do not, however, provide a means of composing a sermon.

More than eight hundred years after Augustine had written the first book of *De doctrina Christiana,* a prescriptive, theoretical treatise on sermonizing had yet to emerge. By the fourteenth century, however, hundreds of preaching manuals had appeared. The thirteenth century was marked by a multiplicity of treatises on *ars praedicandi.* Among them, the earliest is generally thought to be Alexander of Ashby's *De modo praedicandi* (ca. 1200). Other representative early works on sermonizing are Thomas of Salisbury's *Summa de arte praedicandi* (ca. 1210–1215), Richard of Thetford's *Ars diltandi sermones* (ca. 1245), and Jean de la Rochelle's *Ars conficiendi sermones* (ca. pre-1245).[41]

The *artes praedicandi* were generally uniform in content. Camargo offers a concise explanation of their typical content:

> The sermon is divided into four parts . . . ; *Thema*—a passage from the Bible that is the main subject of the sermon; *prothema* (often a sermon in miniature)—a second biblical text, related to the *thema,* but serving mainly as a transition to an invocation of divine aid through prayer; *divisio*—the breakdown of the *thema* into its constituent parts; *distinctio*—subdivisions introduced in the course of developing the *divisiones* of the *thema.* Any given *thema* has several *divisiones,* each of which is taken up in turn with its *distinctiones.* Having described this format, the typical *ars praedicandi* goes on to treat the modes of amplifying the last two parts.[42]

Thus, the sermon was given a format that is relatively unvaried throughout the *artes praedicandi.* The *thema* was the sermon's all important component, the Gospel that served, in essence, as a proverb (*sententia*) on which the whole sermon was based.

More than format was prescribed in the manuals, however; most treatises featured topical modes of expanding or amplifying sermon material. Richard of Thetford, for example, offered eight methods of expanding sermons: using a locution instead of a name; using division; using reasoning; using authorities; using roots of the known; proposing metaphors; exposing the theme in diverse modes; and attributing cause and effect.[43] Also frequently seen are the four levels of scriptural interpretation, which served as ideal vehicles of amplification. The fourteenth-century author, Robert of Basevorn even analyzed the methods of preaching used by St. Bernard, St. Gregory, St. Augustine, St. Paul, and Christ.[44] Yet another frequent feature was the picture tree (*arbor picta*), in which the development of the sermon was charted on a three-branched tree.[45] No longer was sermonic material provided through divine inspiration alone. Formulaic treatises were developed that essentially required the preacher only to have a knowledge of scripture—the preaching manual would provide the rest.

According to Murphy, the *ars praedicandi* provided the preacher with five elements: scripture, examples, concordances and other bibliographic aids, collections of sermons and outlines suitable for all occasions, and the manual itself that contained the prescriptive format.[46] Thus, the *ars praedicandi* represents a complete rhetoric (from the classical perspective) embodying principles of invention, arrangement, style, and delivery. For the most part, however, the appropriation of classical rhetorical doctrine in *ars praedicandi* was largely in the literal/grammatical mode. Augustine used figures grammatically to analyze texts, but he also used them rhetorically to compose. That composition was for transmission of a fixed doctrine, but it was still based on negotiation with an audience.

Ars praedicandi represents a significant intellectual development. Denied the use of extrinsic evidence, the *auctores praedicandi* faced a rhetorical challenge entirely different from conventional Roman oratory and developed methods of intrinsic demonstration and interpretation. These methods coupled with a prescriptive method of presentation formed a unique genre of discourse.

Ars dictaminis

Although letter writing was an implicit part of the classical system of rhetoric, a formal treatment of the subject did not appear until the fourth century in Julius Victor's *Ars rhetorica. Ars rhetorica,* however, does not contain a systematic treatment of the subject.[47] In the sixth century, Cassiodorus Senator published a book of his letters, however his work served more as a model of eloquence than as a preceptive treatise. The first theoretical treatise on letter writing appeared at Monte Cassino in the late-eleventh century.

Alberic of Monte Cassino's *Dictaminum radii* and *Breviarium de dictamine* are generally accepted as embodying the first *ars dictaminis.*[48] *Dictaminum radii* represents a traditional rhetorical approach applied to letter writing. As the title clearly identifies its subject as letter writing, several internal references to writers and readers further indicate the work's scope. The treatise consist of a discussion of the divisions of oration (principally the *exordium*); the vices of diction; the figures of diction; and tropes and figures. Alberic identifies four parts of speech, *exordium, narratio, argumento,* and *conclusio,* but spends a good portion of his time distinguishing between the *exordium* (introduction) and *salutio* (greeting). The *salutio* was not considered part of the letter proper.[49] Murphy regards the distinction between *exordium* and *salutio* as the "hallmark" of the *ars dictaminis.*[50] The *Breviarium de dictamine* adds examples of *formulae* and a discussion of *rithmus* (rhythmic writing). *Rithmus* or *cursus* was to be an important part of later treatises on letter writing.[51]

By the mid-twelfth century, many *artes dictaminis* had been produced in Bologna. Among the eight treaties that survived are works by Hugh of Bologna, Aldabertus Samaritanus, Henricus Francigena, Bernard of Bologna, and several unknown authors. The Bolognese writers crystalized the standard pattern of *ars dictaminis.* The typical format for a letter included five parts: *salutatio* (the greeting); *capitatio benevolentiae* (the introduction, also called *exordium* or *proverb*); *narratio* (the narration); *petitio* (the request); and *conclusio* (the conclusion). The theoretical section of the treatise was known as the *ars* and the section containing the form letters was known as the *dictamina*—together, they formed a *summa dictaminis.*[52]

A good example of *ars dictaminis* is the anonymous *Rationes dictandi,* written in Bologna in 1135.[53] The author defines a letter as "a suitable arrangement of words set forth to express the intended meaning of its sender. Or in other words, a letter is a discourse composed of coherent yet distinct parts signifying fully the sentiments of its sender."[54] The author then proceeds to describe the parts of a letter.

The *salutatio* greets the receiver of the letter in a fashion consistent with the social standing of both sender and receiver. Normally, the name of the recipient is written before the name of the sender. When a superior writes to a subordinate, the sender's name is written first to indicate rank. The *capitatio benevolentiae* is designed to produce goodwill on the part of the letter's recipient. Accordingly, the writer of the letter might praise the recipient or humbly mention their own accomplishments. The *narratio* is simply the orderly account of the matter being discussed in the letter. The *petitio* is the point in the letter at which the writer calls for a particular action to be taken. Finally, the *conclusio* is used to indicate the usefulness or disadvantage of the subject discussed in the letter. Then, the letter is terminated in a way that avoids mentioning the subject of the letter.[55]

Most parts of the letter, such as the *capitatio benevolentiae, narratio,* and *petitio,* may be interchanged to better suit the purposes of the writer; however, the *salutatio* and *conclusio* should retain their assigned places. The author then provides a number of examples showing how these changes may be accomplished. The final sections of the treatise are devoted to discussions on grammatical construction and the various parts of speech.[56]

Ars dictaminis was also treated by scholars in France, England, and Germany. The French–English component of *ars dictaminis* shares some of the same authors belonging to the *ars poetriae*—both John of Garland and Gervasius of Melkley deal with letter writing in their *poetriae,* and Geoffrey of Vinsauf is said to have authored, a now lost, *dictamen.* The *ars dictaminis* eventually reached its peak with the second wave of Italian authors in the late-thirteenth century: Boncompagno, Bene of Florence, and Guido Faba. After that time, the *ars dictaminis* continued to exist only as collections of models.

The *ars dictaminis,* like the *ars praedicandi,* developed from a practical need. Changes in the evolving political division of Europe made letter writing an essential tool of politics and diplomacy. Murphy regards *ars dictaminis* as "an attempt to apply Ciceronian rhetoric to a specific compositional problem—that of writing letters."[57] Over the course of its development, *ars dictaminis* seems to have embraced the structural component of classical rhetoric, but ultimately, it discarded the other rhetorical trappings. As Murphy wrote, "the art always faced the inherent dilemma of formalism versus invention."[58] In the end, formalism prevailed.

The evolution of *artes praedicandi et dictaminis* from classical rhetorical doctrine shows a strong reliance on *dispositio* (arrangement). These arts are somewhat narrow genres in that the nature of their enterprises often places much more emphasis on form than substance—the substance being predetermined. *Ars praedicandi* offers a little more creativity in its levels of interpretation, but those levels led toward a predetermined end. Where the *auctores praedicandi et dictaminis* nearly ignore invention, *ars poetriae* champions and expands it. To better see that expansion, it is first necessary to consider later developments in grammar—developments that Murphy categorized as preceptive.[59]

Preceptive Grammars

Donatus and Priscian were generally viewed as the authorities on medieval grammar until two new works (*Doctrinale* by Alexander of Villedieu and *Graecismus* by Evrard of Bethune) appeared in the twelfth and thirteenth centuries. Alexander and Evrard take a more compositional focus on grammar than Donatus or Priscian. Moreover, Alexander and Evrard cast their works, particularly the accounts of the figures, in the form of a rhetorical demonstration of the precepts they teach. Significantly, Evrard begins rather than closes his grammar with an account of the figures.

The *Doctrinale*[60] is written in some 2,650 hexameters of verse and, over the course of twelve chapters, covers: the parts of speech, syntax, etymology, accent, meter, and figures of speech.[61] Alexander's work was popular; it was printed in over 260 editions between 1470 and 1530[62] and was used in European universities as late as the seventeenth century.[63] Abelson attributed the work's attraction to four factors: it was written in verse; it recognized the changes the Latin language had experienced since the time Priscian's grammar had been written; it recognized that Priscian's system of syntax was no longer applicable to the twelfth century; and it included improvements and additions to previous accounts of prosody and figures.[64]

The utility of its format in verse is demonstrated in this sample of Alexander's treatment of first declension nouns, provided by Orme:

> The nominative ends in as, es, a,
> but certain Hebrew proper nouns in am.
> The genitive and dative end in ae,
> The accusative in am, but en or an
> For nominative es or as, and an
> For Greek nouns with a nominative a.
> The vocative is a, but es makes e;
> The ablatives are also a and e;
> But nominative am remains the same
> In both the vocative and ablative.[65]

Thus, Orme notes, Alexander has offered the singular form of every Latin noun of the first declension, as well as Greek and Hebrew derivatives. The hexameter form rendered the text chantable and therefore memorable.[66] The text is terse and in many cases the descriptions are so brief as to be enthymematic; the reader is forced to provide a grammatical context to comprehend the text.

Alexander generally followed Donatus' account of the figures, discussing schemes, tropes, *metaplasms, solecisms,* and *barbarisms.* Alexander's treatment, however, included fewer schemes (dropping *anadiplosis, epanalepsis, polyptoton, polysyndeton,* and *asyndeton*) and eliminated all but *antiphrasis* from Donatus' subtropes. *Acyrologia, pleonasmos,* and *eclipsis* were dropped from the *barbarisms* and *solecisms;* he also dropped *episynaliphe* from the *metaplasms* and added *antithesis, cynaresis, metathesis,* and *synthesis.* In addition, Alexander discussed some twenty-four miscellaneous devices at the end of the text: *protheseos paralange, liptota, topographia, chronographia, hypallagia, prosopopoeia, apastrophe, conversio, ebasim, emphasis, efflexigesis, euphonia, anitosis, antitheton, anthypophorum, anticlasis, aposiopesis, euphemismus, synepthesis, oliopomenon, homophesis, epimonen, anthropospathos,* and *homopathios* (2573–2639).

Many of *Doctrinale's* devices are familiar figures that were discarded by Donatus as inappropriate to grammar: *liptota* (litotes), *prosopopoeia, apastrophe* (apostrophe), *conversio, emphasis, antitheton,* and *aposiopesis.* Other devices are not as familiar, and the definitions of many of them are vague because of the terseness of the text. The figures are diverse, covering emphasis, variation, description, and strategies. Their presentation hardly reflects the systemization of Donatus. Indeed, the free-flowing presentation of the *Doctrinale* resembles *Rhetorica ad Herennium* more than Donatus. For example, *protheseos paralange* (the practice of substituting one preposition for another; 2573–74) is followed by *litotes* (the practice of using fewer words to say more), and then by *topographia* and *chronographia* (descriptions of place and time; 2577–78). *Epimonen* (the repeated emphasis of a phrase or points; 2630–33) is followed by *anthropospathos* (the assignment of human traits to a deity; 2634–35). And finally, *anthropospathos* is then followed by *homopathios* (the use of an expression having both literal and figurative meaning; 2639).

Alexander edited and redistributed some of Donatus' figures and added others to them—apparently from Greek sources. He expanded the scope of the grammatical figures beyond their status as permutations and variations from the foundations of grammar. His account included descriptive devices such as, *topographia* and *chronographia,* as well as strategic devices—including some of the rhetorical figures discarded by Donatus. The brief, enthymematic form of the *Doctrinale* suggests it is almost a gloss of more particular and detailed grammars. Its verse format, furthermore, allowed it to serve as a mnemonic device, helpful in remembering the basic rules of grammar that were treated in detail elsewhere.

Also noteworthy is the *Doctrinale*'s pedagogy. Dietrich Reichling cites a gloss of the work that notes that "grammar is triplex, that is, preceptive, permissive, and prohibitive."[67] Thus, the function of these grammars was to offer rules and to allow for their strategic violation, within limits. The threefold function is developed further in *ars poetriae,* particularly Eberhard the German's *Laborintus.*

Doctrinale moves away from the grammatical and toward classical notions of rhetoric. It is expressive rather than analytical. The early grammars of Donatus and Priscian were closed systems of analysis, *Doctrinale* was more of an open system. Finally, Alexander's work was oriented toward the composition of discourse and as such its metrical format demonstrated many of the very principles it elucidated. This function can be seen more readily in Evrard of Bethune's *Graecismus.*

The Graecismus[68] was written circa 1212 and is said to have approached the *Doctrinale* in popularity.[69] The work postdates the earliest of the *artes poetriae,* Matthew of Vendôme's *Ars versificatoria,* and is roughly contemporary with Geoffrey of Vinsauf's *Poetria nova.* The foundation of the work differs from Donatus', Priscian's, and Alexander's works in that *Graecismus* opens with a consideration of the figures. The first three of the *Graecismus*' twenty-seven chapters feature *metaplasms,* schemes, *barbarisms, solecisms,* and the colors of rhetoric. Chapter 4 then moves to the metrical feet: *spondee, trochee, iamb, dactyl, anapest,* etc. Chapter 5 discusses the various letters in the alphabet; while chapter 6 features the monosyllabic nouns. The muses and their clans are discussed in chapter 7, and chapters 8 through 12 discuss the various nouns. Chapters 13 and 14 cover adjectives and pronouns, and chapters 15 through 19 go over the various forms of verbs. Adverbs and participles are featured in chapters 20 and 21. Conjunctions, prepositions, and interjections appear in chapters 22 through 24; while chapter 25 discusses the species of nouns and chapter 26 the accidents of verbs. Finally, chapter 27 discusses diasyntastics, the phenomenon surrounding words that represent multiple parts of speech. As one may see, Evrard's progression is nearly the reverse of Donatus' treatment of grammar.

Evrard's account of the figures is designed to add order and consistency to the burgeoning doctrine of grammatical figures. He tries to classify the various devices in groups according to their function and attempts to indicate a number of equivalents. He discusses *metaplasms* first, then schemes, tropes, *barbarisms, and solecisms,* and finally, Evrard discusses a new category, *colores rhetorici.*[70]

Evrard's account of the *metaplasms* includes thirteen of Donatus' original fourteen *metaplasms;* however, Evrard drops *episynaliphe* in his treatment (as Alexander did) and includes Alexander's additions to the *metaplasms*: *antithesis, metathesis, synthesis,* and *cynaresis.* Evrard also names sixteen other *metaplasms*: *anastrophe* and *aposiopesis* from *Rhetorica ad Herennium; pleonasmos* from Donatus' *barbarisms and solecisms; temesim* (*tmesis*) from Donatus' subtropes; and five of Alexander's miscellaneous devices: *protheseos paralange, epibasim, epimone, hypallage,* and *antitosis.* Finally, he includes six figures not previously discussed: *diastole, elipsis, hysteron proteron, metabolen, epizeuxis,* and *exallage.*

His explanation of the various figures is developed from the basis of oppositions, contraries, and similarities. Like Alexander's, Evrard's definitions are terse, providing little context or explanation. For example, the opening lines in the section on *metaplasms* read as follows:

> *Prothesis* places at the beginning and *auferesis* takes away. *Syncopa* takes from the middle what *epenthesis* adds. *Apocope* takes from the ending what *paragoge* gives. *Sytole* produces brevity, *diastole* length: what nature commands brought out *systole* shortens, *Extasis,* on the contrary, brings out what is taken away. *Elipsis* destroys m, *synalimpha* destroys a vocalization. (1.7–13)

This passage discusses briefly the relationship between *prothesis, auferesis, syncopa,* and *paragoge.* Through the comparison between *diastole* and *sytole,* the meaning of *diastole* becomes apparent. Likewise, *extasis* adds to a word, while *elipsis* and *synalimpha* remove letters and vocal distinctions from words.

Evrard explains *hysteron proteron* as the placing of the end of a thought or expression before its beginning; he compares it to placing nursing before birth (1.26). *Metabolen* and *epizeuxis* are then discussed together with *epimone*—all three of which are repetitive devices. *Metabolen* is a type of varied repetition, *epizeuxis* is repetition of one word, and *epimone* is the repetition of a phrase or assertion (1.31–38).

His account of schemes includes the five schemes dropped by Alexander and adds others taken from Alexander's miscellaneous category; Evrard's list includes the following: *liptotes, chronographia, topographia,* apostrophe, *anthypophorum, antithesis,* and *efflexigesis.* In addition, he appends *dialyton, parenthesis, hendiadys, prophonesis, etymologia, synacrysmos, dyasmos, cosmographia, catatyposis, characterismos, idiopasis, allopasis, epilogus, epitrochasmos, brachylogia, teretema,* and *tropologia* to his treatment. He also includes the traditional scheme, *gradatio,* and the trope *periphrasis.*

Evrard refers to the *ornatus verborum* as "scema" because "it removes the tediousness associated with the various devices forming grace and expression" (1.43–45). His method of disposition is the same: he groups the devices according to functional relationships and includes a definition of *asyntheton* that is also an example of the device:

> You may say what follows makes *asyntheton* . . . and *dialyton* is a similar figure. *Polysyntheton* is the opposite. . . . And *zeuma* is itself with *polysyntheton* one figure. *Anadiplosis* stands with its ending as beginning. Beginning and ending are the same word in *anapolensis.* . . . If reckoning intercedes, *parenthesis* results. *Hendiadys* is made loose in a moveable place. . . . If you say less and more is signified, *liptotes* is produced. And when you cry out to God, *prophonesis* is made. . . . Restore the cause of a thing, thus *etymologia* is made. An expression that brings together praise and blame at one and the same time, thus *synacrismos* is made. (1.46–64)

These figures, Evrard notes, are under the same jurisdiction in that they render expressions in a more graceful form. As such they could be seen as examples of the rhetorical color, *correctio.*

Antithesis (*antitheto*) and *syndyasmos* are equated as the same figure and are written through the use of a *tmesis:* "Uteris *antitheto* dicens contraria dicto, *syn*que *dyasmos* erit similisque figura" (1.68–69). The conjunction, *que,* is inserted into the word *syndyasmos.*

Cosmographia, a description of the world, is added and grouped with Alexander's schemes *chronographia* and *topographia* (1.72–73). *Catatyposis* is a device by which a person is indicated under the name of their father or mother. *Characterismos* is a similar figure (1.74–78).

Idiopasis and *allopasis* deal with references to self and another. *Idiopasis* is used to refer to one or the other, whereas *allopasis* refers to both (1.80–81).

Evrard regards *epilogus* and *epitrochasmos* as identical figures, in that they are both used to summarize many previous expressions (1.82–83). When one is questioned many times it is an example of *teretema* (1.86). *Tropologia* and apostrophe are departures from direct discourse (1.90–91).

Evrard's tropes include the traditional ones found in *Rhetorica ad Herennium*, except *periphrasis*, and append the subtropes *antiphrasim*, *paradigma*, and *parabole*. In addition, he adds the subtropes *prosopopoeia*, *ethopoeia*, *antitheson*, *emphatice*, *phantasiam*, *somatopoeia*, *evocitatio*, and *conceptio*.

Prosopopoeia and *ethopoeia*, generally not included as tropes, much less figures, are discussed together. *Prosopopoeia* is a device by which inanimate objects are given voice. Similarly, *ethopoeia* is used to give voice to someone other than the writer (1.105–8).

Evrard then discusses *antithesis* (defined in the usual sense of opposition), *antiphrasis*, and irony (1.109–12). He then follows with a discussion of *emphatice* (a means of emphasizing one word over another; 1.113). *Phantasia*, *somatopoeia*, *epithet*, and *evocitatio* are discussed in conjunction with one another: "You make *phantasia* by attributing to the inanimate what is animate: Forests and waves are amazed. And *somatopoeia* is the same thing made inwardly. If you relate characteristics properly, this is *epithet*. *Evocitatio* joins similar characters" (1.114–18). He then discusses *conceptio* (a device involving the combination or omission of premises) and then moves to contemplate allegory (1.119–20).

Evrard's treatment of *barbarisms* and *solecisms* is identical to Donatus' and Alexander's treatments, with the exception of the restoration of *acyrologia* and *pleonasmos* and the addition of Alexander's miscellaneous devices—*anthropospathos*, *euphonia*, and *alleotete* (2).

Finally, in his category of colors of rhetoric Evrard adds most of the *exornationes verborum: repetitio, conversio, complexio, traductio, contentio, exclamatio, ratiocinatio, sententia, articulum, adnominatio, subiectio, gradatio, definitio, transitio, correctio, occulatio, disiunctum, coniunctum, adiunctum, conduplicatio, commutatio, dubitatio*, and *praecisio* (3). Missing from his account are *interrogatio, contrarium, membrum, continuatio, isocolon, interpretatio, permissio, expeditio*, and *conclusio*.

Evrard increased the number of grammatical figures by combining Donatus' and Alexander's accounts, adding other grammatical devices, and including the rhetorical figures heretofore seen as beyond the province of grammar. In placing the various figures at the opening of his treatise rather than at the end and then following the figures with an account of metrical feet before proceeding to the parts of speech, Evrard identified the function of grammar more specifically with the composition of poetry and prose. His concern with the divisions of speech is secondary to the figures themselves. This method is nearly the opposite of the incremental, microscopic approach to composition evident in Donatus' approach to grammar. Evrard's concern with the larger picture represents something of a shift in emphasis that culminates more fully in the *ars poetriae.*

Like the *Doctrinale,* the *Graecismus* seems oriented toward readers who have already met the various devices and concepts presented in the treatment, perhaps in an elementary grammar similar to Donatus' study. Again, the work seems exemplary; it demonstrates many of the principles it relates. Indeed, where Donatus described the various figures in flat, analytical language, Evrard described the figures by means of the figures themselves—including *tmesis. Tmesis*—a device used in Virgil—was one figure Donatus was almost apologetic for having used.

For Donatus, the figures were important only insofar as they related to, and stemmed from, the parts of speech. His exclusion of, what later became known as, the rhetorical colors clearly reveals this focus. For Alexander and, most particularly, Evrard, the figures are foregrounded as the means of producing discourse. Again, this is a shift from a literal, analytical, and closed system of grammar to a compositional, inventional, open system.

The verse formats of *Doctrinale* and *Graecismus* show a shift in pedagogy and art. Their brief accounts of the figures allow them to display the art they explain in a game of wits with their readers. Instruction shifts from a listing of principles supported by examples to examples that explain the principles. The pedagogy of the time has shifted to one that is designed "to teach by word and example" (*docere verbo et exemplo*).[71] These shifts are soon followed by a different though similar genre, *ars poetriae,* which evolves from a marriage of the late-grammatical tradition and the inventional focus of classical rhetoric.

Part 2

Ars poetriae

Auctores poetriarum

Biographical information on the *auctores poetriarum* is sparse at best. What follows is an attempt to provide an overview of the authors with the data that is known. Matthew of Vendôme (ca. 1130–1200) was born in Vendôme and educated in Tours under the tutelage of Bernard Silvester. He taught school in Orléans, where he wrote *Ars versificatoria* before departing for Paris around 1175. Matthew was also the author of *Milo, Pyramus and Thisbe,* and *Tobias.* All three works are used as examples in *Ars versificatoria.*[1]

Geoffrey of Vinsauf was born in Normandy, educated at St. Frideswide, Oxford, and later studied in France and Italy. The exact dates of his life are unknown. It is known, however, that he was sent to Rome by Richard I as a papal ambassador (sometime before 1199) and wrote *Poetria nova* between 1208 and 1213 as a gift to Pope Innocent III. His *Documentum de modo et arte dicandi et versificandi,* extant in short and long versions, has been dated both before and after *Poetria nova.* Geoffrey authored a poem ("Causa magistri Gaufredi Vinesauf") and a short treatise on the colors of rhetoric (*Summa de coloribus rhetoricus*).[2] He is also said to have been the author of an *ars dictaminis*—now lost.[3]

John of Garland was born in England circa 1195 and studied at Oxford around 1210–1213. He taught at the University of Paris and, from 1229 to 1231, was master of grammar at the University of Toulouse. He was the author of numerous works on subjects as diverse as rhetoric, grammar, medicine, and music.[4] He is believed to have died after 1258, and perhaps even as late as 1272. His work *De arte prosayca, metrica, et rithmica,* or *Parisiana poetria,* was written between 1220 and 1231.[5]

Virtually no biographical detail exists for Gervasius of Melkley. His work can only be dated after those of Geoffrey and Matthew, because he cites both authors in his work. Details on Eberhard the German are likewise fugitive. His work has been dated as late as 1280 and he certainly seems to be the last of the Latin writers on the subject; he uses examples found in Geoffrey, Gervasius, and John.

The *auctores* saw their works as extensions of Horace's *Ars poetica.* The influence of Horace, however, can be a little hard to fathom. The work—amounting to no more than ten pages and written as a letter—offers little advice and is not fully developed. Murphy sees its appeal in its compositional focus; its focus on the future.[6] But it is also Horace's dedication to unity and clarity that attracted the attention of the *auctores poetriarum.* Horace's letter opens with an unsightly image that he compares to faulty composition:

> Imagine a painter who wanted to combine a horse's neck with a human head, and then clothe a miscellaneous collection of limbs with various kinds of feathers, so that what started out at top as a beautiful woman ended in a hideously ugly fish. . . . Let me tell you . . . a book whose different features are made up at random like a sick man's dreams, with no unified form to have a head or a tail, is exactly like that picture.[7]

Horace also shows a sensitivity to the rendering of words in a striking fashion: "As to words: if you're delicate and cautious in arranging them, you will give distinction to your style if an ingenious combination makes a familiar word new."[8] Later, he strikes a blow for clarity melded with beauty: "It is not enough for poetry to be beautiful; it must also be pleasing and lead the hearer's mind wherever it will."[9]

Ultimately, however, the Horace of the *auctores* is one who is as contemporary as the *poetriae* themselves. He is the one transmitted through the lens of medieval hermeneutic, rhetorical theory. Karsten Friis-Jensen has edited a twelfth-century commentary on Horace's *Ars poetica,* which he believes is the basis for Matthew's, Geoffrey's, and John's attributions to Horace.[10] The commentary explicates Horace with the aid of *Rhetorica ad Herennium* and *De inventione.* Accordingly, the doctrine which the *auctores* attribute to Horace comes with a liberal dose of Cicero and *Ad Herennium.*

The *artes poetriae,* then, are a conglomeration of various doctrines gleaned from ancient rhetoric, grammar, and poetic, medieval commentaries, along with *artes dictaminis et praedicandi.* Each treatise after Matthew's and Geoffrey's builds from their predecessors, absorbing and refining the previous doctrine. Simultaneously, the *artes poetriae* are unique. Each author has his own particular focus, highlighting certain doctrine and presenting that doctrine in his own way. The following section, then, surveys each of the treatises, emphasizing their particular contributions to composition theory.

Chapter Three

Matthew of Vendôme's *Ars versificatoria*

Matthew of Vendôme's *Ars versificatoria*[1] is a pastiche of grammar, rhetoric, and poetics that were modified and transformed into a system for generating verse. Matthew took Horace as his point of departure and interspersed general sentiments from *Ars poetica* with the *topoi* of classical rhetorical invention; the parts of speech used in antique grammar; and the schemes, tropes, and colors of medieval grammar and rhetoric. All the components in *Ars versificatoria* are charged with the oral/literal tension; none exists in its pure state. Grammatical units (the parts of speech) are used as a means of composing verse. The methods of rhetorical invention (the topics of arrangement) are used as a means of poetic description. Beyond the doctrine created and transmitted via *Ars versificatoria,* the treatise serves to display many of the ideas it addresses and demonstrates Matthew's compositional abilities.

Matthew was apparently a participant in an intense feud with another teacher at Orléans, Arnulf de Sancto Evurciu, whom he calls Rufus. Matthew refers to Arnulf in his preface and makes him the subject of several derisive and even lewd examples throughout his work.[2] Matthew's use of his own text as a means of quarreling with a rival is reminiscent of Anselm de Besate's *Rhetorimachia.* The quarrel, coupled with his later allegory featuring Philosophy, Satire, Tragedy, Comedy, and Elegy suggests a connection with the tradition of Menippean satire.[3] The derision aimed at Rufus also demonstrates more of an oratorical focus on the part of Matthew.

The work is also apologetic; Matthew repeatedly asks his readers not to regard his examples as indicative of his poetic abilities. Many of his examples are lewd, but there is a reason behind such techniques. After a particularly vivid example, in which he refers to a "belly swollen like the testicles of Saturn" (2.34), Matthew explains his occasional, vivid, vulgar examples: "I have introduced a number of examples akin to the subject under discussion, it has been done as a diversion to refresh dainty ears" (2.35). He justifies his practice with the authority of Cicero, whom, he remarks, wrote that "a little monotony goes a long way, while variety relieves boredom" (2.34–35). One can imagine that *Ars versificatoria* was popular with schoolchildren.

Though the manuscript tradition of the work contains four parts, none of the divisions is particularly clean. Matthew seems to wander from his stated organizational pattern and repeats himself or picks up a previously abandoned topic at odd times. The meandering format suggests an oral tendency that makes *Ars versificatoria* difficult to summarize. The work itself is not easily sectioned. The organizational structure is also incremental in the grammatical mode with each section building upon the other. The basis of the entire system is verse; thus, the first section provides the foundation for a line of verse.

Matthew opens the treatise by offering a definition of verse that dissects it into its constituent parts and then fuses the parts into an organic whole:

> Verse is metrical discourse advancing in cadenced periods with the restraint that meter demands and made charming by a graceful marriage of words and by flowers of thought. It contains in itself nothing deficient and nothing redundant. For it is not the accumulation of words, the counting of feet, and the knowledge of meter that constitutes verse, but the elegant combination of words, the vivid presentation of relevant qualities, and the carefully noted epithets of each single thing. (1.1)

This aesthetic appreciation of verse seems to move away from the grammatical, analytical orientation and presents verse as a subjective phenomenon. In spite of this aesthetic orientation, however, Matthew's method of developing verse is both mechanical and grammatical. The ultimate enactment of the mechanical parts, though, becomes quite organic. The definition of verse also displays the oral/literal tension. One can teach the analytical parts of verse, but they alone are insufficient to its production. One must go beyond that focus and blend those constituents together as an elegant whole.

Reversing the order of his discussion, Matthew quickly defines epithet, the final element of his definition. An epithet, he notes, is an expression that indicates an attribute belonging to some noun and may display qualities that are good, bad, or indifferent (1.2). Matthew then moves to the elegant combination of words, which, for a versemaker, involves the means of beginning a verse. It is this essential means of beginning that is the foundation on which Matthew has based his system.

Matthew identifies four ways of beginning: *zeugma, hypozeuxis, metonymy,* and proverbs, but he places most of his emphasis on the first two. *Zeugma* is the use of a single verb to serve multiple clauses. The verb may be placed at the beginning, middle, or end of the clause (1.4–12). For example, *Tu mihi dominus eras, tu vir, tu frater* (to me you were master, husband, brother).[4] *Eras,* the verb that ends the first clause, serves the second and third clauses as well. The same meaning could be rendered by moving *eras* to the middle clause (*Tu dominus, tu mihi vir eras, tu frater*) or end clause (*Tu dominus, tu vir, tu mihi frater eras*). Conversely, *hypozeuxis* provides each individual clause with its own verb (13–14). For example, *Bella cupit laxatque genas et temperat ungues* (she yearns for war, and she loosens her jaws, and she trims her talons). A passage employing *zeugma* can easily be converted to one employing *hypozeuxis* and vice versa.

The twofold method of beginning, also employed by Eberhard the German, has been something of a mystery to scholars, especially when compared to Geoffrey of Vinsauf and John of Garland's works that speak of natural and artificial order. Kelly explains the problem as follows:

> How, in fact, does one explain two fundamentally distinct ways to begin a poem, the one pure embellishment and related to the sentence structure of the first few lines, the other more truly compositional in that it is concerned with the orderly arrangement of the poem's contents? That Geoffrey of Vinsauf and John of Garland say nothing of *zeugma* and *hypozeuxis* may not seem surprising. But how is one to explain the total silence of Matthew of Vendôme on natural and artificial order?[5]

The answer, Kelly argues, is that Matthew and Eberhard were concerned with the more particular task of instructing beginning students to compose individual lines of verse, rather than entire poems. Matthew and Eberhard therefore confined their treatises to the explication of versification and ornamentation, while Geoffrey and John were concerned with the total composition of a poem. Thus Geoffrey's and John's treatises were expanded to include all the divisions of rhetoric, most specifically invention and arrangement.[6]

Missing from Kelly's account, however, is an explanation of why *zeugma* and *hypozeuxis* are so important to the practice of versification. The answer is to this question is that use of either of the devices allows the writer to match her or his sentence structure with the demands of the particular meter in which it is written. If one is constrained by a particular literary genre to use pentameter or hexameter, it is necessary that instruction in versification include a method of converting one's thought to the appropriate form. The emphasis on sentence structure as a way of beginning orients the versemaker to the constraints of his or her particular genre and provides a method for working within those constraints. The meter and the required sentence structure are scaffolds from which one builds a line of verse. Recognition of those constraints and the emphasis on working within them is repeated throughout the created text. The basis of a verse is set upon a frame of verb placement. This beginning allows the composer to select other words that fill in and complete the frame.

Matthew writes that one may also begin by using *metonymies* or *sententiae.* When using a *metonymy,* one begins by attributing the characteristics of an object to its container or identifying the characteristics and then the container (1.15). Matthew's treatment of this method, however, is brief—covering only ten lines of text—and his examples are obscure.

Matthew of Vendôme's account of proverbs or *sententiae* provides more information, but only in its abundance of examples. He defines the devices as "universal sentiments in which common opinion agrees, and in which the purity of unalloyed truth inheres" (1.16). His examples are a series of *sententiae* that are virtually undeveloped. For example, to demonstrate the effect of custom he writes: "Custom tastes of nature; an unglazed jar does not lose the taste of what it first held" (1.26). The limited discussion of *metonymy* and proverbs, along with the examples, implies that these devices are concerned with beginnings—but, on a macroscopic rather than a microscopic scale. The *metonymies* and proverbs set the tone for a whole composition rather than lines of verse. Thus, Matthew acknowledges thematic concerns in composition, but his particular focus is the verse. The importance of *sententiae* in developing prose and poetry, however, is developed further in Geoffrey of Vinsauf's *Poetria nova.* After giving two examples of *metonymy* (1.15) and twenty-five examples of *sententiae* (1.17–29), Matthew returns to methods of beginning—specifically *zeugma* and *hypozeuxis.*

The reference is a transition to the discussion of the three faulty styles that may occur in working out the material: drifting and slack, turgid and inflated, and dry and bloodless. Matthew attributes the faults to Horace, but they actually come from *Rhetorica ad Herennium* (4.10) via commentaries on Horace. The drifting and slack style, he notes, is marked by inconsistency; the composition moves from one style into another (high, middle, and low) so that it lacks unity: "The beginning does not agree with the middle nor the middle with the end" (1.30–31). The turgid and inflated style is one begun in a manner that is so lofty and ornate that it cannot be sustained to the end of the discourse (1.32). The dry and bloodless style features the excessive use of low style. This type of composition is so conservative that it can never hope to reach eloquence. As Matthew quotes Horace (*Ars poetica* 28): "Overcautious and fearful of the storm, he creeps along the coast" (1.33). The faults are ones of beginning, and each fault arises in a faulty beginning that traps the composer in a stylistic morass. Essentially, they are the antitheses of the elegant combination of words. Matthew underscores this view with apt quotes from Horace, including the following: "Remain to the end even as it came forth at the first and have it self-consistent" (*Ars poetica* 27; *Ars versificatoria* 1.34). The beginning sets the tone for the larger work and must be well considered lest it set a faulty tone. Thus, Matthew has not only addressed the mechanical beginnings, but he has discussed the thematic and stylistic ones as well.

Other, perhaps lesser, faults are the use of varied verb tenses and improper word order (1.36–37). In regard to the latter, Matthew cites Donatus' grammatical fault, *cacosyntheton.* Just as in the grammatical notions behind *metaplasms,* schemes, and tropes, Matthew allows rules to be broken when there is good reason to do so, because a rule loses force when it is made absolute (1.36). The most egregious faults of diction thus delineated, Matthew moves on to description.

The source for most of the various modes of description is Cicero's *De inventione*—though the examples used to exemplify many of the principles come variously from Horace, Virgil, Ovid, Statius, Juvenal, and Lucan. Descriptions are used to explain the actions of a person, as well as their extrinsic and intrinsic qualities.

Extrinsic qualities serve to differentiate one person from another: status, age, occupation, gender, geography, and native land (1.42–43). Matthew provides descriptions of a variety of persons: the pope (1.50), Caesar (1.51), Ulysses (1.52), Davus (1.53), Cartula (1.54), Marcia (1.55), Helen (1.56–57), and Beroe (1.58). He asserts that the descriptions offered are meant as examples that would apply to other people of the same rank, social status, etc. His use of names is intended to refer to one from that particular class. The epithets by which he refers to specific people are to be interpreted as symbols of that particular class (1.60–62). As Gallo wrote, "The purpose of description is a *manifestatio,* a demonstration, a declaration of the nature of some person: and that person will be a type, not an individual."[7] Matthew further writes that many qualities should be offered, as people are seldom identified by a few characteristics. Just as a rose is not seen when surrounded by brambles nor a pearl when still in the marsh "so a person's worth is not sufficiently proclaimed by ascribing to him a single or even a few good points, when perhaps a host of vices may outweigh the scanty praise thus given" (1.64). So, while the descriptions are stock, the aggregate combination of the various stock descriptions is what distinguishes the particular person.

Epithets, of course, also aid in description and certain epithets should be restricted to certain kinds of persons—a pastor, prince or emperor; a beautiful woman; a wife; or a man (1.64–71). Matthew writes that the craft of versification consists largely in the skill of description.

To this point, Matthew has addressed external description, but, after a brief reorientation, he moves to internal description (intrinsic qualities). Internal descriptors speak to the qualities of the inner person. They describe such aspects as "reason, faithfulness, patience, honesty, double-dealing, arrogance, or prodigality and other characteristics of the inner mind" (1.74). One may also address the various personal attributes: name, nature, way of life, fortune, character, goals, appetites, judgement, luck, exploits, and eloquence (1.75–92).

Matthew then moves back to external descriptors, addressing Cicero's attributes of action (1.93–113; *De inventione* 1.24–28). Ultimately, he appropriates Quintilian (5.10.32) in summarizing the attributes of actions and persons: who, what, where, with what aid, why, when, and in what manner.

Matthew's opening section is an extraordinary blend of poetic, rhetorical, and grammatical lore. He mentions Horace most frequently, but he is perhaps more reliant on Cicero's *De inventione* and the pseudo-Ciceronian *Rhetorica ad Herennium.* Though attributed to Horace, and unquestionably present in *Ars poetica,* the three faulty styles are a prominent feature of *Rhetorica ad Herennium.* The qualities that differentiate one person from another come from *De inventione,* as do the eleven personal attributes. Matthew's list of the attributes of action is also from classical rhetoric, particularly that of Quintilian. Matthew's work provides support for the contention that ancient authors understood poetry "from the precepts of rhetoric rather than grammar."[8]

Equally important to Matthew's account of beginnings are medieval grammars, though unacknowledged in his text. True to its mixed heritage, the work wanders from the neat categories of literacy to the repetitiveness of orality. On the one hand, the treatise categorizes and separates its doctrine; but on the other, it blurs its categories by doubling over and under those distinctions. That nonlinear pattern is consistent throughout the work. Indeed, Matthew revisits his ideas of *hypozeuxis* and *zeugma* in his closing passages.

Matthew briefly moves away from the business of setting the meter of his verse when he raises the issue of description. Description is discussed here because the descriptors themselves are necessary before one can select the various grammatical units in which to depict them. The next section, therefore, addresses further construction of the basic frame, the line of verse.

Part 2 focuses on the threefold elegance of versification: polished words (*verba polita*), color of expression (*dicendi color*),[9] and inner sentiment (*interior favus*). As a way of introducing the subject, Matthew tells the reader that he will relate a dream that came to him the night before so that he might charm his readers and make them receptive, sharpen their attention, foster their good will, encourage them to listen, avert their boredom, and whet their appetites for instruction (2.1). His announced motivation displays Matthew's rhetorical sensitivity and is reminiscent of Cicero's and Augustine's duties of the orator. The allegory itself, however, moves into the literary tradition. Matthew's dream places him before Flora, the gatekeeper of spring, who has adorned the earth with fresh flowers and also adorned the places of learning with her favor (2.2). The pleasing environment inspires Matthew to write a description of nature (2.3). In nature's realm, he encounters Philosophy and her handmaidens. Philosophy is a remarkable and serious woman who is practically indescribable. Nonetheless, Matthew employs some of the descriptive techniques he has previously outlined in order to offer a portrayal of Philosophy. By describing her expression, facial features, demeanor, stature, and clothing, Matthew underscores the nobility of her character. Three of Philosophy's handmaidens (her foster daughters) provide comparisons to her own personality. Tragedy is ferocious and shouts warnings, "bombast, and jawbreaker words" (2.5). Satire's "downcast eyes" demonstrate the "slyness of her mind." She constantly chatters and "makes a big show of her modesty which has never blushed at the naked body" (2.6). Comedy appears in ordinary clothes and with bowed head, showing no merriment (2.7). A fourth daughter, Elegy—the hexameter-pentameter couplet toward which most of Matthew's instruction is focused—comes forward, pleasing in appearance, but limping because of her unequal feet (2.8). Elegy then explains the threefold elegance of versification.

Polished words derive their elegance from the ideas found in the expression: "Thus the beauty of what the words signify overflows to grace the very words themselves" (2.10). Color of expression is elegance derived from exterior sources and results from such eloquent expression that requires the reader to think of it favorably by virtue of the manner in which words are arranged. The mere arrangement of words cannot make up for ideas that lack at least some elegance, however. The arrangement serves only to reinforce the beauty of an idea (2.11). Nonetheless, Matthew is not so concerned with polished words as he is with color of expression and interior sentiment. Color of expression seems more concerned with the selection of grammatical devices while interior sentiment deals with the various figures.

The remainder of the section deals with the colors of expression that enable one to shape material to produce the desired form of versification. Attention to the particular parts of speech (adjectives, participles, and verbs) is an essential tool that allows the versemaker to further arrange the frame of the meter previously set by means of *zeugma* and *hypozeuxis*. The various *topoi* of description provide the raw substance in which to fill the frame; the attention to adjectives, participles, and verbs with particular endings provide the writer scaffolds on which to build the composition. The approach uses the incremental system of language analysis provided by ancient grammarians, but it is used for compositional rather than analytical purposes. The introspective move of grammar is thus focused outward toward the construction rather than the deconstruction of discourse.

Lines 13–38 are a series of examples of various adjectives (14–21, 24–35), participles (22–23), and verbs (36–38) which are most helpful in producing meter. Most of Matthew's examples are pentameter so that the reader may see how the various devices are used in construction of this difficult meter (2.40). As Aubrey Galyon observed:

> The metrical demands of the pentameter placed a premium on words ending in *-alis, -osus, -atus, -uus,* and *-aris.* The adjectives whose use Matthew discusses are those having these desirable endings. He points

> out that the restrictions of the pentameter make certain words unsuitable for poetry, particularly those ending in *-ativus.* (9)

Likewise, words ending in *-uo,-uro, -ivo, -ulo, -apo, -isco, -ico, -ivus, -icus, -ior, -ale, -ales, -iosa, -iosus, -ata, -ulosa, -ulosus, -ata, -atus, -ativo, -ativa, -ivas,-are, -iore, -icus, -tus, -icus, -igus, -ius, -ica, -iga, -eat, -erat, -uare, -urat, -ivant, -ulat, -at, -icare, -erare, -inat,* and *-eare* are also useful in poetry. Matthew again uses the grammatical tradition for compositional purposes. He shows how useful an understanding of grammar can be; it allows one to generate verse.

Just as the placement and use of verbs in the conceptualization of a line helps the versewriter meet the generic demands of meter, so does the choice of adjectives, participles, and verbs. By becoming familiar with the various endings most suitable for facilitating the particular meter, the student is equipped with a repertoire, albeit a mechanical one, which assists in the composition of the meter. Again, one must remember that Matthew's dictates are written for novices. The examples he creates using his suggestions work, however a glance at most classical elegiac poetry shows that Matthew's recommended endings appear rather infrequently.[10] True art, therefore, involves the ability to learn from the rules rather than being confined by them.

Part 3 of *Ars versificatoria* deals with the quality or manner of the expression (*interior favus*). The manner of expression frequently adds grace more than substance to an utterance. Matthew offers the example of *zeugma* from 1.11, *Tu dominus, tu vir, tu mihi frater eras* (my master, my husband, my brother were you), and notes that its elegance is not derived from its inner sentiment or figurative expression, but from the manner in which it is expressed. His example features three schemes: *zeugma,* because of the use of one verb for three clauses; *repetitio* (the color of rhetoric), because *tu* (my) is repeated three times; and *dialyton* or *asyndeton,* because it features a series of clauses joined without a conjunction (3.1). He likens the function of the various figures to that of the sculptor transforming rough material into a pleasing shape. In composing poetry, he writes, language "is rough and awkward until it is arranged through the artful employment of some scheme, trope, or rhetorical color" (3.2). Grammatical and rhetorical lore are therefore the tools of the versifier.

Matthew cites Isidore in equating schemes to figures and notes that although seventeen are often listed, he himself is only discussing the ones most useful in versification. Having previously discussed *zeugma* and *hypozeuxis,* he proceeds to define and exemplify twelve schemes: *anaphora, epanalepsis, anadiplosis, epizeuxis, paronomasia, paranomeon, schesis onamaton, homoeoteleuton, polyptoton, polysyndeton,* and *dialyton* or *asyndeton* (3.3–17). As in the grammatical tradition, the rhetorical colors are missing. Matthew notes that there are thirteen tropes, but again he focuses particularly on those tropes helpful in versification: *metaphor, antithesis, metonymy, synecdoche, periphrasis, epithet, metalepsis, allegory,* and enigma (3.18–44).

His account of the schemes and tropes may come from Isidore, but Isidore's account is taken from Donatus. Thus, Matthew's compositional focus sees the grammatical figures most helpful. His inclusion of *antithesis* is unique, it being listed as a trope in neither the previous grammatical nor rhetorical traditions. Epithets, he notes, may be composed from phrases, verbs, and adjectives (3.38–41). This notion is not fully developed in Matthew's treatise, but does receive more attention from Geoffrey of Vinsauf and Gervasius of Melkley as the doctrine of determination.

Moreover, Donatus and Isidore do not mention the rhetorical colors. It is worth noting, however, that a contemporary of Matthew's (Evrard of Bethune) includes colors of rhetoric in his *Graecismus.* Matthew omits a detailed discussion of rhetorical colors because he says they have been discussed elsewhere. He does observe, however, that certain rhetorical colors correspond to some schemes and tropes: *antithesis / contentio, anaphora / duplicatio, paronomasia / annominatio, epanalepsis / repetitio, schesis onamaton / membrum orationis / articulus, dialyton / dissolutum, polysndeton / conjunction,* and *metalepsis / climax / gradatio* (3.45). He spends some time in discussing climax, noting that a treatise strung together from climaxes is not poetry (3.46). Climax, though, is included in Matthew's account of tropes. He nonetheless lists the rhetorical colors: *repetitio, conversio, complexio, traductio, contentio, exclamatio, ratiocinatio, sententia, contrarium, membrum orationis or articulus, similiter cadens, similiter desinens, commixtio, annominatio, subjectio, gradatio, diffinitio, transitio, correctio, occupatio, disjunctio, conjunctum, adjunctum, conduplicatio, commutatio, dubitatio, dissolutio, praecisio,* and *conclusio* (3.47).

In closing part 3, Matthew again complicates his system of composing verse by noting that the three divisions (*verba polita, dicendi color,* and *interior favus*) are not mutually exclusive. Indeed, in the following example he shows that all three are featured: "*Non parcit populis regnum breve*" (a brief kingship spares not the populace; 3.48). He writes:

> We have here the beauty of the line's inner meaning according to the first part of the division, for it is a universal sentiment. In accord with the second part the words are elegant, and in accord with the third part there is beauty in the manner of speech. For there is a type of *metaphor,* since that which a quality of animate beings, that is, "to spare," is attributed metaphorically to an animate thing, that is "kingship." Or it is possible that here there is *metonymy,* for the possession is used in place of the possessor, that is, "kingship" for "king." (3.49)

One of the three characteristics, he notes, is rarely used in poetry without the others being present (3.50). So, while Matthew's account often seems to reduce the art of versification to a highly mechanical and artificial enterprise, he mitigates the potential woodenness of such an approach by interweaving the three divisions of expression in an organic, undissectable way. His *Ars versificatoria* allows the student to build a frame and scaffold from which fine verse may be constructed, but the frame and scaffolds alone are insufficient to produce verse.

Each of the previous three sections addressed various components that can be used to construct verse. The final section, part 4, addresses how all those pieces may be put together. Matthew's advice is varied, ranging from a means of rewriting existing themes to a discussion of faulty language use. The writer, Matthew notes, will either treat fresh material or material that has been treated by others. Previously treated material constrains the writer in regard to theme, but the author is not constrained by other concerns. Faulty language used in the original need not be followed (4.3). Again, the medieval authors placed less emphasis on originality than do authors of our own times. Much of the versemaker's art consisted in the ability to rework old material in new ways or, conversely, to use commonplaces to render new material.

Matthew also warns his contemporaries that certain ancient language practices are inappropriate. Matthew feels that his peers should use comparisons sparingly, because tropes create such turns of a phrase (4.4). Ancient authors, he says, were required to adorn their compositions with "artificial luxuriance," but Matthew and his contemporaries are not allowed such practices (4.5). Moreover, these authors are admonished not to practice excessive "poetic license in quantities of syllables." In other words, the liberties allowed for the sake of meter in Donatus' *metaplasms* are not permissible for the authors of Matthew's time. Vague syntactic relationships should also be eliminated, except to quote the works of the ancients (4.7); and, of course, one should avoid improper word usage (4.8).

Matthew summarizes his introductory remarks on faults in language use, asserting that these aspects of expression must always be considered: art, error, and figures. "We ought to imitate art, fault ought to be eliminated, and figures indeed ought to be restrained" (4.9). He then addresses a number of the *barbarisms* and *solecisms* identified by Donatus in the *Barbarismus: perissologia, tautologia, macrologia, acyrologia, amphibologia, eclipsis, tapinosis, cacosyntheton* (4.10–12). Having discussed faults to be avoided, he goes on to offer ways of avoiding them. Matthew argues that human actions have a natural order of progression. Likewise, the poet should allow materials to be related naturally (4.13). Thus, Matthew is an advocate of natural order. His endorsement simply comes at the end of his treatise rather than in the beginning.

Matthew writes that the versemaker may also improve upon material that has been used previously by other poets. Rather than incorporating the ambiguity of an existing theme, Matthew believes his contemporaries should rewrite the material to provide a clearer statement possessing the original meaning (4.14–15). According to Matthew, the rewriting of existing material may be accomplished by paraphrasing, using synonyms and periphrasis, changing grammatical constructions (from active to passive and passive to active), and by amplifying sentences and clauses (4.20–23). In treating fresh material, however, Matthew states that one should consider the attributes of the person or thing to be described. The attributes should make the character of a person evident through the use of words (4.18). When describing, the writer should use restraint to render the attributes clearly—unless the need for stylistic grace requires that the description be supplemented by quotations, metaphor, epithets, and similes (4.19).

Failure to recognize the various distinctions in language may result in ten particular faults: "Wrapping ideas in obscure brevity"; "digressing into superfluous loquacity"; "worrying over accepted language"; "wondering because of a doubtful mind"; "an overly scrupulous concern with meaning"; "boundless confusion of speech"; "a barren waste of talent"; "an unseemly hastening into linguistic disasters"; "confused agitation over words"; and "overloading the meaning of expressions" (4.25). Matthew also notes that equivalence may be achieved by rendering the peculiar properties of a person, providing similar expressions, referring to antecedents, referring to causes and effects, or by means of *synecdoche* or metaphor (4.31).

Working out the written material, both existing and new, requires correction. Matthew's advice on correction clearly shows his focus on verse—particularly single-line verse. Correction involves two functions: marking of faults and producing a remedy for them (4.32–33). In verses that are complete sentences, faults may be corrected by use of *zeugma* or *hypozeuxis.* Moreover, an idea should rarely be completed in one line of verse unless it is a proverb. Matthew states that the idea begun in the hexameter should extend into the pentameter or the clause of the pentameter should begin in the hexameter: "In fact, the hexameter and the pentameter serve a joint function, for the pentameter ought to serve and wait upon the hexameter, either by explaining or concluding its idea" (4.34). Further, he decrees that ideas should not extend into a third line of verse and monosyllabic words should not be the final word in a line. Matthew goes on to advise that a pentameter should end in a disyllabic word except when this impossible (4.37–39). The writer should always be attentive to the ease with which the verse may be recited for the distinction of separate sentences within the verse (4.40). Matthew's advice on correction is again grammatically based. But it is not so much correction of language to the rules of grammar as it is the use of grammatical principles for the better construction of verse. Again, verb placement via *zeugma* and *hypozeuxis* allows the writer to set the metrical frame.

Matthew then changes his focus concerning correction from particular faults in composing verse to students' faults in pursuing their education. In summation, he writes that three areas of correction should concern students: "Confession of error, not hiding behind excuses, and accepting blame." Confession, of course, leads to forgiveness; but one will not be forgiven if he or she errs too often. Avoidance of excuses prevents excessive pride and avoids the placing of blame upon the innocent. Ultimately, acceptance of blame bodes well for the student's improvement (4.43).

Matthew makes it clear that error must be dealt with in an appropriate way:

> Those for whom error is a daily affair and who need a curb more than spurs ought to be severely upbraided often lest the silence of the teacher be taken as a form of approval. For when error goes unreproved, more error is bred. The correction must be very careful

in this area, for we have Ovid's testimony that: This work is harder than writing. (4.44)

In concluding his comments on correction, Matthew notes that words that please in prose will please more in verse. And of course, Matthew emphasizes the importance of proofreading by quoting Horace's admonition that writers must have the spirit of an honest censor and remove unworthy words (4.45–46).

He summarizes his work and then moves to conclusions. Several modes of ending may be used: a summary of ideas, emendation of the speech, a plea for indulgence, a display of boasting, an abrupt conclusion produced by the death of the author, an expression of gratitude, or a praise of God (4.49–51).

Matthew closes his work with thirty-four lines of elegiac verse that exemplify many of his principles, including the last injunction. It begins:

Christe, tibi sit honor, sit laus, qui cum patre regnas,
Rex cum rege, Deus cum sine fine Deo.
[O Christ, may honor be yours, may praise be yours, who rules with the father,
King with king, God with God, without end.]

Matthew has begun the elegy with the use of *hypozeuxis* and the three clauses served by the verbs *sit, sit,* and *regnas.* The second, pentameter, line of the couplet completes and elaborates on the thought begun in the hexameter line. The fifth and sixth lines of his closing passage feature *zeugma, polysyndeton,* and *asyndeton:*

Et pater et natus et spiritus est Deus, unum
Non unus, tres sunt non tria, tres et idem.
[And the father and the son and the spirit is God,
a unity not one, a trinity not three, three
yet one and the same.][11]

Moreover, the clause of the pentameter line begins in the hexameter. The remaining lines feature a variety of the other devices, including a number of words with the recommended endings. Finally, the holy trinity, the three yet one, also applies to versification. *Verba polita, dicendi color,* and *interior favus* are fused as one to produce elegant verse. Thus, Matthew demonstrates in this example how his precepts work: practically, theoretically, and spiritually. The modeling of precepts of a text in the text itself is seen again in the other *artes poetriae* (particularly, Eberhard the German's *Laborintus).*

Matthew closes the work by recalling the length of time taken in its composition: "Little book written during the course of two months. I recall what is pleasant to have recalled: 'The meadows have drunk enough.' Here ends Vendôme's completed work" (4.54).

Matthew of Vendôme combines elements of rhetoric, grammar, and poetics into a treatise on versification. Though he emphasizes the organic, oral, indissectable nature of verse, he stresses mechanical elements in his means of composition. Although his move is oriented more toward the literal, Matthew has a constant awareness of oral constraints. Moreover, he has taken the grammarian's focus on the parts of speech as a mode of compositional invention. All these components are added, modified, and transformed into his system in a way suited to his unique purpose—to write a treatise on versification that provides a means of generating verse. Matthew's focus is also shared by the last author to be discussed—Eberhard the German. The next four authors, however, shift the focus from the line of verse to the entire composition.

Chapter Four

Geoffrey of Vinsauf's *Poetria nova* and *Documentum de modo et arte dictandi et versificandi*

Matthew of Vendôme drew on the varied resources of grammar, rhetoric, and poetics to focus his *Ars versificatoria* on the composition of a line of verse. His work represented a literary approach to an oral phenomenon. Geoffrey of Vinsauf, as Kelly aptly noted, focused his attention beyond the line of verse toward the larger work.[1] Geoffrey employs many of the same grammatical, rhetorical, and poetic resources to develop the ideas expressed in a text; yet in many ways his treatise represents an oral approach to a literary problem. Understanding the innate beauty of an expression, he picks up Matthew's concept of polished words, provides instruction in the use of *sententiae,* and gives substantive methods for reworking sources by means of the figures. He uses the tropes and their master concept of *transsumptio* to develop a type of expressive invention. He also uses grammatical categories to develop his concepts of conversion and determination to arrive at means of apt expression. Moreover, Geoffrey goes beyond Matthew of Vendôme's pedagogic modeling by smoothly and unobtrusively depicting his own doctrine in *Poetria nova.* As an early commentator wrote of *Poetria nova:*

> The author is both a rhetorician and an orator: a rhetorician is one who teaches the art of beautiful expression; an orator is one who acts in accordance with the art that Cicero teaches. It is one thing to speak about rhetoric, another to speak rhetorically. Similarly, it is one thing to write about verse, another to write in verse. Virgil wrote in verse, but not about verse; Donatus wrote about verse, but not in verse. This author does both. Similarly, it is one thing to speak about an art, another to write artfully. To speak about an art is to give the precepts of the art. To speak artfully is to imitate the precepts, which is more

> difficult, just as it is more difficult to write verse than to give the precepts of verse. This author does both: he says about his art what he demonstrates from it; he writes verses while giving the precepts of verse. And thus he does what he teaches, which is the custom of a good teacher.[2]

Indeed, *Poetria nova* is a masterpiece of instruction and exemplification.

The *Poetria nova* survives in over two hundred manuscripts, twenty of which are of English origin. The work was highly influential in its time and has been found in bound copies along with Horace's *Ars poetica,* Virgil's *Georgics,* and Boethius' *Philosophiae consolatio.* It was an influential textbook, cited in works by John of Garland, Gervasius of Melkley, Erasmus, and Chaucer.[3]

Though his particular focus is on the composition of complete poems, Geoffrey is concerned with careful versification, as his opening passage shows:

> O Pope, wonder of the world, if I call you 'Pope 'Nocent,' I will be rendering your name without a proper beginning, but if I attach the beginning, it will be unfriendly to my meter.
>
> Yet the name "Innocent" has in mind to be like you, not as likes the meter; nor will virtue as great as yours be confined by any measure. There is nothing by which to measure that virtue: it transcends the measures of men.
>
> Yet divide the name—divide it thus: place "In" first and then add "Nocent"—and it is made a sociable participant in my meter.[4]

Geoffrey thus draws attention to the difficulty of beginning in, and adhering to, meter. Nonetheless, compared to Matthew of Vendôme's *Ars versificatoria,* Geoffrey's work does not offer much instruction on methods of achieving particular metrical lines, rather its precepts focus on thematic and expressive concerns.

The play on the pope's name, however, also serves to draw attention to Geoffrey's poetic abilities, as Alexandre Leupin has written, by transforming "the pope / dedicatee into a pawn of his own poetic game."[5] This exemplary mode provides the work with a type of absolute reflexivity; which, Leupin writes, "glistens in doctrine."[6] The examples are indistinguishable from the text and its message; the message is the example and the example is the message: "This dynamic force functions reflexively to collapse or otherwise blur the distinction between the text's writing and its 'content.' The reflexive movements of this specular dynamism are not truly separable."[7] The text, its expression, and message are all the same. Each underscores the other.

Unlike Matthew of Vendôme's *Ars versificatoria,* Geoffrey's *Poetria nova* follows a careful structure that is maintained throughout the treatise. *Poetria nova* consists of roughly seven sections that deal with arrangement, amplification and abbreviation, style, conversion, determination, memory, and delivery. Invention is discussed briefly in the opening where Geoffrey compares composition to laying the foundation of a house. Even though it is not addressed in any detail, invention pervades the entire work. As an early commentator wrote, the work includes all five canons of rhetoric, "and all the parts of rhetoric invoke, basically, invention."[8] The means of Geoffrey's invention go beyond the categories of classical rhetoric, including much of the doctrine of ancient grammatical theory. The inventional aspect, as well as Geoffrey's concern with performance, infuses the work with an oral focus. As one may see, in the opening section (43–86), which provides a statement of purpose and a preview for the work, Geoffrey professes to instruct his reader on how to order material, how to balance material, how to use words that are not "wild but domesticated," and how to combine a well-modulated voice with an appropriate facial expression and gesture.[9] Thus, in an ostensibly literal work, *Poetria nova*'s final manifestation is viewed as an oral performance. *Poetria nova* is an example of how a work can reduce composition to the idea of a text, but still consider itself oral.

Contrary to Matthew's view, Geoffrey is a proponent of artificial order. He notes that nature follows order. Natural order, however, he regards as barren, while artificial order is fertile. Art may invert things to arrange material for better effect. Therefore, one may begin a work by starting in the middle or at the end of a story. The preference for art over nature again displays a literal focus. One manipulates natural thought patterns for more effective presentation. Geoffrey's treatise also differs from Matthew's in that *Poetria nova* offers specific instruction on developing the thematic dimension of a story. He writes that one may achieve "greater splendor" by beginning the composition with a *sententia* pertaining to some universal sentiment. Likewise, one may begin with an *exemplum* that illustrates some general point. By combining the various methods, Geoffrey offers eight ways of beginning: from the middle of the story, from the end, from the beginning of the story with the aid of a *sententia,* from the middle with a *sententia,* from the end with a *sententia,* from the beginning with an *exemplum,* from the middle with an *exemplum,* and from the end with an *exemplum* (87–201).[10] Gallo writes that the first two forms of beginning come from Horace and Quintilian, respectively. He regards the notion of beginning with a *sententia* or *exemplum* as being derived from the *ars praedicandi et dictaminis*—since both genres emphasize such beginnings.[11] Gallo also sees it as a variation of the *progymnasmata* or *praeexercitamina* exercise, *chria.* Most importantly, he asserts the use of *sententiae* or *exempla* as an opening that creates an enthymematic premise on which the subsequent composition is to be based.[12] By beginning a treatise with a *sententia* or *exemplum,* the work becomes more of an oration, a demonstration of a particular principle brought to greater splendor. Beginning with a *sententia* also allows the rhetor to expound upon a thematic moral principle—a technique particularly attractive to the Christian rhetor. In essence Geoffrey seems to regard composition as argumentation.

Amplification and abbreviation (202–741) are compared to the molding of wax: "The subject . . . is at first resistant to handling; but if diligent application kindles the intellect, suddenly the material softens under this fire of intellect and follows your hand wherever it leads, docile to anything."[13] Amplification and abbreviation are achieved by means of the figures and the categories of grammar. Geoffrey spends lines 219–694 explaining amplification through the use of periphrasis, comparison, apostrophe, *prosopopoeia,* description, and opposition. His section on abbreviation is appropriately brief (695–741) and extolls the virtues of emphasis, comma, intimation, the ablative absolute, the elimination of repetition, the elimination of conjunctions, and the combination of many ideas into one statement. As Marjorie Curry Woods has written, Geoffrey offers "an amplified treatment of amplification" and "an abbreviated discussion of abbreviation."[14] Appropriately, the amplified treatment of amplification features a discussion of rhetorical categories, while the brief discussion of abbreviation is achieved by means of the categories of grammar. Thus, the rhetorical techniques lead to expansiveness, while the grammatical techniques lead to restriction. Similar modeling of their principles takes place throughout the work.

Geoffrey's section on style (742–1592) is devoted to schemes and tropes. Style for Geoffrey, however, is not merely ornamentation. He warns that effective use of style involves much more than simply embellishing: "First, muse upon the spirit of an expression, and only lastly upon its countenance; and be not credulous about the color of the latter: unless the inward color conforms to the outer, it is insulting to the intelligence. To paint the surface of an expression is like a picture made of mud."[15]

Like Matthew, Geoffrey admonishes his reader to rework old material in new ways. Much of his exposition employs the figures and tropes as a means of amplification. Prominent in that discussion is *transsumptio*—a doctrine virtually overlooked in previous studies of *Poetria nova* in particular and the *ars poetriae* in general.

Transsumptio

Several factors have obscured past understanding of *transsumptio* as used in the *artes poetriae*. Four of the six works that comprise the *artes poetriae* (Geoffrey of Vinsauf's *Poetria nova* and *Documentum de modo et arte dictandi et versificandi,* Matthew of Vendôme's *Ars versificatoria,* and Eberhard the German's *Laborintus*) were edited by Faral. Faral assumed a strong classical influence on the *artes poetriae,* particularly in the sections about schemes and tropes. Faral attributed the treatment of schemes and tropes in the *artes poetriae* solely to *Rhetorica ad Herennium*. Thus, his edition of the *artes poetriae* features marginal notes identifying the figurative principles from *Rhetorica ad Herennium* found in those works.[16] Although Faral's marginalia are helpful in places, they have fostered a misunderstanding of *transsumptio.* Indeed, Faral equated *transsumptio* to metaphor.[17] Subsequent translators and editors of the *artes poetriae* have followed Faral's classical interpretation, as well as his mistaken interpretation of *transsumptio.*

Until Gallo's study in 1971, Faral was the sole authority on *Poetria nova.* The danger in singular reliance on Faral, however, is aptly shown by Gallo: "His [Faral's] method is to group similar comments made by the medieval authors, and then to cite parallel passages in classical sources. These general references are often not specifically relevant to Geoffrey's teaching, and cover only a small part of the passages which Geoffrey employed."[18] In spite of Gallo's warning, Faral's analysis has influenced subsequent translations and analyses of *Poetria nova,* including Gallo's own translation.

The first of three translations of *Poetria nova* was published by Nims in 1967. Nim's edition features two aspects in particular which obfuscate Geoffrey's account of *transsumptio:* (1) she includes the Faral marginalia in the text without an explanatory note indicating that the items did not originate in *Poetria nova*, and (2) she consistently translates *transsumptio* as metaphor. Inclusion of Faral's marginalia creates the impression that they are a part of Geoffrey's treatise and without a doubt derived from *Rhetorica ad Herennium*. Such an impression is tenuous if one considers that the only tropes specifically named in *Poetria nova* are *transfero* (metaphor), *permuto* (allegory), *pronomino* (antonomasia), *nomino* (onomatopoeia), *yperbolicus* (hyperbole), and *abusio* (catachresis)—only six of the ten tropes or special *exornationes verborum* listed in *Rhetorica ad Herennium*. The repeated translation of *transsumptio* as metaphor conceals a lengthy discussion (lines 765–948) of *transsumptio* and its various uses. Gallo's translation of *Poetria nova* also equates *transsumptio* to metaphor and identifies the *exornationes verborum* in brackets. Both translations are misleading.

Kopp provided the most accurate account of *transsumptio*. She translated *transsumptio* as "transsumption," rather than metaphor,[19] as in the following passage: "When you transsume your own material, it has more pungency because it derives from what is your own. Such a transsumption of language is like a mirror for you, since you see yourself in it and recognize your own sheep in a strange field."[20]

Transsumption therefore seems to be an integral part of *Poetria nova*. In order to best understand *transsumptio* it is necessary first to consider previous uses of the term in the rhetorical/grammatical corpus—beginning with Quintilian.

Transsumptio first appears in *Institutio oratoria*, 3.6.46. There, Quintilian discusses the various legal stases used by the followers of Marcus Antonius: conjectural, legal, and juridicial. Species of the juridicial *stasis* include: definition, contradictory laws, *metalepsis* (which is equated to the various terms of *translativus*, *transumptivus*, and *transpositus*),[21] *ratiocinatio*, and ambiguity. No clue to the meaning of *metalepsis* is given in the passage. Later, however, in 6.3.52, reference is made to a witticism formed by *metalepsis:*

> In metalepsis a reckoning of remarks descends, as when Fabius Maximus, complaining of the meagerness of the *congiarium* of Augustus, which he owed to his friends, said it was a *heminaria*. For *congiarium* draws us to what is common of generosity and of measurement. *Heminaria* draws us from that meaning by a lessening of things.[22]

In this example, *congiarium* (a term which refers to the sum of the dole, or *congius,* given to the poor) is referred to as a *heminaria.* A *hemina* is equal to six *cyathi,* while a *congius* is equal to seventy-two *cyathi*. Therefore, to refer to the *congiarium* as a *heminaria* (a word coined for this occasion by Fabius Maximus) diminishes the value of *congiarium.*

The next example of *transsumptio* or *metalepsis* gives a clearer sense of its meaning. In 8.6.37–38 of *Institutio oratoria,* H. E. Butler translates:

> Metalepsis or transumption . . . provides a transition from one trope to another. . . . It is the nature of metalepsis to form a kind of intermediate step between the term transferred, having no meaning in itself, but merely providing a transition. It is a trope with which to claim acquaintance, rather than one which we are ever likely to require to use.[23]

At this point an example is given:

> The most frequent example
> is: I sing [*cano*]. I chant [*canto*]. I speak
> [*dico*]. Therefore: I sing [*cano*]. I speak
> [*dico*]. *Canto* is the intermediary between them.[24]

Now the sense of *transsumptio* or *metalepsis* is more evident. A *transsumptio* or *metalepsis* provides the explicit link between two expressions possessing a common quality, but not being synonymous. In Quintilian's example, "I sing" is similar to "I chant," but not to "I speak." Chanting, however, bears a commonality to both singing and speaking because, it is a form of both. Quintilian's example reveals a pattern in which *canto* serves as the middle term in a three-term syllogism and produces major premise, minor premise, and conclusion:

> *Cano* (*A*) is *canto* (*B*).
> *Canto* (*B*) is *dico* (*C*).
> Therefore, *cano* (*A*) is *dico* (*C*).

A similar pattern is seen in the previous example from book 6:

> *Congiarium* (*A*) is derived from *congius* (*B*).
> *Congius* (*B*) is a form of measure as in *hemina* (C). Therefore,
> *congiarium* (*A*) is *hemina* (*ria*) (C).

A *transsumptio* or *metalepsis*, then, can be likened to the middle term of a syllogism in that it provides the connection between the major and minor premises.

After his discussion of *transsumptio*, Quintilian notes that the remaining tropes to be discussed "are employed solely to adorn and enhance our style without any reference to the meaning."[25] Thus, Quintilian designates *transsumptio* or *metalepsis* and the six tropes discussed before it—metaphor, *synecdoche, metonymy, antonomasia, onomatopoeia, and catachresis*—as tropes involving changes in meaning. Moreover, he identifies *transsumptio* or *metalepsis* as the intermediate element in those tropes.

Transsumptio is absent from stylistic rhetorics produced before the thirteenth century. *Metalepsis,* however, does appear in Donatus,[26] Bede,[27] Alexander of Villedieu,[28] and Matthew of Vendôme.[29] Each time the device appears in these texts, it serves as a sort of syllogistic device which connects unrelated expressions through intermediate terms.

Metalepsis is a means of connecting dissimilar terms or expressions that retain some similarities or relationships. In the words of Donatus and Bede, it is a "stairstep" between expressions. In the usage of Donatus, Bede, Alexander, and Matthew, *metalepsis* appears to be a means of developing climax. In Quintilian's usage, *metalepsis* or *transsumptio* is not explicitly linked to climax; rather, it appears to be restricted to providing relationships between words. In each treatise, *metalepsis* or *transsumptio* takes the form and function of the middle term in a syllogism. Therefore it seems that *metalepsis* or *transsumptio* may be used as an argumentative device and an inventional one as well.[30]

Geoffrey's treatment of *transsumptio* commences with line 765, where he explains how to transsume words properly (*transsumere verba decenter*).[31] He believes that speech should transfer its subject to something bearing similarities to itself. For example:

> In strictly correct speech one says "yellow gold," "white milk," "scarlet rose," "sweet flowing honey," "fiery flames," "white mass of snow." Say therefore: "snowy teeth," "flaming lips," "honied taste," "rosy face," "milky forehead," "golden hair." Well suited to each other are: "teeth" and "snow"; "lips" and "flames"; "taste" and "honey"; "face" and "rose"; "forehead" and "milk"; and "hair" and "gold."[32]

Each of the above expressions is apt and understandable because of their common terms: snowy (white) teeth, flaming (red) lips, honied (sweet) taste, rosy (red) face, milky (white) forehead, golden (yellow) hair. The transsumption is achieved through the syllogistic pattern: *AB* (snow white), *BC* (white teeth), and therefore *AC* (snowy teeth).

Geoffrey goes on to explain how *transsumptio* can be used with verbs. Verbs associated with human actions can be used to convey nonhuman actions. For example, "springtime adorns the earth" can be substituted with "springtime paints the earth" because when one produces adornment one often paints.[33] Again, the pattern *AB, BC, AC* is seen.

A transsumption may be made more evident through the use of adjectives. Thus the expression, "The earth drank the dew out of the sky more than was meet, and the rainstorm doled it out irresponsibly," would best be stated, "A sottish earth drank the water more than was meet, and the spendthrift rain distributed them irresponsibly."[34] In the second example the relationship between a "drinking earth" and "doling rainstorm" becomes quite clear when the earth becomes a sot and the rainstorm a doling spendthrift. An adjective ensures clarity by providing explicitly the *transsumptio* used in the figurative expression.

Finally, Geoffrey demonstrates three methods of transsuming nouns that Faral and others correctly identify as examples of onomatopoeia, antonomasia, and allegory (Geoffrey later identifies them as *nomino, pronomino,* and *permuto* in lines 949–54).

Onomatopoeia is shown by the following: "The people's 'thunder' struck the city . . . , a thunderbolt's 'trumpet,' the air's 'attack,' 'quarrels,' of the winds, the 'crash' of the sea, the 'wrath' of the storm."[35] A storm (*A*) can be violent (*B*) just as the wrath (*C*) of an angry man can. Therefore, the wrath (*C*) of the storm (*A*). None of Geoffrey's examples is overtly onomatopoeic, but they are transsumptive.

Antonomasia is exemplified as follows: "You may praise with such words as 'that Paris,' similarly you may blame by saying 'that Thersites.'"[36] Thus a praiseworthy person is lauded by being compared to the noble Paris, while one worthy of blame is compared to the foul, unpleasant, and ugly Thersites. The pattern is: *X* (*A*) is worthy (*B*), Paris (*C*) was worthy (*B*), therefore *X* (*A*) is Paris (*C*).

Geoffrey then likens allegory to *antiphrasis.* He exemplifies this comparison by calling a deformed person "Paris"; a person savage at heart "Aeneas"; one of little strength "Pyrrhus"; a rude speaker "Cicero"; and an unpleasant person "Hippolytus".[37] The *AB, BC, AC* pattern is again used, though with some explanation in the minor premise: *X* (*A*) is an ineloquent speaker (*B*), *X* (*A*) is as ineloquent (*B*) as Cicero (*C*) is eloquent, therefore *X* (*A*) is Cicero (*C*).

Geoffrey gives some final advice on the use of *transsumptio* before explaining the relationship between *transsumptio* and *transfero, permuto, pronomino,* and *nomino:* "These verbs produce from themselves further words, and they are the names of rhetorical colors, all of which *transsumption* alone includes in itself."[38] Before proceeding to his discussion of tropes and figures, he states: "There are ten such bouquets of words, counted on this side and that: six on one side and four on the other."[39] Thus concludes Geoffrey's discussion of *transsumptio* and its relationship to tropes.

In *Poetria nova, transsumptio* is a concept that subsumes the tropes of metaphor, allegory, *antonomasia,* and *onomatopoeia.* The term *transsumptio* refers to an enthymematic method of connecting words for figurative use. A transsumption is achieved when one word or expression is used to provide a link between the term used and the term supplanted. The mode of reasoning used in transsumption is syllogistic, and *transsumptio* can be equated with the middle term in a syllogism. Geoffrey observes that transsumption can be unclear and he shows how adjectives can be used to enhance the clarity of a transsumption. Beyond its fusion of argument and invention into stylistic devices, Geoffrey's doctrine of *transsumptio* repeats the inventional use of the parts of speech seen in the Latin grammatical tradition.[40]

Geoffrey's use of *transsumptio* is based on the same logic used in Quintilian, Donatus, Alexander of Villedieu, and Matthew of Vendôme. Whether his treatise is based on those works or a subsequent tradition is uncertain. The conceptual meaning of Geoffrey's tropes, however, surpasses those of *Rhetorica ad Herennium.* Geoffrey offers a clear rationale for the use of each of his tropes. *Auctor ad Herennium* simply presents a list with little justification or explanation. Reliance on *Rhetorica ad Herennium* in lines 765–948 of *Poetria nova* is minimal.

Having partitioned the transsumptive tropes from the remaining six, Geoffrey provides examples of five of these tropes: hyperbole, *synecdoche, metonymy, catachresis, and hyperbaton. Periphrasis* is omitted from the traditional list of ten tropes, but is included earlier in Geoffrey's eight means of amplification.[41]

Geoffrey closes the section on a cautionary note. While he believes that these various types of expression are meant to be keys that can unlock a closed mind, he also holds that faulty use of the devices can make a lock out of a key. Thus the writer must always be mindful of how words are used: "For if a speech enters through the ears into the mind's sight without light, it builds on river water, it plants in dryness, it flogs air, it draws a furrow in sterile sand."[42] Throughout the section, Geoffrey refers to the various methods of transsumption and use of tropes as serious (*gravis*). This reference seems to refer to their nonliteral use of language.[43] This is contrasted by the so-called *ornatus levis* (light figures) that retain the literal sense of words.[44]

In treating the other various *exornationes verborum et sententiarum* Geoffrey relies almost entirely on examples. His account of the thirty-five *exornationes verborum* that *auctor ad Herennium* designated beyond the tropes is delivered only through one lengthy example. Gallo describes it quite nicely: "The figures are all woven into a discourse on the Fall and Redemption—something of a *tour de force,* since Geoffrey did not feel free to vary the order in which he presented the figures."[45] A similar *tour de force* is performed later by Eberhard the German in *Laborintus.*

In the following section Geoffrey defines, but does not name, the nineteen *exornationes sententiarum,* which he says may be studied further in Cicero (*Rhetorica ad Herennium*). Again the devices follow the exact order of *Rhetorica ad Herennium,* omitting only *commoratio*—a device marked by an entire discourse rather than a short example.

The next section treats Geoffrey's doctrines of conversion (*conversio,* lines 1593–765) and determination (*determinatio,* lines 1766–846),[46] concepts that are also arrived at by means of *transsumptio.* Gallo describes conversion as "a systematic method of varying an expression in order to find its most apt and euphonius form."[47] The method begins from three *loci:* grammatical tense, cases, and through uninflectable words. The method is very much the same as those seen previously in the grammatical tradition and in *Ars versificatoria.* One may consider the different verb tenses available for a particular verb, but also the declension of the noun forms of each verb. Geoffrey instructs: "Collect beforehand in your mind all the various grammatical modes." Then one should decide which case will be most pleasant to the ears.[48] For example, Geoffrey considers the conversion of the verb *doleo* (I grieve/feel sorrow):

> Sorrow [*dolor*] flows to me from this fountain. Hence arises to me the root . . . of sorrow [*doloris*]. This shows the substance and cause of my sorrow [*dolari*]. It produces . . . my sorrow [*dolorem*]. O anxious sorrow [*dolor*], you injure me with grievous wounds. My ill-fortuned mind lies ill, sick with sorrow [*dolore*].[49]

One may also take other verbs equivalent to grieve or the particular verb being converted and generate a variety of expressions that pertain to the phenomena being described or expressed, such as: sigh, lament, moan, or weep. Then one may convert these verbs to nouns: "From my soul come sighs; from my mouth lamentations; tears pour down upon my face; and my moans I renew continually." Thus, an expression is unified by bonding nouns and verbs through art. Geoffrey continues: "There is a pleasant enough charm in words used literally, but in things well transsumed we know a pleasure more complete."[50] The doctrine of conversion, then, also pertains to *transsumptio.* One considers the root of an expression and considers its various grammatical variations as a means of generating the word appropriate for the particular expression. Similarly, one may take an adjective, convert it to a noun and generate a number of expressive options. Nondeclinable words, according to Geoffrey, are best eliminated by substituting them with verbs, nouns, and adjectives that equal their functions. Though the method of conversion is not emphasized as much as similar methods in *Ars versificatoria,* it is still a means by which a composer meets the constraints of meter.

Geoffrey introduces the idea of determination (*determinatio*) as follows: "Add these principles to those preceding: since a word that is heard by itself is, as it were, raw material, stuff crude and formless, give it a helpmate: the addition will give it beauty."[51] Thus, determination simply involves the modification of its meaning in an expression through the apt choice of adjectives, adverbs, and qualifying phrases. This method involves the various parts of speech and is also referred to by Geoffrey as transsumptive. It is transsumptive in that the combined parts of speech (the determinations) help provide the missing term in the syllogistic, transsumptive expression. This form of transsumption is further developed by Gervasius of Melkley.

Lines 1847–973 of *Poetria nova* address a variety of concerns; the most significant of which concerns the fit of language to its subject matter and genre. The writer should always be aware of the differences between prose and poetry. The methods Geoffrey has offered apply to both, still he writes: "Meter is straitened by laws, but prose wanders in a freer road: the public thoroughfare of prose admits both wagons and carts at random; but the narrow footpath of a line of verse does not want things so gross."[52]

The remainder of the work consists of standard miscellaneous advice concerning composition. He notes that there are times when colors should be avoided altogether—for example, when one is writing comedy. It is in comedy that the plainest language often suffices, and this is why humorous speech is designated as light. Geoffrey also offers a short section on various vices of language: one should avoid hiatus; excessive alliteration; mindless repetition of the same word in different senses or meanings; excessive repetition of the same word ending; excessively long, periodic sentences; and awkward variations from normal word order. Each of the six devices represents the extreme use of devices that are often quite elegant. Geoffrey refers to the consideration of such vices as a comb, which, after use, allows the poem to gleam.[53] Finally, Geoffrey suggests that one should always consider an expression in three ways: mentally, orally, and, ultimately, in usage.

Geoffrey cautions his readers to master the art of poetry in sections. This will allow composition to be a pleasure rather than a burden. The process should be deliberate and, the author should reflect upon a section while it is still fresh and then leave it to consider another section.[54]

As far as methods of composition are concerned, Geoffrey notes that Tully (Cicero) has a system that is suitable for Tully and not necessarily for others writers. Likewise, Geoffrey allows that his system may not be suitable to all, but believes that each person, should adopt a system that is suitable for themselves. Geoffrey then offers a short section on memory and recitation and closes his work as he began—in praise of the pope.

Documentum

The *Documentum de modo et arte dictandi et versificandi* parallels *Poetria nova* in most ways; however, there are a few differences between the two works. First, the *Documentum* is more explicitly reliant on Horace's *Ars poetica* than *Poetria nova* and repeatedly refers to the authority of Horace (much in the same manner of Matthew of Vendôme). Second, the *Documentum* offers more techniques than *Poetria nova.* Where the *Poetria nova* offers the various methods of beginning a work, the *Documentum* goes further by offering various artistic means of continuing the composition. When beginning from the middle or end of a narrative, the writer is advised to use "relative pronouns, such as *who, which, what* (*qui, quae, quod*)." These allow the writer to refer back to some of the events that transpired before the point in the narrative where the writer began—for example, in this account which begins at its end: "'Scylla is smitten by the comeliness of Minos, etc.' Therefore it should continue: 'Whom, being King of the Cretans, in sorrow for his son earned against King Nisus; for although the death of his son was plotted by the envious Athenians, Minos nevertheless wished to avenge the crime of the members on their chief.'"[55] Thus, the pronouns allow the writer to gracefully summarize the action.

In the *Documentum,* Geoffrey features more discussion on the use of *sententiae* (proverbs). The artistic beginnings from proverbs[56] should be followed by words that indicate some form of demonstration: *fatetur, docet, probat, et attestur.* This is further development of the enthymematic nature of the proverb or *sententia* that Gallo observed in *Poetria nova.* Indeed, Gallo's analysis was developed in part from this remark in the *Documentum:* "For a proverb is a universal statement, and what is proposed through a universal statement 'teaches,' 'proves,' 'cites,' through something particular which is connected with it."[57] Similarly, a beginning from an *exemplum* should continue with some kind of word that leads to a comparison between the *exemplum* and the phenomenon (2.1.1–12). Again, the focus on the use of *sententiae* allows the development of a moral theme.

The *Documentum*'s section on difficult ornaments features what is clearly a discussion concerning metaphor, but the operation to which Geoffrey attributes the production of metaphor is *transsumptio* (2.3.8–47).

The *Documentum* treats specifically the problem of reworking familiar material. Though Geoffrey offers four methods, the principle one seems to focus on the practice of varying the material by amplifying it when the original material is brief, or vice versa (2.3.132–36). He also discusses the three levels of style and their attendant faults—a concept found in Matthew of Vendôme, but not in *Poetria nova* (2.3.145–57). Finally, Geoffrey offers specific ways of ending a composition: from its natural order, from a proverb, and from an exemplum (3.2).

There is a longer version of the *Documentum* that is neither edited nor translated. This so-called long *Documentum* includes a discussion of *cursus*[58] and a short section on *dictamin.*[59] Camargo writes that the long *Documentum* seems to be the treatise perused by both Gervasius of Melkley and John of Garland in preparation for their own *artes poetriae.*[60] Further study of the *Documentum* awaits the production of an edition of the long version and a careful comparison of the two versions.

Geoffrey of Vinsauf is a significant figure in the development of medieval compositional theory. From a strictly rhetorical focus, Gallo credits Geoffrey with three innovations: (1) equating the literary use of *sententia* and examples used in opening passages to the stating of major premises in enthymemes, (2) giving "theoretical expression to the medieval method of reworking one's sources," and (3) advocating the use of figurative language for amplification rather than the commonplaces.[61] Moreover, Geoffrey melded the categories of rhetorical invention and grammatical analysis into a generative system for developing beautiful poetry and prose. His rhetorical use of grammar opens a textual and analytical doctrine. Likewise, his generative use of the figures stresses the role of elegant, aesthetic depiction in poetry and prose rather than the substantive, quantitative depiction used by Matthew of Vendôme. Geoffrey's master doctrine of *transsumptio* exploits the enthymematic dimension of tropes to provide yet another means of generation. His theories of conversion and determination (executed by means of transsumption) further provide the composer a means of beautiful expression. Conversion and determination seem to follow from the grammatical tradition, but are fused with the rhetorical by their enthymematic flavor. Geoffrey's innovations amount to a significant change in invention. Beginnings, *sententiae* or *exempla,* amplification, abbreviation, schemes, tropes, conversions, and determinations are all elements of invention in Geoffrey's *Poetria nova.* If the sections in *Poetria nova* on arrangement (114 lines), amplification and abbreviation (522 lines), style (850), and conversion and determination (253) are added together, 1,739 of the work's 2,117 lines are dedicated to inventional concerns. The *Poetria nova* might well be termed *Inventio nova.*

Geoffrey moves from the oral to the literal in two ways: first, he shifts the focus of invention from the discovery of material for purposes of creating a narrative to the discovery of material with which to rewrite or recreate a narrative. Rather than placing emphasis on oral performance by means of the rhetorical categories, the site of performance is textual. As Copeland wrote: "In transforming invention into a hermeneutical procedure they [*auctores poetriarum*] prize the ingenuity of the exegetical performance that can disguise its own moves through a consummate act of textual appropriation."[62] The means of grammatical analysis become a means of discursive production. The discursive production, however, is totally literal. The material on which the expanded inventional categories are applied are extant texts and are rewritten into texts by means of textual analysis. This is very different from the use of rhetorical or grammatical categories to produce a text *ab origine.*

Second, Geoffrey's orderly and elegant production of existing materials of rhetorical and grammatical discovery into a smooth, coherent discourse clearly made the compositional treatise a text. The meandering, chatty format of early rhetorical treatises was more in the style of lecture notes or transcripts than texts. These treatises were understood at first hearing/reading and did not stand up to textual scrutiny. Geoffrey's treatise requires a careful and reflective reading/hearing. Like its means of production, the emphasis on *Poetria nova* is on its text; the text is to be analyzed to be understood.

There is an irony in Geoffrey's shift to the literal. He still sees his end product as something to be recited even though his mode of composition is literal. Though *Poetria nova* was not printed until 1721, it continued to be transmitted via manuscript copies well into the fifteenth century. Moreover, the *Poetria nova* exerted a twofold influence during that period: on the one hand it was perpetuated as a compositional text for school children, while on the other it contained sophisticated theoretical insights seen as important in the university classrooms.[63]

Beyond its doctrinal innovations the *Poetria nova* is significant for its pedagogical form; Geoffrey illustrates the very principles he offers in his work in a smooth, unobtrusive way. Leupin views the *Poetria nova* as a "triumphant manifesto" in which the "ancient of the absolute takes on a new sparkle, and the Lost Paradise of old poetic words is recuperated in modernity's most dazzling mirror."[64] I will return to Leupin's insight in the conclusion. First, however, I will consider how these pedagogical precepts and the custom of modelling are seen again in the other *artes poetriae.*

Chapter Five

John of Garland's *De arte prosayca, metrica, et rithmica*

De arte prosayca, metrica, et rithmica lacks the grace, clarity, and innovation of Geoffrey of Vinsauf's *Poetria* and *Documentum* and lacks the inventional focus on verse developed by Matthew of Vendôme. Indeed, the very sections John devotes to rhyme and meter are virtually void of inventional schemes. Nonetheless, his treatment shows a fresh approach to composition—he rejects some Ciceronian methods of invention and arrangement, and substitutes his own. His methods, however, are borrowed extensively from others. He follows the grammatical tradition in his use of the parts of speech and the rhetorical tradition in his treatment of the topics.[1] He borrows Geoffrey's notion on beginnings, proverbs, easy and difficult ornaments, determinations, amplification, and abbreviation. Also significant is that John includes *transsumptio* as a category of invention rather than style. This clearly shows a focus on style as a means of initial composition, rather than an "add on." While absorbing those innovations, however, John of Garland still offered a faithful account of the *exornationes verborum et sententiarum,* including the tropes. Moreover, he uses the method of beginning with a proverb as the basis of a type of moral argument on which the composition is to be based.

John's work was an ambitious attempt to meld together both of the genres of *ars dictaminis* and *ars poetriae,* along with assorted other compositional tasks. His work's dual nature is indicated very clearly in the introduction to the manuscript tradition, which may or may not have been written by John, but is certainly written in the voice of a nonauthor: "The subject matter is the art of writing letters, of quantitative verse, and of rhymed syllabic verse; but behind these three lie five others, which are: the art of invention, of selection, of memory, of arrangement, and of embellishment" (1.3–6). Though the introduction suggests a rhetorical focus represented by the five canons, his inventional categories are primarily grammatical. He goes on to note that the work encompasses the fields of grammar, rhetoric, and ethics. More specifically, the introduction states, the work's focus is invention: "This is the approach: the author teaches how to invent, according to the categories of invention, words, that is substantives, adjectives, and verbs used both literally and [transsumptively], in any kind of composition, whether it be a legal or academic letter, or an elegiac poem, or a comedy, or a tragedy, or a satire, or a history" (1.11–16).[2] The aim is admirable, but the work falls short in coherence. The early focus on discovery soon lapses into a listing of everything possibly related to the various types of discourse. This is again indicative of the meandering format of orally oriented works—works not composed in the literally reflective fashion we associate with the composition of contemporary discourse.[3] He follows the pattern of orality in offering lists of relatively independent examples. His presentation can be rather maddening to the contemporary reader, particularly one attempting to summarize his ideas. He mentions some concepts tangentially and returns to them, if at all, later in the treatise. As Traugott Lawler observed, John had "an associative rather than an analytical mind."[4] At best, John offers a number of key concepts from each of his previewed concerns. Murphy cautions the contemporary reader from being too critical, however, in noting that John's goal of a unified language art—his "meta-genre"—was nearly impossible.[5]

John of Garland's work is composed of seven chapters that cover invention, selection of material, arrangement, parts of a letter, vices of writing, rhetorical embellishment, and examples of legal and academic letters in various styles (1.15–25). The final section also includes a lengthy passage on *rithmus* and meter. He covers the previewed topics and also additional material. He provides commentary on comedy and tragedy at various times. Again, however, he is never constrained by his announced pattern of organization. The presentation of his work leans more to the oral than the literal.

John's treatise is an important one, however, in that he expands the scope of invention in theoretical terms. John organizes the composition of oratory, prose, and poetry around the rhetorical canons with some success, while absorbing Geoffrey of Vinsauf's contributions. Interestingly, he provides a number of visual illustrations for his work which show a literal tendency. On the other hand, he hardly matches Geoffrey's feat of illustrating the very principles he states in the form in which he expresses them.

John defines prose as "pithy and elegant discourse, not in meter but divided by regular rhythms of *clausulae*" (1.28–29). He identifies four types of prose: technographic, used in technical manuals; narrative (*ystoralis*), used by the church, writers of comedies and tragedies, and by learned men; *dictamen,* employed by courts and schools; and *rithmus,* used in sections of the liturgy (1.49–62). Meter is defined as "a certain series of uniform feet, divided into verses." A foot, in turn, is "a certain length of syllables and quantities. A verse is a regular grouping of these feet" (1.64–67). Meter thus involves the relationship between patterned long and short syllables gathered into a verse, or meter, of a particular quantitative beat. It is distinguished from *rithmus,* a topic he discusses at the end of the treatise, which focuses on rhymed patterns.

His notions on invention are influenced by both Horace and *auctor ad Herennium;* indeed he quotes from both authors verbatim. His own definition is as follows: "To invent is to come into knowledge of an unknown thing through the agency of one's own reason" (1.84–85). He carefully outlines his notions on invention, but presents them inconsistently. John uses Quintilian's inventional questions: where, what, what kind, how, and why (1.88–89). As Copeland has written, though, John's use differs from that of the classical rhetoricians:

> [C]lassical theorists used the circumstances to describe an action performed which is the *res* or the case to be argued . . . , John uses the circumstances to describe the process of writing itself, to describe the text that comes into being through invention, so that "where" and "what" describe the author's own action, where he can look for a subject and what the subject will be.[6]

Moreover, each of the species of invention, with the exception of "how," is related to moral concerns. "Where" is divided into three sources: character, examples, and etymological explanations of words (1.90–91). Only character, however, is explained under the heading of "where." Character pertains to three basic types of people: courtiers (*curiales*), city dwellers (*civiles*), and peasants (*rurales*) (1.124–34). "What" concerns the actual topics of discovery: "Seditions, murders, wars, thefts, plunderings, simonies, presentations, friendships, petitions, and the activities of ecclesiastical personages." The subdivisions are the same as in "where": persons, examples, and etymologies. Thus, persons and characters are conflated. They are essentially considered according to the quality of their actions—whether they do something well, poorly, good, or noble. For example, in regard to peasants the concern is whether they are "sweating over rural duties, or giving up" (1.135–46). The very use of description involves the relation of a basic moral lesson.

Examples perform a similar function by involving the discovery of a saying or action of an authoritative person who is worthy of emulation. These examples are developed from expressions, actions, authorities, and proverbs. When proverbs are not available, they may be developed according to the following method. One considers what is praiseworthy or blameworthy about the person/phenomenon at hand and, by considering the dichotomy, develops similarities and comparisons through which a proverb may be formed. John defines a proverb as "a brief statement, moral in purpose, setting forth what is good or what is bad in an important matter." It may concern natural things, both animate and inanimate, and moral truths taken from classical authors (1.147–309). Similar to Geoffrey of Vinsauf, John employs the proverb as a major premise on which the discussion is based. John identifies his discussion more specifically with moral persuasion, however. Similar to Matthew, John offers a number of examples of proverbs with relatively little explanation. Etymologies also involve the dichotomy of praise and blame. Essentially, one dissects the meaning of a word etymologically for purposes of amplification. John uses "pope" to illustrate the practice, noting that the pope is the holiest of fathers. The word derives from *pape* (governor, tutor) in Greek, *admirabilis* (admirable) in Latin. Thus, the pope may be described as a "most admirable priest" (1.310–15). Likewise, "what kind" involves whether or not the matter under discussion is honorable or dishonorable, praiseworthy or blameworthy (1.316–26).

John of Garland reverses the order of his fifth and fourth previewed species by discussing "why" first, which indicates the purpose for which a particular action is taken. It is concerned with what is "useful and right," even when one intends to accuse or condemn because one accuses or condemns, ultimately, for some good purpose (1.327–30). Again, use of the device allows the rhetor to develop a moral lesson. It also allows the orator to investigate the motivations for an action.

John's species of "how" takes a somewhat inconsistent and different approach. He divides it into seven colors by which material is "embellished and amplified": *annominatio* (*paronomasia*), *traductio* (transplacement), repetition, *gradatio, interpretatio* (synonymy), *definitio,* and *sermocinatio* (dialogue) (1.331–80). Copeland regards this approach as grammatical—merely foregrounding the "formal properties of textual production."[7] Ironically, however, John's grammatical move is made using the colors of rhetoric—devices eschewed by the strict grammatical tradition. John then moves to invention by means of pure grammatical categories: nouns, adjective, and verbs (1.381–93). From there follows a discussion of cognate words appropriate to the material exemplified in an "Elegiac, Amoebaean, Bucolic, Moral Poem" (1.406–56). He goes on to speak on the invention of adjectives and verbs. Their creation can come from the following rhetorical categories: effect, outcome, dress, place, family, size, and quality. John cautions that invention of verbs should rarely be done, except by necessity. When needed, it may be done by transforming old, familiar nouns (1.457–90). John's category of "how" seems to deal with the means of achieving the various purposes found in the earlier categories. Again, grammar and rhetoric are combined in a fashion that allows the author to forge a personal agenda.

John then speaks on *De arte transumendi verba* (the art of transsuming verbs). Of this, he notes, some words pertain to the mind and some to the body. The various words may be transferred to one another providing adequate similarities are related between the two. This may also be accomplished through the use of paraphrase. Additionally, one may produce variation in words transsumptively by using them in the six different cases: nominative, vocative, genitive, accusative, dative, and ablative. Finally, one may consider the matter according to the logical categories: efficient, material, formal, and final causes (1.491–523). Copeland writes that John uses the scholastic devices as hermeneutical devices.[8] This is true, but the logical categories are also a means of compositional invention. Ultimately, the art of transsuming verbs melds rhetorical invention and style along with categories of grammar and logic.

The methods of rhetorical invention are inverted by John. Rather than applying the categories of invention to particular rhetorical situations and developing materials from the situation into a speech, John considers the categories as a means of generating ideas to serve his purposes.[9] The author has become more important than the situation. Though the first chapter is ostensibly focused on invention, it also deals with the disposition of material. Ultimately, John cannot be bound by his own organizational scheme. Rather, he consistently moves beyond his announced category to the next step. Thus, he seems oriented to the form of literacy, but expresses himself on the model of orality.

Chapter 2 moves into the selection of material. John observes that he differs from Cicero's teaching by considering the selection of the subject matter after the discovery of it (2.2–5). He does this deliberately, because poets and letter writers will find it most useful. John's basic criteria for selection of material is governed by qualities of entertainment, attractiveness, and utility. Entertaining material strikes the mind because it is pleasant; attractive material grasps the mind because of its beauty; and profitable material is that which is useful (2.6–9). John goes beyond a strict, classical notion of invention by incorporating some stylistic and conceptual categories in his inventional scheme. He continues an inventional tack in the sections that follow.

Shifting from the selection of material, John considers how it is presented. First, he offers ways in which light (*levis*) material can be made more serious and authentic (*gravem et autenticam*) through the use of nine devices known as the *difficili ornatu,* substituting property for subject, material for the thing made with the material, consequence for the antecedent, part for the whole, whole for the part, cause for the effect, container for the thing contained, genus for the species, and opposites for the proper expressions (2.44–50). This is essentially the same as Geoffrey's notion, but John avoids mentioning any particular tropes although he seems to be addressing the functions of metaphor, metonymy, and synecdoche.

John supports his doctrine on selection with techniques of memory. These techniques are the typical ancient notions of associational memory operationalized in this case by the three categories of character / persons (courtiers, city dwellers, and peasants), along with their implements and duties. John provides two visual aids to his system—a three-columned device and Virgil's wheel (a circle divided into three sections) (2.87–123). He moves on to a discussion of simplifying difficult subject matter, which simply amounts to the avoidance of the *difficili ornatu* (2.124–27). He then writes of easy or light ornamentation by means of determination (*De facili Ornatu per Determinaciones Verborum, Adiectiuorum, et Substantiuorum*) (2.147–265). Finally, he returns to the discussion of the transsumption of verbs (2.280–310).

John also offers some of his own notions like the criteria for selection of material and the technique for memory, but otherwise the section features the wholesale adoption of the doctrines of Geoffrey of Vinsauf. In essence, the selection of material in chapter 2 consists of ways of rewriting and reworking themes. One does not select material on which to base a story, rather one selects options for converting the story and the means for taking possession of it.

Chapter 3 consists of only ninety-seven lines. Here, John continues to use all of Geoffrey's innovations in addressing the eight methods of beginning developed in *Poetria nova* and *Documentum.* He closes the chapter by noting a ninth method not used by his contemporaries—beginning by placing a proposition, invocation, and plot motivation first. The final topic of discussion, bearing some resemblance to contemporary practice, is intriguing, but John fails to expand upon it with discussion.

Chapter 4 is much longer than the previous ones. This chapter professes to address the parts of a letter, but focuses only on the introduction. John of Garland notes that the salutation differs according to the rank of the correspondents and that the parts of the letter vary according to the type of letter. He then discusses a variety of ways of beginning the exordium of the letter: with a proverb, with an example, with a comparison, from a similitude, from a condition, with the adverb *cum,* with *vel,* or with the ablative absolute (4.17–75).

Eventually John uses every conceivable mode of beginning by borrowing forms of speeches, letters, literature, and the *thema* from *ars praedicandi.* He notes that an *exordium* may be defined as all material that precedes the narration or in a more narrow sense. Various types of beginning include the *exordium,* narrowly defined as a rhetorical beginning aimed at persuasion; a *proemium,* a preview of a work aimed at instruction; a prologue, a preliminary discussion of a work to follow; an epigram, "a beginning that states a cause and a similitude, and that explains the approach"; a theme (*thema*), the beginning of a sacred discussion; and a preface, the beginning of sacred songs and services (4.92–102). The emphasis is again on ways of developing an existing theme. He then addresses the greetings appropriate for people of various stations (4.103–192) and discusses the six parts of a Ciceronian oration, which he exemplifies with an oration aimed at gaining support for the Crusades (4.193–284).

He moves on to a standard discussion of amplification and abbreviation of material. Like Geoffrey, he mixes various grammatical concepts and figures as his means. Abbreviation is achieved by means of emphasis, *disjunctum,* participles, ablatives absolute, and by choosing words that "express the essence of the subject matter." Amplification may be achieved through the use of *digressio, descriptio, circumlocutio, prosopopoeia,* and apostrophe. Apostrophe is in turn divided into five parts: *conduplicatio, exclamatio, subiectio, dubitatio,* and *interpretatio* (4.285–416). Finally, John notes that material may be amplified by converting to each of the various levels of style: high, middle, and low (4.417–464).

The exemplification of the levels of style through a comic example brings John to a parenthetical discussion of comedy. The number of acts in a comic drama is five, according to Horace. A correct comedy, John maintains, consists of five characters—husband and wife, adulterer, the adulterer's accomplice or critic, and the servant of the wife or adulterer. Technically, John writes, a comedy focuses on low and humorous material, though it has come to be applied to a variety of humorous situations. John goes on to discuss briefly the parts of a narrative and the characteristics of tragedy, but then concludes the section with brief accounts of various legal documents: deeds, indentures, suits, and summons (4.484–514).

This fourth chapter is perhaps the most diverse in the work. John discusses everything from tragedy to deeds, though very few of the concepts are discussed in detail. It is an oral / rhetorical display of erudition that focuses not so much on the edification of its reader, but on the display of the writer's range of knowledge.

Chapter 5 begins with a discussion of six vices that can appear in verse: incongruous arrangement of parts, awkward digression from the subject, obscure brevity, unwieldy variations of styles and subject matter, and awkward endings. As far as the variation of style is concerned, they must correspond to the three types of characters / persons: the low style is suitable to the pastoral life, the middle style for farmers, and the high style for prominent persons. Style, thus, becomes a means of moral argumentation signaling the character of the person being portrayed in the presentation. John also mentions the various faulty styles associated with each: turgid and inflated, drifting and slack, and dry and bloodless. Other vices included are the *barbarisms* and *solecisms,* which he does not list. He does mention *synalimph,* however, because it has become permitted under contemporary practice (5.1–191).

John identifies a number of vices pertaining to meter: the elision of vowels; awkward pauses; elision of consonants; immediate repetition of a phrase; and the addition, removal, change, and transposition of letters and syllables (5.192–234). John's vices show a clear rejection of many of the *metaplasms* allowed by Donatus, Alexander, and Evrard (5.192–234).

John also suggests certain vices of word order that should be avoided in meter. A hexameter should not feature a long word at its end, nor should it end in a three or four syllable word. The *arsis* of the third foot should never coincide with the end of a word. Conjunctions should not join verbs of different tenses unless they follow logically. Tenses should not be changed frequently (5.235–259). It is interesting that much of the compositional doctrine of early grammars focused on how one could reasonably break the rules of grammar for expressive purposes. John shows a movement toward a literal emphasis by using certain rules and by avoiding rule-breaking strategies.

He goes on to discuss faults in composing letters. Faults, he writes, can occur in all parts of the letter: the salutation, supersalutation, proverb, narration, request, and conclusion. John does not discuss the proverb, presumably because it was treated earlier, but he does discuss the other elements at least briefly. The salutation and supersalutation both can be either too wordy, too abject, or simply used inappropriately. He writes that one should avoid a salutation entirely when writing to a nonbeliever (especially if one mentions the grace of God), an enemy, and a superior. The same is essentially true of the supersalutation (5.260–303)

He then provides definitions of dictamen and epistle. "Dictamen is a letter marked off by clausulae and embellished by figures of words and sentences. An epistle . . . is a letter directed to certain persons, laying bare the mind of the sender, sometimes containing a salutation, sometimes not" (5.265–70). The definitions are terse and without further elaboration.

In addition, John identifies a variety of narrative forms: dramatic or deitic, which is imitative or interrogative writing; exegetical or apangeltic, which is expository or interpretive; and *mictic* or *koinon,* which is didactic or instructive writing (5.303–310). Cicero, he writes, saw a division of the narrative forms, distinct from the legal causes, that deal with plot and character. Those forms dealing with plot include fable, history, and argumentum. Beyond those, John offers many subdivisions of history: *epithalium* (wedding poem); *epicedium* (plain song); epitaph (poem uttered over a dead body); *apotheosis* (song that celebrates the coming of a soul to glory); bucolic (poem about cowherding); georgic (poem about farming); lyric (poem about drinking, eating, and love of the gods); *epode* (poem about horse racing); secular songs; invectives; reprimands; tragedy; elegiac; and *amoebam* (song which focuses on a lover's spat) (5.311–372). His categories of history go a little beyond Cicero's, but he also borrows *topoi* for development of character from Cicero such as: social position, age, sex, occupation, nationality, and manner of speaking (5.373–381).

John moves on to faulty dimensions of poems. Five things that cause a poem to be criticized harshly are excessive length, too much haste, carelessness on the part of the writer, ignorance of his or her art, and malice on the part of the critic. Other faults occur in the development of beginnings. One should be careful to employ a beginning that allows the work to take a rising course or to build to a climax (5.382–389). John then moves rather abruptly to engage in a discussion of *cursus*—the system of rhythmical patterns employed in prose composition. He identifies four types: the Gregorian, Ciceronian, Hilarian, and Isidorean (5.402–467). The chapter closes by discussing briefly the request and asserting that a conclusion is bad if it is longer than the narrative (5.468–481).

Chapter 5 begins and ends with a discussion of vices in writing, but packed in between are a variety of other considerations. Again, the person expressing the ideas is not constrained by structure—even his own intended structure. Intent and expression of that intent can be remarkably different things.

Chapter 6 focuses on the ornamentation of meter and the art of ordering the parts of speech in dictamen. It consists of a number of doctrines: grammatical parts of speech, colors of rhetoric, and rhetorical categories of description (appropriated from the canon of arrangement). John addresses the placement of particular parts of speech—substantives, adjectives, verbs, adverbs, conjunctions, prepositions, interjections—in their most pleasing and effective order. Proper nouns, for example, should precede nouns that suggest office or rank: Donatus the Grammarian and Cicero the Rhetorician. He closes his section on grammatical ornamentation by allowing one of his few exceptions to the rules of grammar—that it is artful to express emotion by means of an incomplete sentence (6.1–69).

John goes on to list, define, and provide examples for the colors of words and thoughts (*De coloribus verborum et sententiarum*). John's *colores* are essentially the *exornationes* of *auctor ad Herennium* using the same Latin terms given in the same order, with a couple of exceptions. John omits *continuatio,* places *conduplicatio* and *conclusio* at different points in the list, and reverses the order of *translatio* and *abusio* (6.71–393). He offers yet another visual aid to illustrate *similiter desinens.*[10]

John closes the chapter with Cicero's eleven attributes of description (*De XI Attributis Persone ex Quibus Loci Rhetorici Eliciuntur*): name, nature, social position, wealth, character, motives, disposition, occupation, circumstances, actions, and words (6.394–416). Though each of John's ornamental systems is suitable for various circumstances and each involves a different type of phenomenon, all are used in a way that facilitates more elegant language through the choice of expressive options. Thus, the impetus of his method is compositional and inventional.

Though it was previewed as focusing on letter writing, chapter 7 begins with a consideration of the various properties of tragedy illustrated by a somewhat off-color example involving soldiers, washerwomen, a lover's quarrel, and a murder. John's synopsis begins as follows: "Sixty soldiers were besieged in a certain castle. With them were two washerwomen; one furnished the services of laundry and copulation for thirty soldiers, the other for the other thirty." One of the washerwomen falls in love with a man outside her assigned group. She quarrels with the other woman and, eventually, finds her in bed with her loved one. She kills the two and, to conceal her crime, lets the enemy into the castle. All the men are killed, including her own brother. Having rendered his synopsis, John notes the essential characteristics of tragedy: "It is written in the high style; it deals with shameful and criminal actions; it begins in joy and ends in tears" (7.1.26). He then offers an extended version of the tragedy that spans more than three pages (7.29–153).

This section on tragedy is followed by examples of various types of letters: one from the pope to the emperor, one to a person undertaking a crusade, one from the pope to his delegated judges, and a summons from those delegated judges (7.155–246). John interrupts his examples to offer general rules for the composition of a variety of legal documents: deeds, indentures, reports on the examination of witnesses, contracts (*transactionibus*), letters of record, summons, and letters of privilege. The discussion of the last type of document is accompanied by a description and illustration of a seal that is appended to the letter.[11] He then continues with his sample letters: a recommendation for a teaching position, a petition to the pope, a letter from the bishop granting alms, a letter for a convert to the church, a letter granting indulgences, and one granting ordination (7.246–466).

John ends his treatise with a treatment of rhymed poetry (*rithmica*) and hymns. He defines *rithmus* as "a harmonious arrangement of words with like endings, regulated not by quantity but by number of syllables [*pedibus ordinata*]" (7.480–481). He then lists and exemplifies forty-six different types of rhyme. He follows his account of *rithmus* with *Ars De Hymnis Usitati*—a discussion of three types of meter used in hymns and then the nineteen types of meters used in Horace's odes.[12] The final section is rather awkward and, indeed, may well be an addition to the original manuscript.[13]

John's treatise is a transitional work in a transitional genre. He reflects on the process of composing literal works, but with many of the techniques of oral composition. Moreover, though his work features an attempt at the classification and division of literacy, his presentation is through the meandering and repetitive digression of orality. His account of the inventional options for literary composition utilizes options from both grammatical and rhetorical works. Interestingly, he uses the rhetorical colors that had been excluded from grammar, while rejecting the *metaplasms* that had been allowed in grammar. He distributed the various doctrines to a great degree, yet his presentation of it is disorganized. His independence from authority and his systematic tendency sets the stage for Gervasius of Melkley to present a literal systematization of *ars poetriae.*

Chapter Six

Gervasius of Melkley's *Ars poetica*

Matthew of Vendôme, Geoffrey of Vinsauf, and John of Garland blended the doctrines of rhetoric and grammar together to form arts of composing poetry and prose. In many ways, their innovative work was unreflective and atheoretical. Matthew's and John's work manifests the loose, repetitive, and demonstrative format of orality. Indeed, each, in varying degrees, is written as a demonstration of their knowledge and abilities. Geoffrey offers his work as an example of the very principles he proposes. Though borrowing heavily from both rhetoric and grammar, each of the previous authors is deferential to the authority of certain doctrines—particularly the figures of speech. The figures are deemed so important to the various authors that, apart from the tropes, they present them virtually verbatim and in the same order found in *Rhetorica ad Herennium.* Gervasius of Melkley takes a step beyond his predecessors in presenting a more theoretical, though still practical, treatise. Gervasius abandons much of the terminology of the classical notions of style and reorganizes the figures into a coherent, consistent, and modern account that blends the systemicity of *stasis* with the efficiency of a contemporary vocabulary.

Gervasius of Melkley's *Ars poetica* is the most theoretical of the *artes poetriae* and perhaps the most literal. The first of its three sections comprises the bulk of the treatise and discusses principles common to all species of discourse. The second section deals with the specifics of composition. Among its subtopics are proverbs, elegance of style, arguments, rules of verse composition, and rules of prose composition. The final section contains a very short treatment on letter writing.[1]

Gervasius views his treatise as a practical handbook for composition. He uses the knowledge and authority of such scholars as Matthew of Vendôme, Geoffrey of Vinsauf, Bernard Silvester, Horace, Donatus, Priscian, Cicero, and his own master, John of Hanville. Gervasius notes that their works are complex and rather difficult for the less advanced student. His work therefore attempts to be more particular than general by offering rules, explanations, and examples that allow knowledge to be gained both directly and indirectly.[2] Gervasius' task, then, is to present a complex body of knowledge in a simple, streamlined fashion. Compounding the difficulty inherent in his task is the fact that the Greek terminology used to describe the various aspects of composition was largely unfamiliar to thirteenth-century students and teachers alike. He accomplishes his task by presenting the concepts in increasing levels of difficulty and through ordinary and descriptive Latin language.

Gervasius outlines four ways of understanding the nature of composition: through knowledge of prohibitions (*prohibitiones*), permissions (*permissiones*), rules (*precepta*), and strategies (*consilia*). Prohibitions are lists of faults or instances of faulty composition; permissions are figures that may be used in composition; rules consist of the elements of proper grammar; strategies outline the way elements of grammar and composition may be used to achieve eloquence.[3] Prohibitions, permissions, and rules are both standard categories of medieval grammar, but strategy (*consilium*) is the province of rhetoric.

Gervasius writes that knowledge may be gained directly through lists of rules, faults, and figures. Knowledge may also be gained indirectly by observing examples of discourse composed in accordance with the rules of grammar and through the use of the various figures and strategies. The direct type of knowledge is gained through the prohibitions, rules, and permissions. Both are necessary in teaching composition.[4] Gervasius' treatise, however, deals primarily with figures and strategies.

Gervasius' system begins as follows: once the subject matter of a discourse has been decided upon, separate clauses are generated. A clause is an utterance that provides explicit or implicit understanding. Clauses may be generated from three *loci* (sources of discourse): *identitas* (identities), *similitudo* (similarities), and *contrarietas* (contraries).[5]

The *loci* amount to three progressively sophisticated levels of expression and meaning. *Identitas* involves instances of the use of language that are linguistically simple; utterances mean what they would be interpreted to mean within the limits of normal usage. *Similitudo,* on the other hand, involves an extension of meaning wrought through similarities found in both utterances and the phenomena utterances represent. In *contrarietas* one goes beyond *similitudo* by using utterances in a way that is contradictory to their meaning in normal use. Each source of discourse includes a number of figures and tropes. Gervasius does not pay particular attention to conventional terms used to refer to many of the operations he describes. Many of the conventional terms could be classed appropriately in more than one of his three *loci*. Therefore, rather than using the traditional names of the various figures, he describes each linguistic dimension by a term that is descriptive of its function.

Identitas

Identitas (see figure 6.1) occurs in utterances possessing neither transsumption nor contradiction of thought. *Identitas* is either rough (*rudis*) or polished (*polita*).[6] Rough *identitas* is a narrow category that is divided into three basic types: *rudis* (rough), *rudior* (more rough), and *rudissima* (most rough). Polished *identitas*, on the other hand, consists of two main categories, seven subcategories, and at least thirty-two lesser categories.

Rudis Identitas

Rudis identitas consists of simple utterances that are grammatically and linguistically correct. Anything added to a clause of this type either obscures or decorates it. *Rudior identitas* is a statement containing a required imperfection—something required for the sake of lyric, rhyme, meter, or rhetoric. *Rudissima identitas* involves the use of an inexcusable fault. It is an imperfection that cannot be justified.[7]

These types of rough *identitas* serve to distinguish between purposeful and nonpurposeful variations from the conventions of language use. One may stray from strict usage only if that usage allows one to conform to other necessary conventions—meter, rhyme, or a part of a strategy being pursued in the larger work by which the clause is subsumed.

Polished *Identitas*

Polished or elegant *identitas* is produced through two rhetorical means: colors and arguments. Colors attract and please the ear and the senses. Arguments attract and please the mind and reason.[8] *Identitas*, therefore, may refer to words as utterances or as representations of things. Some attract the appreciation of what is heard. Others attract the understanding of the word itself. *Identitas* is thus colored by two means: *conservantia* (preservation) and *mutatio* (change).[9]

Figure 6.1

- Identitas
  - Rough
    - Rudis
    - Rudior
    - Rudissima
  - Polished
    - Conservantia
      - Simplex Narratio
        - Tautoparonomion
        - Euphonomaton
        - Amphibolum
      - Loquendi Vehementia
        - Correctio
          - Adversative
          - Additive
        - Exclamatio
        - Dubitatio
      - Questio et Responsio
        - Dialogus
          - Ratiocinatio
        - Subiectio
    - Mutatio
      - Subtraction
        - Praecisio
          - Prolempsis
        - Additio
          - Occupatio
          - Coadunatio
            - Of Words
              - Polysyndeton
              - Articulum
            - Of Phrases
              - Aggregatio
                - Disjunctive
                - Conjunctive
              - Reiteratio
                - Repetitio Pr. Dicti
                - Conduplicatio
                - Interpretatio
        - Determinatio
        - Diversio
          - Equalitas
          - Digressio
            - Comparatio
            - Descriptio
          - Transversio
            - Inversio
            - Transmutatio
          - Transcensus
            - Hyperbaton
              - Hysteron Proteron
              - Anastrophe
              - Themesis
              - Interpositio
              - Synthesis
              - Singula Singulis
            - Litotes
            - Hyperbole

Conservantia

In *conservantia* nothing substantive about a clause is altered. It transcends rough *identitas* in that it changes the way in which a clause is expressed—either through sound or emphasis. *Conservantia* may be achieved through simple narration (*simplex narratio*), forceful speaking (*loquendi vehementia*), or question and answer (*questio et responsio*).

Simple narration consists of three types: *tautoparonomion*, *euphonomaton*, and *amphibolum*. *Tautoparonomion* is the use of maxims or proverbs that are relevant to the subject being discussed. They are maxims that underscore the point being made.[10] *Euphonamaton* is a resounding harmony of discourse that is achieved through repetition of sounds, syllables, and words.[11] This includes such figures as *paronomasia*, *paronomeon*, *poliptoton*, *consonantia*, *leonitas*, *similiter cadens*, *similiter desinens*, and *homoeoteleuton*. It may also include forms of *conversio*, *complexio*, *annominatio*, *repetitio*, *traductio*, *gradatio*, *inflexio*, *resumptio*, and *metalepsis*.[12] *Amphibolum* consists of discourse that may take several meanings. It should only be used where the skilled reader can discern the meaning through the position of the words.[13]

Forceful speaking is used in cases in which one speaks as if angry or amazed. This may be achieved through correction (*correctio*), exclamation (*exclamatio*), and uncertainty (*dubitatio*).

Correction is produced through two means: adversative (*adversativa*) and additive (*additiva*). Adversative correction may be achieved in two ways. One is by negating one statement and positing another. A second is to posit two statements that oppose each other (or cancel each other out) and then feature a corrective word that allows them to coexist. "But" (*sed*) may be used to achieve this effect.[14] Additive correction occurs when something new is added to a previous statement. This works best in conjunction with *gradatio*. Additive correction includes *exclamatio* and *dubitatio*. Exclamation is simply an exclamation of grief or anger. Uncertainty occurs when remarks are uttered in a hesitating fashion.[15]

Question and answer is divided into dialogue (*dialogus*) and subject (*subiectio*.) Dialogue is discourse featuring a conversation between two people. A subspecies of dialogue is *ratiocinatio*. *Ratiocinatio* is the practice of questioning a premise and then confirming that premise through reasoning. Subject occurs when a question is posed, but the answer is anticipated and stated. As a result the question is strengthened. Exclamation may also be colored by this device.[16]

Mutatio

Mutatio (change) occurs when a clause is colored by subtraction (*subtractio*), addition (*additio*), or alteration (*diversio*). Unlike *conservantia, mutatio* allows for a substantive change in a clause. Regardless of how the substantive change is produced, however, it must still be within the bounds of conventional language use.

Subtraction is achieved through *praecisio* or *prolempsis. Praecisio* is the truncation of a word or phrase. This may occur by subtraction of a word or interpolation of a phrase. In the first, a word is left out because it may be understood. Interpolation occurs in cases where a person is designated both by his name and the attributes of the proper meaning of that name. Therefore, the name or designation may be left out. In *prolempsis* the addition of a newly added clause anticipates the conclusion of the clause already begun.

Addition is achieved through *occupatio, coadunatio,* and *determinatio. Occupatio* is the modification of one statement by adding another statement indicating that what had just been uttered was not serious. This device is used for humor or to create variety.[17]

Coadunatio is a collection of words or phrases connected by some similarity or dissimilarity. *Coadunatio* of words is achieved by *polysyndeton* and *articulum. Polysyndeton* is *coadunatio* achieved through the use of conjunctions. *Articulum* is *coadunatio* achieved by punctuation.[18]

Coadunatio of phrases includes *aggregatio* and *reiteratio. Aggregatio* is *coadunatio* of phrases without repetition. This is determined according to the use of verbs or conjunctions. *Aggregatio* of a verb is either disjunctive (*disiunctum*) or conjunctive (*coniunctum*). *Disiunctum* occurs when each clause in a phrase has its own verb. *Coniunctum* occurs when clauses are joined by one common verb. *Coadunatio* is also found in forms of *similitudo* and *contrarietas.*[19]

Reiteratio is divided into repetition of the previous utterance (*repetitio prius dicti*), doubling (*conduplicatio*), and interpretation (*interpretatio*). Repetition of the previous utterance is a device by which the end of a clause is repeated for the sake of emphasis. Conversely, doubling is produced when the beginning of a phrase or clause is repeated for emphasis. Interpretation is produced when a previously stated phrase is restated in different words.[20]

Determinatio includes adjectives, partitives, appositives, and relatives. Adjectives and partitives, however, exceed the dimensions of appositives and relatives. Adjectives can note cause, difference, sign, effect, and epithets. Differentiating adjectives exclude some type of characteristic and therefore serve as partitions. Partitions are uniform or nonuniform. Uniform partitions are those made through identical case endings. Nonuniform partitions are made through irregular case endings. Nonuniform partitions may be made through direct and indirect methods. Direct partition occurs when a dividing term precedes and the divided term follows. Indirect partition occurs when the reverse is performed. Direct partition is decorative when an indeclinable word is divided into a term with case endings. Indirect partition is produced through the use of signs. A relative is modified when its contrary or like is placed in close proximity. The clauses should be related in some coherent fashion that is made evident by the context in which they are uttered. An appositive is the joining of two substantives in close proximity. Relative and appositive *determinatio* are often enacted by a juxtaposition that makes a word more specific.[21]

The quality of simplicity (*simplicitas*) is common to adjective determination, relative determination, and apposition. Determination is a way to modify equivocal or nearly equivocal words.[22]

Diversio, alteration of normal word order, is used to ornament a clause. There are four kinds: equal substitution (*equalitas*), digression (*digressio*), *transversio,* and *transcensus.*

Equal substitution occurs when a clause is altered by using substitute expressions or words bearing force equal to the original. This is done for the sake of agreement, reason of hidden argument, or uniform variation. Agreement refers to maintaining a consistent meter or prose style. Substitution by means of a hidden argument may be used when a substitution is consistent with the original utterance because of a necessary relationship between the two. Uniform variation refers to the practice of intentionally varying the form in which the clause is composed. One way to achieve variation is by using a feminine adjective with a masculine noun or vice versa. A second and more appropriate way is to follow a clause with variations of, or synonyms for, the clause previously stated.[23]

Digression is a departure from the subject matter being discussed that is permissible because it is related and appropriate to the subject. It may be achieved through comparison (*comparatio*) and description (*descriptio*). Comparison is addressed more appropriately under *similitudo.* Description is a digression that clarifies or explains an aspect of the subject under discussion. This should be used only when the author means to elicit some argument from the discussion. These descriptions may be intrinsic or extrinsic. Intrinsic descriptions refer to circumstances particular to the phenomenon being described. Extrinsic descriptions refer to external deeds or actions that affect the phenomenon. Description may include *circumlocutio* or *periphrasis,* but it does not include *antonomasia, metonomia, circutio,* or *synecdoche* which are more appropriately classed under *similitudo.*

Transversio is a departure from a word of identity by means of a change in vocalization or alteration of the word form. It is divided into *inversio* and *transmutatio. Inversio* is the warping of the sound of a word so that it resembles a different word of a different meaning. It is used as a means of showing contempt. *Transmutatio* is a *transversio* that alters a word, but does not change its sense. For example, an adjective may be made into a genitive to show emphasis.[24]

Transcensus is a departure from the usual in a word or phrase. It consists of three species: *hyperbaton, litotes,* and hyperbole. *Hyperbaton* is transposition of word order. Gervasius notes that Donatus has divided it into three species: *hysteron proteron, anastrophe,* and *themesis.* He then suggests that one consult Donatus to find out what they are. Gervasius does, however, designate two useful divisions of *transcensus:* parenthesis (*interpositio*) and synthesis. Synthesis is a *hyperbaton* in which all parts of the sentence are confused.[25] It is permissible only when required by meter. Related to synthesis, however, is a very useful device called *singula singulis* that occurs in an expression where subject, verb, object and other various components are listed in uniform series—for example, when five subjects, five verbs, and five objects are expressed successively to represent five sentences:

> Bob, Ellen, Jim, John, Paul,
> took, stole, gave, received, worshiped,
> money, books, thanks, praise, God.

Understatement (*litotes*) occurs when less is said, but more is understood. Hyperbole is a word that overstates a situation for the sake of augmenting or diminishing its significance.[26]

Identitas, then, covers the variety of means one may use to express a thought literally or conventionally. A basic utterance and thought are present throughout. The form the thought takes may be changed to adhere to conventions required by the various forms of literature into which it is encoded (poetry, prose, song, verse, oratory), but the utterance is always intended to convey a clear, unequivocal meaning. It is purposeful composition and each of its devices has a reasoned and intentional use.

Similitudo

Similitudo (see figure 6.2) occurs in discourse that extends the meaning of a word or phrase through implicit or explicit resemblance. It consists of three species: *assumptio, transsumptio,* and *omiosis.*[27]

Figure 6.2

- Similitudo
    - Assumptio
        - Significative
        - Nonsignificative
    - Transsumptio
        - Transsumptio Dictionis
            - Absolute
                - Substantive
                - Adjective
            - Referential
        - Transsumptio Orationis
            - Antismos
            - Enigma
    - Omiosis
        - Icon
        - Paradigm
        - Comparatio

Assumptio

Assumptio involves "the adaptation of a word to a signification or secondary signification which it does not have from its establishment by means of a resemblance other than the one used [originally]."[28] For example, *achillior* is adapted to mean the same as *fortier* (stronger) because Achilles was a strong man.[29] Likewise, *mirrifluus* (flowing with myrrh) could be coined by using a resemblance to *mellifluus* (flowing with honey).[30] Each of the above examples are termed nonsignificative *assumptio*—a word that is adapted to a new meaning. Significative *assumptio* occurs when a word that is significant in one way is used in another way.[31] An example is "three good soldiers" who are referred to as "three Achilles." In this case, Achilles, which is properly used only as a singular, is converted to a plural for the sake of expression.[32]

In each of the examples above, the adaptation is achieved by simple analogy. Because an addition to a term creates a modification of that term, new words are formulated based on the model of another:

strong (*fortis*) (*A*)	Achilles (*B*)
stronger (*fortier*) (*A* plus *X*)	*achillior* (*B* plus *X*)
honey (*mel*) (*A* plus *X*)	*myrrh* (*B*)
mellifluus (*A* plus *X*)	*mirrifluus* (*B* plus *X*)
good soldier (*A*)	Achilles (*B*)
three good soldiers (*A* plus *X*)	three Achilles (*B* plus *X*)

Each *B* plus *X* change is made following the model of *A*, *A* plus *X*. *Assumptio*, then, can be defined as the creation or adaptation of a word through a resemblance in structure.[33] Nonsignificative *assumptio* involves the creation of a new word based on the model provided by an existing word. Significative *assumptio* seems to differ only in that it allows changes in word forms that are proper only through changes in meaning. Thus, it is permissible to refer to three Achilles if Achilles is referring to good soldiers, but not if it refers to the Greek hero. *Assumptio* would seem to include the trope *onomatopoeia*. In *onomatopoeia*, a word is created because of its resemblance to another word or sound. Though Gervasius does not specifically mention sound resemblance, sound and other words imitative of sound would seem to provide the same type of model used in the assumptive creation of words.

Transsumptio

Gervasius defines *transsumptio* as "the transferral of a word from its proper signification to another [signification] by means of an untransformed resemblance."[34] *Transsumptio* has two forms: of a word (*transsumptio dictionis*) and of a phrase (*transsumptio orationis*). *Transsumptio dictionis* involves a transferral through the use of a word—as in "the meadow laughs." *Transsumptio orationis,* however, requires a phrase to achieve clarity—for example, "he plows the shore."[35] The abnormal use of words in *transsumptio dictionis* requires only that the subject and verb be understood. In *transsumptio orationis,* the object must be appended to the subject and verb before the abnormal usage becomes apparent.

Transsumptio dictionis has two divisions: absolute and referential. Absolute *transsumptio* is used appellatively as a substantive or adjective. Substantively, one could substitute "no Hector" or "no Achilles" for "no good soldier." Rather than use the word "mistress," one could substitute the names Phyllis, Corinna, Amaryllis, or Galatea. Instead of the word "tyrant," Herod, Nero, Phalaris, or Busiris could be substituted. Gervasius cautions his readers that substantive absolute *transsumptio* varies according to the intention of its user. Therefore, the condition of a transformed word is addressed at times. At other times, only similarities are addressed. For example, a reference to a person as Pyramus might be intended to mean: "a lover denied his will" (conditional) or "willing in all the things which Pyramus wills" (similarity).[36] The first use of Pyranius addresses a condition shared by Pyramus and its referent. The second usage addresses similarities shared by the two. Both examples follow in the *AB, BC, AC* pattern seen in the earlier discussion of *transsumptio* or *metalepsis:*

CONDITION	(*A*) is a lover denied his will (*B*). A lover denied his will (*B*) is Pyramus (*C*). (*A*) is Pyramus (*C*).
SIMILARITY	*A*) desires things (*B*) (power and wealth). (*C*) desires things (*B*) (wine and song). (*A*) is (*C*).

In conditional substantive absolute *transsumptio,* the *B* term is specific. In similar substantive absolute *transsumptio,* the *B* term is more flexible and less precise. Context, then, is an important element in achieving clear transsumptions.

Adjectival absolute *transsumptio* may be particularly ambiguous. For example, although the intention of saying "Agenor was a Paris" may be to indicate that Agenor was handsome, it may be interpreted to mean that Agenor was lascivious or weak. Therefore, the ablative "in countenance" is added to provide clarity. "In countenance" excludes lasciviousness or weakness, thus focusing the reader's attention on appearance.[37] Using this method, one can praise or blame in a clear, distinctive way. To praise Agenor, one might say: "Agenor was a Paris in countenance, an Achilles in reputation, a Hector in strength, a Croesus in prudence, a Caesar in lineage." Likewise, to blame Davus: "Davus was a Herod in deeds, a Nero in spirit, a Birrea in words, a Synon in deceit, a Proteus in heart."[38] Just as Geoffrey's use of adjectives provided the transsumptive link between terms, so too does Gervasius' use of ablatives. An ablative provides much needed context to an obscure expression and renders its meaning more clearly.

Gervasius also notes that proper nouns, nouns, pronouns, and appellatives are sometimes transformed to act as collectives. For example, the word "king" is sometimes used to represent the monarch and his state, or the king's vestments may be referred to as his state.[39]

Referential *transsumptio* occurs "when two words refer themselves in turn to what each is transformed by." For example, "sometimes he is hot, sometimes he is cold" means that a person is inconsistent.[40] The reference to the same person as both hot and cold causes the transformation of both descriptors.

Transsumptio orationis involves the transformation of a phrase from its conventional meaning.[41] For example, if one were to say "he washes brick," meaning "he makes a futile effort," then a phrase rather than a word is transformed.[42] Phrases are transformed in two ways: *antismos* and enigma. *Antismos,* Gervasius notes, includes all rhetorical devices. Donatus defines *antismos* as anything that lacks rustic simplicity and is described more appropriately as witty urbanity. With a more restricted meaning it is a species of *transsumptio orationis* achieved by appearance, equivalence, or resemblance.[43] For example, one could say "Phoebus emerged from the waves" to express "the sun rises."[44] Another example may be seen when Bernard Silvester said: "The male organ wars against

Lachesis and skillfully re-knots the threads cut by the fates" to express "the male organ prevents the human race from dying [out]."[45]

Enigma is defined as "any obscure statement which tries the cleverness of the one guessing." Two examples of enigma are as follows:

> Who gave light to this work? Do you wish to have his name? Add the peak of Gaurus after having reversed "suis aure."

> I am the daughter of the sun and I am created with the sun. I am called ten times five, and five plus ten.[46]

The answer to the first enigma is Gervasius (*G* added to *suis aure* backwards). The second enigma is answered by *lux* (light). *L,* the Roman numeral fifty, is equal to five times ten. *V* is the Roman numeral five, and *X* is the Roman numeral ten. Together they spell *lux. Antismos* and enigma follow the same pattern seen in *transsumptio dictionis,* except that a phrase rather than a word is transformed. Lachesis, the fate who determines the length of the threads of life, is equated to death. The male organ thwarts Lachesis by reknotting and extending the threads of life, or perpetuating the race. The answer to an enigma represents the common element shared by the two riddles. Who is both the author of the work and *G* plus *suis aure* reversed—Gervasius.

Another principle, *advocatio,* is packed within the discussion of the various types of *transsumptio. Advocatio* is defined as "the referential quality which exists in any word because—by means of the signification of a property which it has—it is harmonious with another word or other words used in the same statement."[47] There are two types of *advocatio:* intrinsic and extrinsic. Intrinsic *advocatio* is exemplified by: "The playfulness of youthful spring banishes the decrepit old age of winter." Playfulness brings to mind the word *senectutus* (old age) by means of extrinsic *advocatio.* Youth is the opposite of old age and old age is something that youth reacts against violently.

Gervasius goes on to note that "a non-transformed resemblance is taken from either the person or from the [characteristic] action. It either goes from the person toward the meaning from which the word is transformed, or from the meaning toward the person to whom the meaning is transformed."[48] Moreover, "transsumptio proceeds most beautifully when the First word of the transformation refers equally to a person and to [characteristic] action."[49] For example:

> Hic est philosophus Veneris, quem mollis pagina lecti non libri reficit, cui dum magis approbat album incaustum tripusque nigrum, nocturna placere non lucis scriptura solet, eubeoque libello inspuitur calamo delectans litere caeca.[50]
>
> This is the philosopher of Venus, whom the soft sheet of a bed not of a book refreshes; to whom the white ink and the black time of night is now more satisfying; who is accustomed to enjoy nocturnal [activities], not the Scriptures of light; who, delighting in a blind letter, spatters the little red book with his reed pen.[51]
>
> See how the two words "philosopher" [*philosophus*] and "Venus" summon successively the words which follow. And see at the end: This phrase "of Venus" [*Veneris*] summons this word "red" [*rubeo*]; this word "philosopher" [summons] this word "little book" [*libello*]; this word "Venus" [summons] this word "spatters" [*inspuitur*] and so on through the order.[52]

A transsumption proceeds beautifully and effectively if the first words prepare for and summon the subsequent words in the expression. *Advocatio* then sustains such relationships.

Gervasius' doctrine of *transsumptio* may best be characterized as the transferal of a word from one meaning to another through the common qualities of the phenomena being signified by the word. Metaphor, allegory, *antonomasia, synecdoche, metonymy,* and *catachresis* are all tropes that seem to be subsumed by Gervasius' *transsumptio.*[53] As seen in Geoffrey's and Gervasius' analysis of *transsumptio,* the mode of reasoning used in *transsumptio* is syllogistic.

Omiosis

Omiosis, the third division of *similitudo,* is defined as "the pointing out of something less known by means of its resemblance to something more known."[54] It consists of three types: icon, *paradigma,* and *comparatio.* Icon is the comparison of one person to another by means of those things characteristic of the better-known person. For example, a description may be more vivid if a person was said to have "face and shoulders like a god."[55] "*Paradigma* is the use of an example in order to deter or to encourage." For example, if one were to try to prevent someone from abandoning his master, one might say: "Judas betrayed his lord and hanged himself with a halter."[56] There are two types of *paradigma: apologus* and *parabola. Apologus* deals with irrational things and *parabola* deals with rational ones. The above example concerning Judas demonstrates *parabola.* An example of *apologus* is shown in the remark that Gervasius attributes to Aristotle:

> Certain citizens were instituting a league with others by an agreement that they would remove from their city some of their citizens whom their enemies considered troublesome. And after they had pointed them out by name, they consulted Aristotle on this, who wrote back saying (by means of *apologus*): "Once upon a time, the wolves instituted a league with the sheep with an agreement that they would keep the dogs from the sheep-fold."[57]

Parabola demonstrates a direct relationship between the situation at hand and the example being used. *Apologus* is less direct. By removing the example directly from the situation to which it refers, the person presenting the *paradigma* is able to present the irrationality of the situation with greater clarity.

Comparatio is similar to icon. However, where icon compares similar things, *comparatio* compares the dissimilar. For example, "as Typhus without a thumb, as Hector without a sword, or Tullius without a mouth" is an instance of icon because it compares things that are similar. An example of *comparatio* is: "As ships without a rower, as a lyre which is silent, or a bow which does not bend."[58] The things compared in the second example bear no commonality; however, there is a certain uniformity among them in that each object is lacking in something. If that uniformity was absent, then the *comparatio* would be meaningless.

The temptation to equate Gervasius' devices with various tropes should be avoided. Repeatedly, Gervasius acknowledges that some refer to particular elements of his scheme by other names.[59] Those names, however, are only significant in that they are elements of the larger principles Gervasius is presenting. His elements of composition represent rationale for invention, not the particular devices of style.

Two things in particular can be gleaned from Gervasius' discussion of *similitudo.* First, he confirms the notions about *transsumptio* that are only suggested in the writings of Quintilian and Geoffrey. *Transsumptio* is a subsuming doctrine that includes the tropes of metaphor, *metonymy, synecdoche, antonomasia, catachresis,* and parts of allegory. Second, he makes a distinction between assumption and transsumption. The implications of Gervasius' distinctions are further discussed in the conclusion of this section.

Omiosis is the demonstration of a lesser-known thing by means of its resemblance to something better known. It has three types: icon, paradigm, and *comparatio.* Icon is the comparison of one person to another by means of the better-known person's characteristics. Paradigm is the use of a well-known example for the purpose of exhorting or deterring. *Comparatio* compares dissimilar things in series to demonstrate a certain sufficiency or insufficiency. As in *identitas, coadunatio* serves to make the comparisons in *omiosis* clearer.[60]

Thus, *similitudo* involves language used out of its ordinary sense. Its intended meaning is perceived through comparisons and resemblances both explicit and implicit. It is a form of purposeful language use, however, and should be composed with various contextualizing devices (except in the case of enigma) to render its meaning clear.

Contrarietas

Contrarietas (see figure 6.3) occurs in discourse ornamented by contraries. It is divided into two species: allegory and enthymeme (*entimema*).[61] Allegory involves utterances that feature contradiction in understanding, but not in vocalization. The utterance itself is coherent and presents no contradiction. The contradiction lies in understanding the utterance. Allegory has five species: irony *(yronia), antiphrasis, carientismos,* sarcasm (*sarcasmos*), and *paroemia. Paroemia* is the same thing as a proverb. Gervasius notes that it is a device subsumed by *identitas, similitudo,* and *contrarietas.* He therefore discusses it in a separate section.

Irony is a trope that conveys meaning through opposites. It seems to confirm the thought that it professes to deny and may also be achieved through exclamation. *Antiphrasis* is irony of one word. *Carientismos* is a trope through which harsh ideas are proffered graciously. Sarcasm is a remark filled with hostile derision.[62] Gervasius' allegory, then, is determined more by its context than its meaning. Emphasis, tone of voice, and the fashion in which an utterance is expressed serve as cues to understanding.

Enthymeme, on the other hand, involves contradiction both in the utterance and its meaning. Gervasius quotes verbatim Cicero's discussion of the enthymeme in *Topica:*

To this [the category of contradictories] belong those forms of conclusions from contraries adopted by teachers of rhetoric, to which they themselves have given the name [enthymemes]. Not that any expression of thought is not properly called an [enthymeme], but just as among the Greeks Homer by his outstanding merit has made the name of poet particularly his own, although it is common to all poets, so although every expression of thought may be called [enthymeme], that one which is based on contraries has, because it seems the most pointed form of argument, appropriated the common name for its sole possession. The following lines will illustrate this form of argument: Fear this, and not dread the other! You condemn the woman whom you accuse of nothing, and do you assert that the one deserves punishment whom you believe to deserve reward? What you know is of no use; is what you do not know a hindrance? This kind of argumentation has doubtless a relation to your discussions when you give answers on legal problems, but it more closely concerns the philosophers, who share with orators that method of drawing a conclusion from contradictory statements which the logicians call the third form, and the teachers of rhetoric, the [enthymeme].[63]

Figure 6.3

- Contrarietas
  - Allegory
    - Irony
    - Antiphrasis
    - Carientismos
    - Sarcasmos
    - Paroemia
  - Enthymeme
    - Contrarium
    - Conversio
    - Adversitas
    - Metathesis
    - Contentio
    - Antithesis

Thus, his account of enthymeme is rather narrowly defined. Gervasius then divides enthymeme into six species: *contrarium, conversio, adversitas, methatesis, contentio,* and *antithetum.*

Contrarium is produced when two opposing positions are expressed and one is proved or disproved by virtue of the other.[64] *Conversio* results when the logical progression of a clause is changed to explain the absurdity or problem in a particular situation.[65] This device is well demonstrated by the following remark concerning incest: "Others copulate in order to have children; you have children in order to copulate."[66] *Adversitas* is a manner of speaking by which one conjoins two ideas or thoughts as if they were contradictory. This may be done by speaking of two phenomena that are virtually concomitant as if they were incompatible, speaking of a single thing as if it belonged to two separate classes, or speaking of things agreeable as if they were disagreeable.[67] *Metathesis* is the transposition of ideas in order to make a point. Gervasius illustrates this device by recounting a story of a young man who was disowned by his father because he had sired a son by a prostitute. The young man died and his father then adopted his illegitimate grandson. The situation is summarized pointedly as follows: "He adopted the son of her on whose account he cast out his own [son]."[68] *Contentio* is an expression that contains acceptable contradictions. The contradictions are made acceptable through the use of modifiers that define the conflicting terms in regard to place, time, or the thing itself. For example, one could say that "Pompey was happy in Pontus, but wretched in Greece."[69] The contradiction between being happy and wretched is resolved by the modifiers that show that Pompey's condition varied according to his location.

Antithesis is a statement containing an overabundance of contradictory expressions. The excess of contradictions gives an appearance of impossibility that must ultimately be resolved by means of a subtle analysis of the statement.[70] *Antithesis* may be either expressed or unexpressed. Unexpressed *antithesis* is the weaker form because its contradiction must be explained through modification or from external circumstances.[71] Expressed *antithesis* is apparent without the use of an explanation.[72] The difference between the two is apparent in the following examples:

> Whom you accuse of nothing, you accuse of everything.
>
> You condemn her whom you accuse of nothing.[73]

The first sentence is an expressed *antithesis* that presents a paradox of being accused of all or nothing. The second sentence is an unexpressed *antithesis* that shows the consequence of being accused of everything—condemnation. An expressed *antithesis,* therefore, presents a paradox. The unexpressed *antithesis* implies the result of the paradox or resolves the paradox through the use of a modifier. The unexpressed *antithesis* defines the implications of an *antithesis.* The expressed *antithesis* does not.

An expressed *antithesis* may be determined or undetermined. Determination simply focuses the *antithesis* on a particular phenomenon. For example, an undetermined expressed *antithesis* would be: "to serve is to reign." By adding "the Lord" ("to serve the Lord is to reign"), the *antithesis* becomes determined and easier to comprehend.[74]

Contrarietas, again reasoned and intentional, goes beyond *similitudo*'s extension of meaning by ignoring the notion of linguistic or conventional meanings. Thus, the allegory is intended to mean something other than its literal meaning. The enthymeme employs literal meanings, but juxtaposes them in such a way as to render them meaningless. Both devices rely on their contexts to render their meanings clear.

Paroemia (proverb) is produced by *identitas, similitudo,* and *contrarietas.* There are three types of proverbs: *epiphonema, translaticia,* and *entimema. Epiphonema* is a proverb of identity. It is the same thing as *tautoparonomion,* but is called *epiphonema* because the combination of *epi* and *phonos* refer to the sounds in the material itself. It is a proverb that means exactly what it says. Likewise, *translaticia* is a proverb of similarities that does not apply directly to the particular situation, but may be used because of similarities between the situation to which it refers literally and the situation in which it is being used. Gervasius notes that a *translaticia* can easily become an *epiphonema* if its referent were changed. As mentioned in the previous section, a proverb of contraries is an enthymeme.[75]

The remaining sections of Gervasius' work are a collection of miscellaneous comments that lack the systemization of his earlier thoughts. He writes first of the role of uniformity and diversity in producing elegance. Uniformity and diversity, he writes, "walk with equal steps." Discourse is polished by both. They are defined as follows: "Uniformity is observed in the retention equally of actual referents or of words; diversity in the variation of the same things—as shall be clear manifestly in examples."[76] The concept boils down to a sensitivity to the constant tension between the two goals. One wants to be diverse in his or her expression and composition, but also wants to stay close to the conventions of grammar and correctness. One should therefore be attentive to issues such as parallelism, agreement, and word choice.[77]

Elegance may also be achieved through the choice of certain words, which the contemporary reader of Latin will recognize as filler words: *adhuc, porro, ecce, quippe, et, que, quoque, etiam, nec, tamen, vel,* and *atque.* The appropriate use of these words adds elegance to an expression and aids in the goal of reaching uniformity and diversity.[78]

The section on argument is simply a brief account of rhetorical topics (*loci*). He lists the eleven attributes of a person and nine attributes of place, and then refers his readers to the rhetoricians for further details.[79] He then moves into a series of miscellaneous rules concerning verse: the avoidance of too many monosyllabic words, rules concerning the pentameter and hexameter, and rules for the use of multisyllabic words. He cannot address all of the various rules and omits them for the sake of brevity.[80] His section on dictamen speaks specifically to prose. Prose, he writes, should feature filling and lengthy periodic structure that is governed by many of the concerns of verse.[81] Finally, Gervasius treats *ars dictaminis* briefly. He spends most of his time discussing the salutation and then briefly treats the remaining parts: proverb, *exordium,* narrative, *exhortatio,* and *conclusio.* Of the proverb, he acknowledges that some have advocated starting at the middle and end of a proverb, but that this practice is not really appropriate in letters.[82] Gervasius closes his work by thanking God and provides a few samples.

Gervasius' account of figurative language and its use in composition is intentionally different from classical accounts. It was mediated in part by developments in medieval grammar. Indeed, part of Gervasius' reorganization features the fundamental categories of language alteration outlined early in Donatus' *Ars grammatica.* Moreover, he organized the figures under general headings that described their functions in clear, descriptive Latin. He further subdivided the various phenomena under other equally descriptive Latin expressions. This was particularly important for his unpolished audience that had enough trouble understanding Latin, much less the extensive Greek vocabulary of the schemes and tropes. The Greek vocabulary that was meaningful to the bilingual Roman rhetor of the first century was no longer relevant to thirteenth-century students bound to Latin. Gervasius described the various phenomena in terms meaningful to his audience and also arranged them in a literal scheme designed to show a systematic progression of thought.

His account thus imparted an order and conciseness not found in the traditional accounts and placed an emphasis on figurative function rather than names.

Gervasius' organization of the various figures in progressive levels of abstraction amounts to a *stasis* system for rhetorical style. The *locus* of *identitas* begins with the basic notions of functional language found in rough *identitas,* then advances to the changes of sound and emphasis outlined in *conservantia,* and then ends with the substantive changes provided for in *mutatio.* The *locus* of *similitudo* allows language contrary to convention that: uses other word forms as precedents for change in *assumptio;* departs from the literal meanings of words and phrases through implied comparisons and relationships in *transsumptio;* and employs explicit models, examples, and comparisons in *omiosis.* The *locus* of *contrarietas* takes language one step further from convention by allowing seemingly explicit language to mean something other than what it appears to mean (allegory) and allowing contradictory utterances (enthymeme) to be used in a meaningful and constructive fashion. Each *locus* and its subdivisions present the rhetor with a different and varied way to craft an utterance. Thus the inventional search for the devices of style moves continually and systematically until it comes to rest on the device that best suits both the rhetor's purpose and the genre in which it is to be uttered. The merging of *stasis* and figures clearly places stylistic composition as a strategic process of invention.

Far from being a list of schemes and tropes under pseudonyms, Gervasius' terminology and *stasis* provide the stylistic enterprise with a system that could be taught to schoolchildren in simple Latin. Its basic vocabulary and system no doubt made it an effective pedagogical tool for schoolchildren, but probably did not endear it to masters who well knew that rhetoric was defined by classical sources. Moreover, his abandonment of the classical vocabulary made him an anomaly rather than innovator to his successors. Thus, a treatise on composition, truly made medieval by its vocabulary and rhetorical by its inventional method, was probably of little interest to contemporaries or the humanist heirs who sought a rebirth of classical learning. The paucity of manuscript copies of *Ars poetica* attests to its limited impact.

Nonetheless, the work is significant in at least two respects. First, it demonstrates that Gervasius was a rational, thinking, and creative individual who sought to develop a coherent rhetoric that focused on the students' rather than the master's pedagogical needs. His vocabulary was different, but with purpose. Moreover, his alternate vocabulary represents an organization of the figures into a systematic inventional scheme that also reflects increasing levels of abstraction.

Finally, Gervasius demonstrated a strong literal orientation in a genre otherwise marked by an oral one. His crisp, diagrammable means of presenting the various grammatical and rhetorical options show an orientation toward literal developments in the future. His text is analytical and self-consciously reflective rather than spontaneously expressive. He displays virtually none of the hermeneutical orientation of the other authors. Thus, Gervasius shared in common much of the doctrine advocated by the other *auctores poetriarum,* but displayed it in a markedly contrary method of disposition. His work shows neither the extemporaneous oral expression of doctrine and example seen in Matthew and John nor the carefully reflective and exemplary discourse of Geoffrey which is constrained, but oral. Rather his work resembles the carefully outlined and organized treatise of modernity.

Chapter Seven

Eberhard the German's *Laborintus*

While Gervasius of Melkley had clearly moved in a literal direction with his analytical and logically progressive treatise, Eberhard the German moved back to the looser format of orality in his *Laborintus.* As in each of the earlier works, grammatical and rhetorical categories are fused in *Laborintus* as a set of compositional options. Eberhard follows Matthew of Vendôme's lead in focusing his treatise on the writing of verse, but he also follows Geoffrey of Vinsauf in depicting portions of his work as a carefully planned demonstration of the *exornationes verborum* depicted in the exact order found in *Rhetorica ad Herennium.* At times Eberhard uses a literal sense of composition; portions of his prose are carefully worked out before being written. Other parts of his work display the meandering, digressive format of orality and the bawdiness of Menippian satire—the tensions at the margins of literacy.

Laborintus bears the distinction of being the first of the *artes poetriae* to be mechanically printed. *Poetria nova* is generally regarded as the most influential work in the genre, but *Laborintus* was the only one of the *artes poetriae* to be printed in the incunabular period (1465–1500).[1] Indeed, *Poetria nova* was not printed until 1721.[2] Moreover, manuscript copies of *Laborintus* have been found bound with copies of *Poetria nova,* and the treatise is recommended in some university statutes from the fifteenth century as an alternative to *Poetria nova.*[3]

Yet *Laborintus* has received relatively scant scholarly attention. Baldwin and Murphy have written brief synopses of the treatise that give little indication why it was popular.[4] Douglas Kelly has examined a part of the work in relation to Matthew of Vendôme's *Ars versificatoria,* arguing that Eberhard and Matthew differ in focus from their counterparts in the *ars poetriae,* particularly Geoffrey of Vinsauf and John of Garland. Kelly contends that Matthew and Eberhard were concerned with the more particular task of instructing beginning students to compose individual lines of verse rather than entire poems.[5] Kelly's observation advances an understanding of *Laborintus,* but still addresses only a small portion of the work. In concluding his essay, though, Kelly suggests that Eberhard may differ from Matthew in that *Laborintus* appears to be written for instructors of grammar rather than for students.[6] Kelly relates this directly to Murphy's observation that Eberhard devotes nearly half of *Laborintus* (494 of its 1,005 lines) to "pedagogical matters." Much of Murphy's brief analysis then addresses the apparent bitterness of an experienced teacher of grammar and rhetoric.[7] Despite this presumed bitterness, Eberhard's work portrays certain realities of both the life of a master and the practice of teaching that are still relevant.

The significance of *Laborintus* does not arise solely from its nature as a manual for teachers of verse, grammar, and rhetoric; the work itself is a delightful maze—a labyrinth of learning containing an allegorical account of grammar, poesy, and rhetoric. The very examples used in Eberhard's account of the rhetorical figures contain Christian homilies on faith and action that are exemplary primers for teachers. The homilies also underscore Eberhard's pedagogical theory, which is ultimately the key to his labyrinth.

The title of the treatise, *Laborintus,* is the first clue that Eberhard's purpose is different from the five other works in the genre called *ars poetriae.* Each of the earlier treatises includes poetry or versification in its title. *Laborintus,* on the other hand, is something of a play on words—a shortened version of *labor habens intus* (having work / struggle within).[8] It is similar to the Latin *labyrinthus* (labyrinth)[9] and identical to the middle English *laborintus* (labyrinth).[10] Thus, the title implies that it goes beyond the scope of *ars poetriae.* The double entendre seems to refer to a difficult maze, the winding passage of the school master and, more particularly, the grammarian.

Laborintus consists of 1,005 elegiac lines. It is written chiefly in the form of an allegory with Grammar and Poesy presenting the majority of its doctrine. Eberhard is careful to voice most of his precepts from the mouths of Grammar and Poesy, but when he writes of the problems of the master he clearly drops into his own voice. Though it could be said that the treatise features four principal parts, it does not adhere to a four-part structure.[11] It opens with an account of Mother Nature considering the fate of new born infants. She sees one destined to become a school master and laments his fate (1–105). Philosophy then enters and addresses the seven liberal arts (106–34). She soon gives way to Grammar, who briefly presents the basics of her art (135–254). The remainder of the treatise, with one exception, is presented in the voice of Poesy. She explains methods of beginning, amplification and abbreviation; the figures of speech; which authors should be studied; and precepts for writing in meter (255–1005). At two points (240–253 and 835–990) the voice of Eberhard breaks into the allegory to depict rather awkwardly the unpleasant side of the master's life.

The labyrinth begins allegorically with Mother Nature considering the fates of unborn infants, still in their mother's wombs. She is reluctant to prepare those destined to be masters, but she is commanded by the "Highest" to execute her duty. Written in the stars for these future masters are such things as poverty, abundance, a life of ease, the irritating burden of toil, the hazards of fame, a pinnacle of glory, a flame of envy, a love of favor, the shame of vice, and both the long and brief duration of life. The skies offer no constellation of good fortune for the master to be. Indeed, they prophesy nothing but hardship. Mother Nature gives the child's mother the books on which his life shall focus. The child's misery is shown by a list of the books he shall not read: the Pentateuch and the books celebrating the Holy Spirit, Ptolemy on astronomy, Euclid on geometry, Guido of Arezzo on music, a book on arithmetic, Cicero's two treatises on rhetoric, the philosophy of Aristotle, Galen on physics, Gratian's *Decratales,* the Code of Justinian, the dream of Scipio, astrology, and Plato's cosmography—all of these are denied (11–66).[12] He is destined to a life of narrow specialization.

This child, who was born wailing, is forced to read Donatus (the fountain of tears). This child is destined to see many a tear in his life, but they shall not move him to lenience. A normal child cries "a" when it is born, but this child, destined to be a master, cries "alpha" (67–79). The goddess who determines fate warns that life is fickle:

> Through me the flower of rhetoric withers, the grammarian's toil is vain and the art of speaking is entombed. The acquiescent flatterer is subservient to the one whom I favor, the common people are respectfully compliant, and the cloak of fortune envelopes him. . . . I prophesy that very arduous tasks, which the paltry honor of your Chair will effect, are in store for you. (95–105)[13]

Having been warned of the inconsistency of fate and the thanklessness of his task, the boy is prepared to learn grammar.

The boy's fate to be a master thus decided, Philosophy, who reigns supreme among the arts, summons her seven daughters (the liberal arts) and reminds them that they are dependent on her and she on them: "Without my light your lamp shines not. And still my light has need of yours. What you sow, I reap; what you plant, I gather; whatever you heap up, my treasure chest holds" (129–34).[14] She then addresses Grammar, the eldest sister, and explains the rudiments of her art through an earthy comparison to the nursing of an infant. The image of Grammar is remarkably fertile, especially when compared to the elderly and relatively sterile Grammar depicted in Martianus Cappella's *De nuptiis Philogiae et Mercurii.*[15] Eberhard's Grammar, with breasts full of the milk of knowledge, stands at the threshold of learning. She implants the seeds of word formation and explains which letters can produce musical sounds and which cannot. She designates a group of five letters from which sounds are made (vowels). The remaining group (consonants and diphthongs) is greater in number. She explains syntax and how schemes and tropes are fashioned from the parts of speech (135–44).

Grammar, Philosophy continues, cannot thrive without the aid of the master. Therefore, she must compel him to do his duty. Grammar must "let him cultivate the wild vine and transform weeds into harvest; let him cause the bramble bush to bear fruit; let him mold your foster-sons on the model of his learning, so they may advance a step" (136–56).[16] Grammar, she notes, is the foundation of knowledge. Until the boy has mastered it, none of the other liberal arts are possible (157–70). Philosophy warns, however, that the would-be master must drink the milk of Grammar in moderation: "Thus your herald . . . may drink temperately from Grammar's full breasts. If he has been sated with milk he will despise the crude pupils and will not feed them, though they are hungry. Be considerate of them!" (171–75).[17] The master, then, is warned that an obsession with grammar alone can be counterproductive. He must not let a concern with grammatical correctness prevent him from teaching less-developed students.

The boy draws milk from Grammar's breast. From the first breast "*A*" is imprinted on his mind. The remaining letters follow along with the fundamental parts of grammar. From the other, richer breast he draws diction and sensitivity to style (176–91).

Again, the master is given advice on teaching, this time from Grammar:

> May my method of giving instruction be pleasing to you. Acquire knowledge before you establish a system of teaching; if you wish to

> lead the blind, have vision yourself; first be a master of yourself, then of your pupils. . . . Mildly and with gently pressing thumb imprint the seal of learning upon the plastic wax. As you feel it becoming hardened, constantly press more firmly upon the wax which you must shape. (193–204)[18]

It is fundamental, then, that the master know his material. If the teacher is a studious model, the students will be studious themselves. Grammar states succinctly: "Precepts warn, example inspires; precept strikes the ear, example steals into the depths of the heart" (210–16).[19] Poesy later emphasizes this pedagogical advice in her account of the rhetorical figures.

Knowledge of the students, however, is equally important to the master. Each student is different and must be treated accordingly:

> If passion for study in a pupil cools, it will glow if you fan the flames. It is your task to stir up this fire of glowing desire. The strong student is to be refreshed in one way, the weak in another. The dull and the ingenious have different needs: the one finds pleasure in weighty problems, the other in simple ones. My faithful companion, Poesy, has something useful for both. (219–24)[20]

The master is therefore exhorted to develop a sensitivity to the needs of the students. No one approach works for all—the master must recognize the difference among students and develop an appropriate teaching strategy for each.

The teacher is further admonished to maintain the steady ones with pleas, call back the fugitive ones with promises, and hide the lash from the timid. The teacher must also cheerfully encourage the timid, wrathfully flash fire on the undaunted, curb the unrestrained, love the gentle, disclose to the foolish, guide the devoted, and gather in the wanderers. Offenses are to be corrected with both words and whippings, but the master is admonished to be milder with the switch than with the word.[21] Masters who are prone to anger must learn to become mellow; those who are prone to mellowness must learn to become angry. They must be conscientious (*pius*) in their severity and remember that hope of reward encourages effort (224–39).

Speaking now of effort, the voice of Eberhard, the experienced master, breaks into the allegory and warns of the student's fathers. Rich men seem to be "sparing of pay and prodigal of promise." The master is more sure of payment from a man in "moderate circumstances."[22] He should, therefore, give priority to that man's son (240–53).

At this point the allegory resumes and Poesy, who has been attending Grammar, comes forward and explains her duty. She briefly explains meter, foot, tempo, the time value of each foot, the difference between short and long syllables, the nature and number of feet in each metrical scheme, and permissible variations. She notes that there are certain meters appropriate for particular fields. The hexameter is used for history; the pentameter is used for lamentations; and other meters sing praises. Her power, Poesy notes, encompasses all. It is to the master's advantage to learn it. Indeed, she asserts, even Philosophy must play in compliance to Poesy's game (254–68).

Poesy continues to explain the components of her art, starting, appropriately enough, with ways of beginning. Her ways of beginning are the same ones emphasized in Matthew of Vendôme's *Ars versificatoria: zeugma* and *hypozeuxis.*[23] Poesy states that a passage employing *zeugma* can easily be converted to one employing *hypozeuxis* and the combination of the two methods often produces eloquence because of its forcefulness (255–98).

Poesy next moves into a basically traditional account of the components of style. Discussed first are the various modes of amplification and abbreviation. Modes of amplification are the figures *periphrasis, interpretatio, collatio,* apostrophe, *prosopopoeia, digressio, descriptio,* and *oppositio* (299–336).[24] Her prescriptions for abbreviation are appropriately brief. It is achieved in part by avoiding the figures previously discussed. In addition, abbreviation can be achieved through the use of participles, ablatives absolute, emphases, and the omission of conjunctions (337–42).

Poesy further notes that for her speech to be distinguished she must go beyond its ordinary path. This is achieved through the use of novel words (*verbi novitas;* 345–48), the combination of contrary or discordant words (349–52), the use of indeclinable words (353–56), the adoption of famous sayings for distinction (357–60), the change of syllabic and temporal quantity of an expression (361–64), figurative use of nouns and adjectives (365–68), figurative use of proper names (369–72), figurative use of verbs (373–76), simultaneous use of a word in both its figurative and proper meaning (377–80), and the use of several figurative expressions to convey one thought (381–84). The last five operations resemble the doctrine of *transsumptio* developed by Geoffrey of Vinsauf and

Gervasius of Melkley. The word *transumo* is used in the explanation of the figurative use of proper names. Moreover, the examples there, as well as figurative expressions used to convey one thought, are found in Geoffrey of Vinsauf, John of Garland, and Gervasius of Melkley.[25]

Difficult passages may be changed in a variety of ways—reference to the inventor to signify an invention, reference to an invention to signify an inventor, designation of the user of an instrument by means of the instrument itself, effect indicated by its cause, content used to signify the container, reference to the material to show the object from which it is composed, designation of the abstract by means of the concrete, combination of words out of their natural order, exaggeration, use of a part to designate the whole (and vice versa), designation of plural by means of the singular (and vice versa), and misuse of certain similar words (385–430). Faral and Carlson have identified these modes as the tropes *metonymy, hyperbaton,* hyperbole, *synecdoche,* and *catachresis.* Eberhard does not identify the figures by their traditional names; rather, he merely explains the particular modes and provides examples of each as was the tradition of Gervasius of Melkley.

Following this list Poesy notes that distinguished speech may be produced in two ways. The first, although less popular, method may be used when the subject is not weighty or serious. It consists simply of the use of everyday words in the present tense. The present tense is effective because it can make an action from the past seem to be happening now. The second method is achieved through the use of rhetoric (431–38).

Rhetoric allows the simple style to be written in a striking fashion that sounds sweet to the ear. Without naming them, Poesy then provides examples of the rhetorical colors. She notes that she has, with the help of Cicero, composed them into a poem (439–42). What follows is a poem exemplifying the thirty-six figures of diction found in *Rhetorica ad Herennium.* Most striking, however, are the examples used to demonstrate the figures. Rather than a series of unrelated examples, Poesy's figures comprise a coherent poem of hexameter-pentameter couplets.[26] Moreover, the poem is, in essence, a homily on grace and sin that may be applied directly to the example of the teacher. The first part of the poem is a refresher on Christ's payment for humanities' sins achieved through the successive use of *repetitio, conversio, complexio, traductio, contentio, exclamatio, interrogatio, ratiocinatio,* and *sententia*:

> Let there be praise, let there be virtue, let there be honor, let there be glory to Christ!

> Let there be grace. There is grace, without end there is grace.
> Who is good? Christ. Who is born of a virgin? Christ. Who is free from sin? Christ the man.
> Because through disobedience the first parents sinned, Christ died upon the cross.[27]
> The life of the living Christ, extinguished upon the cross, is redeemed from death. In death is life given.
> O wonderful love of the Father by which his Son came from on high to give life to mankind![28]
> Whom better than his son could the Father send to the wretched, whom greater, or even equal?
> Why did he send him? Because the time was right. Why? Because the enemy was wreaking havoc. For what reason? Because he was destructive to mankind.
> The wise man's task is to foresee the weapon of the enemy who is ever lying in wait for him. (443–58)[29]

Contrarium, membrum and, finally, *articulus* are used to expand on the theme of the enemy: "He [the Devil] slays him who spends night and day in deceits, treacheries, and snares; but he flees him who spends his time with psalms and lamentations." The *sententia* then resumes with an exhortation to guard against the temptations of sin: "He who protects himself by the virtue of the Most High cannot be hard pressed by the impiety of the Enemy" (463–66).[30] Ultimate protection from sin, of course, is provided through faith. The lesson on faith, a paraphrase of I Corinthians 13.13, is accomplished through a mixture of *compar, similiter cadens, similiter desinens:*

> Let your faith be pure: the strength of the faithful is in piety; let your hope increase; let your charity be strong. (471–72)
> These three are the seeds of virtue, the way of salvation. (473)
> Overcome flesh by strength of mind; hasten through holy writ to find godly purity of heart. (475–76)[31]

Finally, the reader is warned of the ultimate danger involved in the lack of virtue and exhorted to reform through the use of the figures *annominatio, subjectio, gradatio, definitio, transitio, correctio, occupatio, disjunctum, conjunctum, adjunctum, conduplicatio, interpretatio, commutatio, permissio, dubitatio, dissolutio, praecisio,* and *conclusio. Dissolutio* and *conclusio* are demonstrated as follows:

> You are not intent upon deceit: you are heaping up earthly possessions,
> you guard these closely. The end concerns you not. (515–16)
> Uncertain is the day of death: but death is more certain than all else.
> Abandon, therefore, the error of thy way. (519–20)[32]

After the conclusion of the poem, Poesy notes that there are some thirty-six of these figures (*colores verborum*).

This homily on grace and sin serves to exemplify the *colores verborum*, thus providing religious instruction along with grammatical instruction. The religious message, however, underscores a pedagogical one as well. The poem is an explication on faith and confession well stated in Romans 10.5–10 where it is stressed that faith must not only be believed and felt in the heart, but also confessed: "For one believes with the heart and so is justified, and one confesses with the mouth and so is saved."[33] The pedagogical parallel, then, is one of belief and action, knowledge and practice, and precept and example. The examples underscore Grammar's advice in lines 210–16. The parallel is emphasized further in a second poem where Poesy displays the flowers of rhetoric.

This second poem shows how the internal expression of a subject may be colored by the figures of thought in rhetoric. The second poem goes beyond the homily and exhorts the reader to exemplify faith in actions. In particular, it speaks to the example of a pastor who fails to practice what he preaches:

> You who bear the name of pastor, be an example of the consecrated
> life which the people under your influence should follow.
> By your leave, I speak: you seek not the things of Christ, but of your
> own choosing. Fatal love of money guides you. (525–28)

Having made the first point through the use of *distributio, licentia,* and *diminutio,* Poesy then employs *descriptio* and *divisio* to stress that the pastor teaches and supports Christian teachings by exemplifying them:

> Instruct those under your care or the people, like sheep or kid, will
> go astray; watch over them as an Argus.
> There are these two, example and teaching: the latter instructs, the
> former influences. (531–34)[34]

Grammar's principle of combining precept and example is again underscored.

The error of the pastor's way is further emphasized through the use of *frequentatio, expolitio, contentio, similitudo, exemplum, imago, effectio, notatio,* and driven home through the use of a *sermocinatio* that reiterates the passage from Romans:

> He shouts to others and says openly to the pastor, "Although you teach us very many things, you yourself do few (of them). That which your tongue utters let your hand carry into effect." But the preacher answers: "You should not seek to weigh by hand, but my words." The former suggests: "If you believed what you say to be true, you would fulfill by works what your tongue thunders forth." (553–58)[35]

The effect of his behavior is then made clear through the use of *conformatio:* "Thus your mode of life replies: 'Parishioner, believe permissible for you that which your pastor does without fear'" (559–60).[36] The pastor, of course, is also a teacher. Both teacher and pastor must teach by precept and example. The example is a living model that their parishioners and students may follow.

The pastor's erroneous ways are expanded upon further through the use of *significatio, significatio per ambiguum, significatio per convenientem,* and *significatio per praecisionem.* Ultimately, he and the readers are urged to follow the example of Joseph in Genesis 37–50. The example is first recounted through the use of *significatio per similitudinem, brevitas,* and finally through *demonstratio:*

> If you are troubled not because of your faults, but because of virtue alone, you ought not be unmindful of Joseph.
>
> Brotherly jealously troubles him, Egypt honors him. Famine brings him brothers and he fosters them.[37]
>
> Since complete kindliness of nature favored the boy his father's constant love kept close watch over him. Moreover, because the boy saw apt dreams his brothers were envious at him: anger imbibes treachery. Treachery anticipates snares. As the boy came towards them they said: "Behold here comes he whom sleep favors! Let him die and we shall see what his dreams avail him." But God was truly a means of redress for the innocent boy. Sold, he became distinguished as prefect of Egypt. Our uncontrolled famine afflicted the entire world: there was sufficient bread in Egypt; for indeed, sole charge of deliverance was at the disposal of Joseph.

> Jacob's food supply was failing and when he was fearing for his sons, there came a report to the effect that Egypt was selling grain. Ten brothers on the advice of their father, Jacob, departed. When the food supply failed they came back and said to their father: "Lo, your son lives! His spirit and life revived" and he said: "Let not death prevent me. I am going to see Joseph." Israel went to Egypt and was received by his son, the mediator, and the Lord multiplied him. (569–94)[38]

After the poem is completed, Poesy notes that it contains some twenty figures of speech—excluding *commoratio,* which has no particular place.[39] More particular instruction on the use of these figures, Poesy notes, may be found in the *Summa* of Bernard Silvestri.

Eberhard's examples of the rhetorical figures carry his readers further into the labyrinth. They are lured into a seemingly routine list of examples only to discover that they are snared into a sermon on faith, confession, and action.[40] The religious message, however, cannot be ignored because the example of the wayward pastor is all too similar to that of the wayward master. Moreover, the scriptural example and the use of the sermonic format underscore the pedagogy of precept and example. Eberhard has thus achieved four purposes in the two poems. He has provided coherent examples of how each of the figures may be used, he has used the examples to preach a Christian sermon, he has used his sermon to exhort the teacher to be a living example of his art, and he has underscored just how effective the combination of precept and example can be. Not coincidentally, Eberhard's four purposes correspond with the four levels of scriptural interpretation advanced by the authors of the *artes praedicandi:* historical, literal reading; allegorical, figurative reading; tropological, reading for moral instruction; and anagogical, reading for spiritual enlightenment.[41]

Poesy now moves to recommend authors and works that the students must study: Cato, *Theodolus,* Avianus, Aesop, Maximianus, *Pamphilus,* Vitalis of Blois' *Geta,* Claudian's *Rape of Prosperine,* Statius, Ovid, Juvenal, Persius, John of Hanville's *Architrenius,* Virgil, Gautier de Lille's *Alexandreis,* Claudian, Phyrgian Dares, Homer, Sidonius Appolinaris, Gunther de Pairis' *Solimarius,* Macer Floridus, Marbod, Petrius Riga, Sedulius, Arator, Prudentius, Alain de Lille, Matthew of Vendôme's *Tobias,* Geoffrey of Vinsauf's *Poetria nova,* Alexander of Villedieu's *Doctrinale,* Eberhard of Bethune's *Graecismus,* Prosper, Matthew of Vendôme, John of Garland, Martianus Capella, Boethius, and

Bernard Silvester (599–686). Each author provides examples of various strengths in writing verse. Aesop, for example, "does not lull verse to sleep; his fable brings forth blossoms, the blossom bears fruit, the fruit has taste."[42] Geoffrey of Vinsauf's *Poetria nova* "is resplendent with special beauty equally charming in substance and in words."[43] Though her list is quite lengthy, Poesy concludes this section by marveling at how many other authors have given themselves to her guidance (685–86). Having covered the methods of beginning, the devices of style, and recommended authors as exemplars of particular stylistic qualities, Poesy moves to the specific subject of her art—meter.

Meter, she notes, is troubling to boys. Their inability to master it will always cause them anxiety. The master should therefore instruct the students to compose rhythmic verse in various stages of difficulty (687–98): "An easy path of meter is best for new recruits; on that path let them advance at a tempo suitable for them. As they become older, demand more of them: let them speed along a more difficult path."[44] She then provides examples of verses in which each subsequent word refers to the word that precedes it—leonine verses, verses featuring similar endings, verses which rhyme in the middle and the end of the line, leonine verses which also feature rhyme at the end of the line, and verses whose beginnings recall their endings (699–734). Poesy's specific comments on meter stress, in part, the principles already demonstrated in the rhetorical figures—particularly *gradatio, conversio,* and *transitio.*

Poesy also provides examples of ways in which words may relate to one another: through a pairing of nouns, through the pairing of verbs, through the successive use of individually paired verbs and nouns, and through reciprocal verse (735–74).

Moreover, Poesy notes, nonpentameter poems require different forms. Those forms are shown in an encomium on the Virgin Mary exemplifying some fifteen rhyme patterns that Faral identifies in his *marginalia* as: *dactylici calenati, dactylici disjuncti, versus mixti, versus salii mediati, dactylici dupliciter concordantes alternatim et mediate, dactylici concordantes et immediate, adonici, adonici biformis, adonica triformis, adonici quadriformes, citogradi, bicipites, versus in se redeuntes, versus decisi,* and *reticulati.*

Poesy declares that the previous examples are ones that should be imitated (817). She then lists, but does not provide examples of, faults to be avoided. The pentameter should not be joined to a following hexameter line. Rather, it should be joined to a preceding hexameter. A word of one or five syllables should seldom end a hexameter line. A pentameter should end only on a disyllabic foot. Hiatus, alliteration, and repetition should be avoided. Frequent use of words with the same ending should be avoided. Finally, figures of speech should always be rendered clearly (818–34). The avoidance of these faults, particularly the one referring to hexameter/pentameter couplets, is exemplified throughout the treatise.

When Poesy finishes her instruction, the master then sits in the snare of the labyrinth and is visited by the mother of elegy. She speaks to him with compassion for his misfortune. Some students, their fathers, and their lawyers will cheat the master out of his pay (835–70). Other students are perverted: "They age other boys by corrupting them with their faults; thus a sheep infects sheep with scurvy" (871–82).[45] Some are simply insane. For these boys "disputes are wont to be the lesson; insults, their recitation; fighting their metre, quarreling, their rule."[46] Some students are deceitful. Some are haughty: "They scorn the humble and tolerate no equals; . . they wish to dominate the rest, to be venerated more than the others, to enjoy more liberal authority."[47] Still others are dullards (88–914).

Working with the students, the mother of elegy states, dulls the mind: "To speak about matters suited to the mental ability of your boys is daily your cross of toil."[48] Although a teacher, the master spends much of his time judging trifles. He must mediate the petty complaints of children and suffer the wrath of their fathers because of his judgments (915–80).

Aside from the problems involved with teaching students, the master must deal with colleagues who are often incompetent:

> There ascend to the chair those who have not learned; they promise very many things, they accomplish few. The ape of a teacher seeks rather the name without the substance than the substance without the name: the latter is apparent, the former conceited. The learned gives place to the unlearned because the other pleases more, and because the group won over by him will belong to the one standing in his place. The parrot gives way to geese, the swan to the raven, the lark to the owl, the nightingale to the crow. Weary with effort I come to the end of my journey. I limp and my tottering foot wavers.[49]

Thus, the allegory ends with a pun referring to both its subject matter and format. Eberhard closes the treatise in his own voice by admonishing his readers not to forget the instruction of rhythm (991–1005). He then provides a list of examples of spondaic verse, iambic verse, combinations of the iambic and spondaic verse, and quatrains.

As the sixth and final treatise in the *ars poetriae, Laborintus* both includes and extends upon the doctrine of its predecessors. Like Geoffrey of Vinsauf, Gervasius of Melkley, and John of Garland, Eberhard fuses grammar and rhetoric into *poetria.* Like Matthew of Vendôme, he focuses specifically on versification. And like Gervasius of Melkley, Eberhard places more emphasis on the particular operations involved in rhetorical style than on the names of its devices. Similarities aside, Eberhard offers considerable contributions uniquely his own.

In Eberhard's educational scheme, grammar is the essence of language and rhetoric the essence of composition. *Poetria,* and more particularly versification, is a hybrid of the two, but grounded primarily in neither form. Poesy, the versemaker, is subordinate to Grammar, yet she must employ the rhetorical figures to execute her art. Thus, grammar and rhetoric, separate but mutually dependent, are intertwined into a genre that unites style and invention.

As his purpose is to produce verse in proper meter, Eberhard uses the rhetorical figures as inventional schemes rather than stylistic ones. He therefore stresses the inventional dimension of the figures rather than the ornamental.

The rhetorical figures are the vehicle for Eberhard's homilies on Christian faith and action. The homilies are, in turn, pivotal in the solution to the labyrinth. The two poems that comprise the homilies are ostensibly traditional lists of unrelated examples. When it is apparent, however, that they are religious lessons the reader moves deeper into the rhetorical maze. The religious instruction emphasizes the pedagogical message that is ultimately the key to the labyrinth.

The labyrinthine structure takes the reader on an educational odyssey that winds its way back onto itself and continually underscores and exemplifies the poetic and pedagogical principles it explains. The pedagogical advice, repeatedly stressed, unlocks the labyrinth. If Eberhard's purpose is difficult to follow at times, it is precisely because of his pedagogy: precept and example. Thus, the lesson is shown in the very words and structure of the treatise. Eberhard does not tell his readers what is to be learned, rather he shows them. That demonstration, however, is not always immediately seen. It is a literate demonstration where the understanding comes from careful and reflective scrutiny of a text—a text rendered as both object and vehicle. Ultimately, then, *Laborintus* is a literate treatise not particularly intended to be understood at first hearing. It is not intended for schoolchildren. Rather, it is a treatise intended for the mature scholar who delights in the unknown and finds pleasure in the challenge of the labyrinth.

Conclusion
The Margins of Literacy

Considering the variegated doctrine found in the *artes poetriae,* one might be tempted to wonder whether *ars poetriae* is a proper genre. Matthew of Vendôme's and Eberhard the German's focus is on the single line of verse, while Geoffrey of Vinsauf, John of Garland, and Gervasius of Melkley focus on the composition of a whole work. Matthew, John, and Eberhard offer faithful accounts of the *exornationes verborum et sententiarum,* while Geoffrey and Gervasius range far and wide, incorporating grammatical lore on figures and creating some of their own. Nonetheless, Geoffrey and Eberhard demonstrate the use of the *exornationes,* in their original order. The long *Documentum* and John's *De arte prosayca, metrica, et rithmica* include sections on *ars dictaminis.* Geoffrey and Eberhard offer their treatises as exemplars of the precepts they taught, while Matthew begs not to be judged by the examples in his *Ars versificatoria.* Except for Geoffrey's *Poetria nova* (the masterpiece of the genre), all of these works have at times become tedious lists of definitions. Geoffrey writes his *Poetria nova* in the most elegant language and examples, while Matthew, John, and Eberhard often employ vulgar examples to maintain the attention of their students.

The variations across the works display an oral/literal tension indicative of the cutting edge of medieval communicative technology. From a contemporary perspective, all of the treatises, except for *Poetria nova* and *Ars poetica,* are unstructured and repetitive. The lack of structure, the repetitiveness, and the bawdiness of Matthew, John, and Eberhard are reflective of an oral tradition—a tradition of spontaneous expression and a stream of consciousness captured in writing. While reflecting on the process of writing in an analytical, textual fashion, these authors express their thoughts in an oral mode. That is to say that the authors were reflective of their thought before expressing it, but not as it was written down. Writing, for them, was a means of recording or storing thought—but not thought itself. There was not yet a "literate consciousness." For Geoffrey, conversely, writing itself was a reflective activity requiring revision and careful depiction in textual form. Repetition in such a work was seen as unnecessary, and bawdiness, upon reflection, was unseemly. His work was crafted in a careful, literal mode that wasted no words and expressed models of how words should be used. His mode of revision was mental, not literal. The written text was a final stage, not a stage for drafting. On the other hand, Gervasius viewed his role as one of analysis. He was not so concerned with substantive presentation—oral or literal—but with analytical, structural presentation. Finally, as oral as Eberhard was in his presentation, he still had enough of a literal orientation to depict a part of his work as a textual puzzle that required careful textual scrutiny.

The works do represent a coherent genre in many important respects, however. All are reliant on both the legacies of grammar and rhetoric, and weave unapologetically the precepts of the various arts into a single body of knowledge. All clearly orient their treatises around the idea of invention, or discovery, of the material of composition. Moreover, they consciously recognize that their ideas are medieval and are suited to their times, rather than the times of the ancients.

In many ways the arts of poetry and prose might be viewed as *poetria nova* (new poetics, in Geoffrey's words) or even as *inventio nova* (new invention). *Ars poetriae* was more of an attitude than a coherent body of doctrine. This attitude was one that saw the classical models of rhetorical invention and grammatical composition as important, but insufficient. The *auctores poetriarum* collapsed the rhetorical and grammatical canons into an interchangeable inventory of concepts. They drew from the classical authorities what was useful and repeated it in and out of its usual context. Thus, John of Garland consciously states that he has gone beyond the precepts of invention stated by Cicero, and Geoffrey writes that Tully's (Cicero's) compositional system was good for Tully, but not necessarily everyone. Moreover, the *exornationes* are used not as means of elaborating thought, as in the rhetorical tradition, but as producers of expression as in the grammatical tradition. That expression is grounded in primary cognitive processes that make invention the art of compositional thinking. The freedom from authority allows Gervasius to restructure invention entirely into a *stasis* system of topics—grammatical, figurative, and argumentative—and thereby create a productive, innovative system of his own.

Beyond the sensitivity to classical genres, the *auctores poetriarum* showed a consciousness of their time and other forms present. Once Matthew and Geoffrey established their genre, later authors borrowed their ideas and cited their authority. Authors repeatedly spoke of how certain historical precepts were not appropriate to their time. They clearly rejected the poetic license—the *barbarisms, solecisms,* and *metaplasms* tolerated by the ancient grammarians. They rejected the notion that ambiguous diction, misspellings, and the overall abridgement of language could be elegant. If anything, their movement was one toward clear, but elegant, verse.

The *auctores poetriarum* showed a remarkable freedom from authority that allowed originality in their theoretical exposition. At the same time, they did not consider it important that an author might be original in the creation of a story line. Their arts of composition were oriented toward the reappropriation of existing themes in metrical and otherwise more elegant forms. As such, they represent a transitional stage in the evolution of literacy. Perhaps it took printed texts to instantiate the story as something that must be original. The aversion to orality and the freedom from authority seem at odds with their presentation of the rhetorical figures. Only Gervasius feels free to present the figures out of the order found in *Rhetorica ad Herennium.* Yet, his treatment follows the organizational pattern of Donatus' system of grammar. Geoffrey and Eberhard, however, do present the figures in novel ways.

Significant too is the pedagogy of the *auctores poetriarum.* Geoffrey and Eberhard, and to a lesser degree Matthew, performed the complex task of offering their principles while exemplifying them in their works. Theory and practice were one and the same. Gervasius wrote of the pedagogy, learning from prohibitions, permissions, rules, and strategies, but did not necessarily follow it. Eberhard advanced the method further in composing his treatise as a puzzling example—a labyrinth of learning. Ultimately, the *auctores poetriarum* exemplified the very art they described. They each related many of the same techniques, but in their own individual ways.

The theoretical contributions of the genre are considerable. The notion of a proverb as a major premise around which the development of a composition is based shows an argumentative, didactic focus on composition. The didactic focus in turn allows for a type of moral argumentation that is used and exemplified by Geoffrey, John, and Eberhard. The various permutations on ways of beginning a composition increase the inventional possibilities beyond its previously narrow bounds. By absorbing Cicero's inventional topics into that development, the composer was presented with a multifold inventional process. The inclusion of grammatical categories into the doctrine of conversion further systematizes and utilizes grammatical doctrine. Above all, the doctrine of *transsumptio* and its related functions, conversion and determination, serve to help the rhetor produce rhythmical, metrical, and prosaic compositions that are both beautiful and clear. Gervasius systematized the various rhetorical and grammatical doctrines in a threefold system of composition. By collapsing that doctrine into a logical scheme, he added to the systematic grammatical tradition and folded it into the *stasis* system of rhetorical invention. Moreover, he took the rhetorical tradition of figures and presented it in a way that gave rhyme and reason to the massive terminology that was the bane of so many generations of students. Indeed, he explicitly transformed the figures from ornaments to procedures of discovery.

What became of *ars poetriae*? As far as the Latin grammatical and rhetorical tradition is concerned, it was discarded in the wake of two trends separated in time by 150 years: humanism and ramism. Those trends became almost calcified in the development of the printing press and the subsequent objectification of texts in mechanically printed form. The humanists, in their enthusiasm to restore the primacy of classical texts, ignored and discarded a unique accomplishment of the medieval world. Just at the time when the medieval world had developed a theory of discourse distinctly its own, the enthusiasm and awe held for classical texts led scholars to abandon medieval doctrines for a style and thought deemed appropriate some one thousand years before. Divorced from its inventional rationale, style (in its Renaissance incarnation) became mere ornamentation. As Geoffrey wrote in the thirteenth century: "To paint the surface of an expression is like a picture made of mud." In the sixteenth century, Henry Peacham planted 191 schemes and tropes in his *Garden of Eloquence* and muddied the true picture of style.

Ramus observed that grammar, logic, and rhetoric shared certain redundancies.[1] Accordingly, he formulated his three basic laws: *lex veritatis* (law of truth), *lex justitiae* (law of justice), and *lex sapientiae* (law of wisdom). *Lex veritatis* decreed that nothing should be included in an art unless it is necessarily and universally true. *Lex justitiae* stated that nothing should be included in an art that is not germane to all of the art.

Lex sapientiae required that general laws should precede and particular laws should follow.[2] According to this system, Ramus placed invention under the province of dialectic, the figures under rhetoric, and the parts of speech under of grammar. The contributions of *ars poetriae* became marginalized by the Renaissance humanists' insistence that the ancients had defined grammar and rhetoric. And the ramistic insistence on exclusive disciplinary boundaries led to the exclusion of invention from style. Thus, the conglomeration that was *ars poetriae* was shattered and its constituent parts redistributed.

On the near horizon, of course, was the development of the printed word. It was certainly not helpful to *ars poetriae* that among the first texts printed, outside of the Bible, were the classical texts—many of which had been rediscovered by the humanists. The development of the printed texts also carried technological implications that eclipsed the viability of *ars poetriae.*

The *ars poetriae* lay at the end of a world whose system of communicative reference was oral, grounded in the dynamics of the human voice, and at the beginning of a world whose system of communicative and intellectual reference was the printed word. The *auctores* viewed language as a vehicle or a tool, not an entity. Stories were meant to be retold in an original fashion. Emphasis was placed on the retelling and the rewriting of an existing story—in a way appropriate to the writer or speaker. The retelling, with its emphasis on rhythm and meter, placed an individual stamp on the language that appealed to the aural; it was language meant to be heard. With the rise of the printed word, emphasis moved away from the original telling of an existing theme to the unique telling of an original theme. The theme, easily frozen in a mass-produced printed text, and its presentation became synonymous. Texts became sacrosanct—the essence of intellectual exchange. Indeed, themes became owned and their reappropriation became a crime. As Ong wrote, "the Renaissance fixed its attention on material visually stored and retrievable. Its lexical and linguistic base was not orally processed language as such, but a body of texts—a controlled and closed field, at least in principle more or less explicitly bounded." Printing standardized texts. It objectified them so that emphasis on language shifted from "the world of sound to the surface of the page, from the aural to the visual."[3] The visual emphasis made language a material thing.

The twentieth century, with the rise of electronic media, has witnessed a return to the oral emphasis on language, an orality preserved through electronic reproduction. Concomitant with electronic reproduction has come an awareness of the tyranny of literacy—the objectification of *logos*. When *logos* was made the printed word, thought became limited by the arbitrary structures and objectification of thought. Twentieth-century rhetoricians and language theorists—beginning at least with Richards[4] and Bakhtin/Voloshinov[5] and carrying on with such thinkers as Burke,[6] Foucault,[7] Derrida,[8] Cixous,[9] Kristeva,[10] and Gates,[11]—have pointed out the limitations of various language constructs ranging from sexism and racism to the abridgement of language and thought by generic forms. The different perspectives—deconstruction, post-modernism, feminism, post-critical—have variously questioned the authority of the author, the text, and forms of rationality. All are reactions to modernism: a phenomenon facilitated by the very existence of texts. How does our world deal with these challenges to modernity? Indeed, how does the human raised with the perception that modernistic constructs are reality adapt to an increasingly less modern world, a world in which standards are increasingly demonstrated to be arbitrary? They embrace the rhetorical tradition and *ars poetriae* as the art of humane thinking.

In the wake of these contemporary movements, however, rhetoric has become grammatical—descriptive rather than preceptive. Rhetoricians in the United States have focused their attention on the rhetorical-critical act, while scholars on the continent have focused more on how discourse affects our lives. Scholars in the United States have embraced the contributions of Europeans such as Toulmin, Perelman, and Olbrechts-Tyteca[12] because their thoughts could be reduced to models and methods. Lost has been the impulse for responding to rhetorical exigencies. Indeed, a very cogent criticism of the post-modern movement is that it is destructive; it destroys a great deal of the status quo, but fosters no tools for living beyond a kind of defensive paranoia. Rhetorical criticism takes us little farther. At best, it fosters a kind of enlightened hindsight.

These contemporary rhetorical turns are themselves subverted by the tyranny of the text. The rhetorical-critical movement, in spite of various attempts to contextualize speeches, has nonetheless frozen and limited the speech as a text. When Wichelns attempted to separate literary criticism from rhetorical criticism, he neutered rhetoric and made its object a text.[13] By deemphasizing the dimension of discourse's enduring qualities and freezing our appreciation of it to a past that cannot again be experienced, we may have denied ourselves any semblance of a rhetorical response or understanding.

When deconstructionists critique discourse for what it is not rather than for what it is, they restore something of a rhetorical response—a response McKerrow and McGee[14] have referred to as "critical rhetoric." Their move, like the rhetorical-critical one, is reactive, not proactive. It is a response to a response (a text) rather than a response to a circumstance. A proactive rhetoric, I believe, is a positive one that builds rhetorical hope, power, purpose, and ownership. As Paul Ricoeur has written, "the tie between critique and rhetoric extends further than tropology and the theory of argumentation: it is the very conjunction between text and action that has rhetorical import to the extent that rhetoric is the *art of discourse aiming at persuading the listener by means of probable arguments.*"[15] In the post-critical, post-modern world the role of the speaker/writer must be one of crafting probable narratives from a sometimes bewildering mass of information. Ricoeur goes on:

> If there is a post-critical moment, it would reside in the moment of selective appropriation by which a reader, instructed by the innumerable texts that nourish his or her culture, interrupts at one point the wandering movements of sympathy in order to say: Here is where I am, this is where I'll stay. Each of us, at one time or another, has to pronounce a verdict like this. What saves it from being merely arbitrary is the conviction of having deepened, through critical work, the even deeper feeling of belonging to the world (to borrow Gadamer's expression) even before I set myself up as judge or arbitrator.[16]

The role of the speaker/writer is one of "selective appropriation." And what the *auctores poetriarum* offer is a proactive rhetoric of selective appropriation. It is ironic that much of Ricoeur's thinking centers around the metaphorical utterance, and that the basis for a part of his thinking on metaphor comes from Konrad's analysis of Geoffrey of Vinsauf and *transsumptio,* yet again misinterpreted.[17]

Leupin argues that Geoffrey's *Poetria nova* possesses a type of "absolute reflexivity" that transcends its doctrinal content and transforms it into a "specular enterprise" that makes it virtually impossible to distinguish between theory and practice.[18] Through Geoffrey's method of reworking old themes, a practice is facilitated that "theorizes the act of writing as a constant and endless transformation of the obsolete, a perpetual relaunching of the old."[19] Essential to the system is *transsumptio. Transsumptio,* in Leupin's view, "designated both the act of taking *and* the act of receiving something from another text, so that it subsumes in one term the notions of borrowing, stealing, and giving."[20] *Transsumptio* fosters a perpetual transfiguration: "Newness thus emerges in a never-ending peregrination from the other to the other, without ever stopping to rest in proper meaning."[21] Ultimately, then, the *Poetria nova* works to undermine the idea of actual reproduction; it creates a text that serves as a mirror—"the mirror becomes the absent locus of poetic language's transformational power and autonomy."[22] It facilitates polysemy as a virtue rather than a vice. It provides a way to make fragments whole. *Transsumptio,* the doctrine so central to the *artes poetriae,* had been discarded by rhetoric, grammar, and poetic, and was eventually absorbed by logic. Unfortunately, the logicians, in their search for empirical demonstration, discarded the rhetorical dimension of *transsumptio* and rendered it as a means of dialectical demonstration.[23]

In their move to absolute reflexivity (pedagogic modeling while doing), the *artes poetriae* provide a rhetoric that empowers and expands, rather than constricts the margins of discourse. They bring rhetor and auditor on the inside, rather than on the outside. They offer a method of expanding horizons and making language once again new. Ultimately, the *artes poetriae* provide a means of linguistic ownership. Words move back to the status of *logos* and away from that of objects or the text.

In effect, the rhetorical movement of *ars poetriae* was a deconstructive, detextualizing one. The thirteenth-century text, vehicle not object, was fair game for whatever purpose the rhetor chose. The rhetor, armed with the various rhetorical and grammatical devices, was prepared to make the text his or hers. The societal values emphasized transactional rather than perpetual ownership of words. All texts were fragments that the rhetor ultimately made whole. Rhetorical virtue was marked by entrepreneurial deconstruction, rather than the carving of paper monuments.

Those paper monuments are on the wane. Our society is becoming increasingly less textual. In the United States, schoolchildren watch videos rather than read books, and those who write and read often have a relationship with a computer screen rather than the printed or handwritten page. Even their games have become a combination of video and computer. Our understanding of public issues and public people is based on visual and audio sound bites. Substantive coverage of a news story on electronic media spans seconds and very few of us have heard a complete speech from a public leader. We respond to fragments, and from those fragments we create our world view.

The textual model leads to a hopelessness in the face of those fragments and we are overwhelmed by the prospect of mastering them. But the model of the *auctores poetriarum,* somewhere between orality and literacy, empowers us to take those fragments and recreate a world that functions. It creates a world that restores coherence—a text that reflects reality, ourselves, and others. The impulse of rhetoric is to provide its users with innovation in the face of uncertainty. The electronic culture, a culture that is moving away from textual literacy and toward uncertainty, will need the rhetor more than ever before.

The connection between *ars poetriae* and contemporary rhetorical theory should not be taken as a reprise of George Santayana's warning that those who ignore history are doomed to repeat it. Rather, the comparison points out the danger in accepting arbitrary and rigid standards of judging intellectual phenomena, particularly those phenomena whose very nature is to change and evolve in accordance with their attendant circumstances. The *auctores poetriarum* followed the innovative and adaptive impetus of rhetoric to appropriate whatever measures necessary—rhetorical, grammatical, poetic, and otherwise—to influence their world communicatively. Their innovation allowed them to adapt to uncertainty and, to a degree, regulate it. Necessity is the mother of invention; invention is the heart of rhetoric. The value of the enterprise known as the history of rhetoric is not merely that it allows one to appreciate rhetorical/intellectual movements of the past, but that it allows us to recognize the variety of discursive options available and realize the intellectual challenges of the present and future.

Appendix A

Rhetorical Figures

The *exornationes* from *Rhetorica ad Herennium* have frequently been listed in tabular form (see James J. Murphy, *Rhetoric in the Middle Ages: A History of Rhetorical Theory from St. Augustine to the Renaissance* [Berkeley: University of California Press, 1974], 365–74, for a recent example). This account provides explanations of the various devices organized by function as discussed in chapter 1. Definitions are from *Rhetorica ad Herennium,* with additional examples taken from Quintilian's *Institutio oratoria* as indicated.

Exornationes Verborum

1. Repetition

Repetitio (*epanaphora*) occurs when the same word is used to begin successive phrases.

Conversio (*antistrophe*) occurs when the repetition ends successive phrases.

Conplexio (interlacement) is the combination of both *repetitio* and *conversio*.

Traductio (transplacement) features the tasteful repetition of the same word. For example, "one who has nothing in life more desirable than life cannot cultivate a virtuous life." *Traductio* also involves the repeated use of the same word, but with a different meaning. For example, "I would leave this place, should the Senate give me leave."

Conduplicatio (reduplication) features the reiteration of one or more words for the purpose of amplification, emphasis, or commiseration.

Interpretatio (*synononymy*) is a related figure that achieves reiteration by using words with equivalent meanings rather than the same word.

2. Opposition

Contentio (antithesis) occurs in utterances consisting of opposites.

Contrarium is the use of two opposite statements for the purpose of confirming one of the two statements and contradicting the other.

Commutatio (reciprocal change) occurs when contradictory expressions are rendered together so that the latter thought follows from the former. For example, "a poem ought to be a painting that speaks; a painting ought to be a silent poem."

3. Strategic Advantage

Interrogatio is the practice of summarizing the case of an adversary in such a fashion so as to support one's own case.

Ratiocinatio is a ploy with which an orator questions the meaning of his or her own statements and then develops the case through the answering of those questions.

Subiectio (*hypophora*) occurs when an orator questions what can be said in favor of an adversary or against him or her. The question is then answered in such a way as to reflect favorably on the orator or negatively on the adversary. This figure differs from *ratiocinatio* in that for *ratiocinatio* one asks for reasons in support of statements. *Subiectio* seeks what amounts to testimony or summary of reputation.

Expeditio (elimination) is the process of listing the various alternatives available and then discarding all but the option favored by the speaker.

Correctio withdraws a statement previously uttered and replaces it with a more appropriate remark. The orator usually expresses the thought initially in rather ordinary language and then utters the correction in a more striking and appropriate form.

Praecisio (*aposiopesis*) occurs when a speaker begins a remark, but leaves it unfinished. This device renders the audience suspicious and maintains their attention in cases where a complete statement might not.

Occulatio (*paralipsis*) is an utterance in which the orator states that he or she will not make a statement about a particular subject. In indicating that the subject will not be discussed, the subject is nonetheless raised. This allows the orator to touch briefly upon a delicate issue without appearing indelicate.

Permissio (surrender) is an *exornatio* by which the orator indicates that he or she will concede the matter under consideration to the will of another. It is particularly effective in soliciting sympathy.

Dubitatio (indecision) is used when a speaker seems to ask which of two or more words should be used. For example, "you have dared to say that, you of all men—by what name worthy of your character shall I call you?"

4. Structure

Definitio is simply a brief statement of the essential characteristics of a phenomenon. Its skillful use results in an expression that appears absolute; to use more words would be excessive and to use fewer words impossible.

Transitio briefly summarizes what has been said previously and indicates what is to follow.

Gradatio (climax) performs a similar function, but in a more artful fashion. It is an *exornatio* by which a speaker moves to a new word or subject in steps, connecting each subsequent utterance with the previous one. For example:

> The empire of *Greece* belonged to the *Athenians;*
> the *Athenians* were overpowered by the *Spartans;*
> the *Spartans* were overcome by the *Thebans;*
> the *Thebans* were conquered by the *Macedonians;*
> and the *Macedonians* in a short time subdued *Asia*
> and joined *her* to the empire of *Greece.*

Gradatio (a stairstep) is a transitionary device that facilitates the production of causal chains.

Conclusio uses a brief argument to determine the consequences of what has been said previously in the speech.

5. Rhythm

Membrum is a unit of words that is brief and complete, but does not express a complete thought without being connected to another unit of words.

Articulus occurs when single words are set apart in choppy, quick speech.

Continuatio is a dense group of uninterrupted words that represent a complete thought.

Each of the previous three *exornationes* has eventually come to be known as punctuation marks rather than linguistic units. Also sharing the linguistic focus is *conpar, similiter cadens,* and *similiter desinens—all of which* facilitate balanced *membra* and *continuationes.*

Conpar (isocolon) is an *exornatio* that consists or two or more *membra* (clauses) that consist of approximately the same number of syllables.

Similiter cadens (*homoeoptoton*) occurs when two or more words in the same group of words (period) feature the same case and case endings.

Similiter desinens (*homoeoteleuton*) features similar but undeclinable word endings.

Disiunctio, coniunctio, and *adiunctio* also involve grammatical/linguistic dimensions. Each is concerned with verb placement.

Disiunctio is a device whereby two or more clauses are presented—each with its own verb.

Coniunctio occurs when two or more clauses are joined by one verb placed between them.

Adiunctio places the verb serving two or more clauses either at the beginning or end of the sentence. Additional linguistic variations are seen in *dissolutum* and *adnominatio.*

Dissolutum (*asyndeton*) is a presentation of a series of admonitions without conjunctions. It presents a thought sharply, forcefully, and concisely.

Adnominatio (*paronomasia*) also features a linguistic bent, but with the flavor of a ploy. It involves the modification of a word through pronunciation—a change in letters, or case, so that the same words mean different things. An *adnominatio* is essentially a pun.

6. Miscellaneous

Sententia and *exclamatio* are a bit difficult to categorize, but are helpful devices used in an oration.

Sententia is a saying based on life that shows briefly what happens or ought to happen in certain situations. A *sententia* may be offered with or without supporting reasons.

Exclamatio (apostrophe) is an expression of grief or indignation to some person, city, place, or object. It tends to render the situation under discussion in a different perspective and therefore can produce indignation on the part of an audience.

7. Special *exornationes verborum* (Tropes)

Nominatio (*onomatopoeia*) involves the coining of a word to describe a phenomenon for which no word exists. The most common usage features words that are imitative of sounds such as roar, bark, or hiss. *Nominatio,* however, is also used to create words that are not imitative of sound. For example, *Sullaturit* was adapted from Sulla to mean "he who wishes to become a second Sulla" (Quintilian 8.6.31). Thus, it may be best to describe *nominatio* as a word coined through resemblance.

Pronominatio (*antonomasia*) occurs when another expression is substituted for the one properly used. The substitution may be made by using an epithet or a striking characteristic for the object being described. Cicero, for example, may be described as "the prince of Roman orators" (Quintilian, *Institutio oratoria,* trans. H. E. Butler (1920, 1921, 1922; reprint, Cambridge: Harvard University Press, 1976), 8.6.29–30).

Denominatio (*metonymy*) results when something closely associated with an object is used to represent it.

Intellectio (*synecdoche*) performs a similar role. It occurs when a part is used to signify a whole or a whole is used to signify a part.

Circumitio (*periphrasis*) is simply the use of many words to express a thought when fewer words will suffice. It serves only as an embellishing function except in cases when more words are needed to describe something that otherwise might seem indelicate.

Transgressio (*hyperbaton*) is the transposition of word order for poetic purposes. It involves no change in meaning, but is designed to make an expression more pleasant to the ear.

Superlatio (hyperbole) is an exaggeration of truth used for the purposes of minimization or magnification.

Abusio (*catachresis*) receives somewhat differing descriptions from *auctor ad Herennium* and Quintilian. *Ad Herennium* cites it as "the inexact use of like and kindred words in place of the precise and proper one" (4.33.45). Quintilian, however, describes it simply as "the practice of adopting the nearest possible term to describe something for which no actual term exists" (Quintilian 8.6.34). Nonetheless, it is inexactness that seems to be the hallmark of *abusio. Abusio* refers to objects or phenomena for which there is no actual word.

Translatio (metaphor) occurs "when a word applying to one thing is transferred to another, because the similarity seems to justify the transference" (Quintilian 4.34.45). It is used to create vivid mental images, avoid obscenity, minimize, maximize, and embellish.

Permutatio (allegory) occurs when an expression is used to represent a meaning different from its literal one. A *permutatio* is often composed from a series of *translationes.* It changes meaning through comparison, argument, and contrast. An example of comparison is: "for when dogs act the part of wolves, to what guardian, pray, are we going to entrust our herds of cattle."

The argumentative *permutatio* is probably best demonstrated by this example that Quintilian attributed to Cicero: "What I marvel at and complain of is this, that there should exist any man so set on destroying his enemies as to scuttle the ship on which he is sailing" (Quintilian 8.6.47).

Contrast occurs when the opposite descriptor is used to describe a phenomenon. Quintilian (8.6.54) refers to a *permutatio* of contrast as irony.

Exornationes Sententiarum

8. Organization

Distributio is the practice of assigning certain functions and duties to a number of things or persons.

Descriptio clearly and perspicaciously depicts the consequences of an action.

Divisio divides an issue and resolves it by reasoning out how the components demonstrate or prove the larger issue.

Frequentatio occurs when the various points contained throughout a speech are collected in one place to make their significance more impressive.

Commoratio occurs when the orator gives great attention to and often returns to the strongest point in a case. This is a figure that pervades an entire discourse rather than being contained in any one part.

Contentio (antithesis), first discussed by the *auctor* as an *exornatio verborum,* is also an *exornatio sententiarum.* The first type consists of the rapid opposition of words; the second depicts the rapid opposition of thoughts.

Similitudo transfers similarity from one thing to another. This may be done through contrast, negation, extended analogy, and brief analogy. The *similitudo* of contrast is used to demonstrate how two seemingly similar things are actually dissimilar. Negation pairs two inappropriate analogies to show the inappropriateness of the case at hand. The remaining two *similitudiones* use analogies constructively—one in extended form and the other briefly.

9. Expression

Licentia occurs when an orator speaks openly on a subject even though he or she speaks to a person or group whom he or she respects or fears.

Deminutio is a figure by which an orator speaks of his or her personal fortune, nature, or advantages, but softens it in such a way as to avoid an impression of arrogance.

Expolitio occurs when the orator continues to speak on the same issue, but appears to be saying something new. This may be done by the choice of words, the delivery of words, by varying the words, by changing the tone or using the words or the character of another, or by appearing excited.

Conformatio (personification) is the practice of making an absent person present or attributing life to some inanimate object.

Significatio is an *exornatio* that implies more about a situation than is actually asserted. It may be produced through *exsuperationem,* exaggeration; *ambiguum,* using words with ambiguous meanings; *consequentiam,* using remarks that imply greater meaning; *abscisionem,* making an incomplete remark that creates suspicion; or *similtudinem,* an implied comparison to something else.

Brevitas is the expression of an idea with a minimum number of words.

10. Comparison

Exemplum is the use of an example from the past to buttress the viability of a contemporary situation.

Imago (simile) depicts a particular activity by comparing it with another.

11. Description

Effictio is the use of a specific description to identify a person in speech.

Notatio is the description of a person by means of certain unique character traits.

Sermocinatio is the depiction of a person by means of language indicative of his or her character.

Demonstratio is a detailed description of an event that seems to depict it in vivid detail.

Appendix B

Grammatical Figures

This account is based on Donatus' *Ars grammatica,* book 3 (see Keil, vol. 4: 395–401).

Barbarisms and *Solecisms*

Acyrologia is inappropriate diction.

Cacenphaton is the use of an expression that may be seen as offensive when expressed.

Pleonasmos is the unnecessary addition of words to an expression that already possesses plenty of significance.

Perissologia is the unnecessary addition of words and elaboration of an expression that add no force to it.

Macrologia is the use of a lengthy expression that is not necessary for comprehension.

Tautologia is an expression featuring repetition of a word or phrase.

Eclipsis is an obscuration of necessary diction that requires precise expression. These are unavoidable expressions in which words may be slurred together without careful enunciation.

Tapinosis occurs when the words used in an expression reduce its dignity.

Cacosyntheton is the faulty gathering together of words in an expression.

Amphibolia is ambiguous diction.

Metaplasms

Addition

Prothesis is the placement of an additional letter or syllable at the beginning of a word. For example, *nato* becomes *gnato* and *tulit* becomes *tetulit*.

Epenthesis is the addition of a letter or syllable to the middle of an expression.

Paragoge is the addition of a letter or syllable to the end of an expression.

Subtraction

Aphaeresis is the removal of the initial letter or syllable of an expression. For example, *contemno* becomes *temno.*

Syncope is the removal of a letter or syllable from the middle of an expression.

Apocope is the removal of a letter or syllable from the end of an expression.

Adaptation

Ectasis is the extension or addition to a syllable contrary to its normal usage (*italiam* instead of *italia*). *Systole* is the lengthening of a syllable.

Diaresis is the division of one syllable into two.

Episynaliphe is the combining of two syllables into one.

Synaliphe is the ellision of two vowels together.

Ecthlipsis is the deliberate combination of harsh sounds.

Transposition

Antithesis is the substitution of one letter for another. (This is a definition of the term that appears to be unique with Donatus.)

Metathesis is the transposition of letters—for example, Evandre instead of Evander.

Schemes

Prolepsis is a form of anticipation by which a scene or situation is set up before relating it.

Zeugma is the use of one verb to serve multiple clauses.

Hypozeuxis is the use of separate verbs to serve each clause.

Syllepsis is the use of one verb to unite dissimilar clauses.

Anadiplosis is the reduplication of a word from its final position in the first clause to the beginning position in the following clause.

Anaphora is the repetition of a word used in the beginning clause into subsequent clauses.

Epanalepsis is the repetition of the first word used in a verse into the final word in a verse.

Epizeuxis is the repetition of the same word in the same verse without other repetition or reduplication.

Paronomasia is a comparison of meaning through similar, but different, words.

Schesis onamaton is the use of a number of names in conjunction with attributes with which they are normally connected.

Parhomoeon is a similar utterance of diverse words: *O Tite tute Tati tibi tanta tyranne tulisti* (thyself to thyself, Titus Tatius the tyrant, thou takest those terrible troubles)—the classic example of alliteration.

Homoeoptoton is the utterance of a series of words with similar case endings.

Homoeoteleuton is a phrase employing a series of similar case endings that are not declinable.

Polyptoton is the use of a number of the same words, but in different case forms.

Hirmos is a series of uninterrupted statements that are continued to the end of the expression.

Polysyndeton is the use of multiple conjunctions in an expression.

Dialyton or *asyndeton* is an expression that forgoes the use of conjunctions.

Subtropes

Hyperbaton is the transposition of word order for poetic purposes. Donatus divides the trope into five types:

Hysterologia is a simple change in word order. For example, *Italiam contra* (against Italy) may also be expressed as *contra Italiam.*

Parenthesis is an insertion into the logical progression of an expression, as in this example from *The Aeneid*: "Aeneas—for a father's love did not suffer his heart to rest—speedily sends Achates toward the ships."

Tmesis is an insertion into a single word. For example, *'septem subiecta trioni' pro septem trioni et 'saxo cere comminuit brum' et Massili portabant iuvenes ad litora tanas, hoc est cerebrum et Massilitanas.* In the example, *septemtrioni* (northern sky) has *subiecta* interjected between its syllables: *septem subiecta trioni. Cerebrum comminuit saxo* (the brain is crushed by rocks) was expressed as *saxo cere comminuit brum. Comminuit* separates the syllables of *cerebrum. Massilitanas portabant iuvenes ad litora* (the Massilitanis were carrying their children to shore) was converted to *Massili portabant iuvenes ad litora tanas. Massili* and *tanas* were separated by the rest of the phrase. Thus, *tmesis* allows the syllables of a word to be interrupted by other words for the sake of meter.

Synchesis is a *hyperbaton* in which all word order is jumbled: *tris notus abreptas in saxa latentia torquet, saxa vocant Itali mediis quae in fluctibus aras* (three ships the south wind catches and hurls on the hidden rocks—rocks the Italians call the altars, rising amidst the waves), *est enim ordo hic, tris abreptas notus in saxa torquet, quae saxa in mediis fluctibus latentia aras vocant* (three ships the south wind catches and hurls on the rocks—hidden rocks called the altars, rising amidst the waves). The first example is convoluted, but pleasing to the ear. The second is more comprehensible, but less metrical.

Allegory consists of seven subtropes:

Irony is an allegory of contrast. It occurs when the opposite descriptor is used to describe a phenomenon.

Antiphrasis is an irony of a single word.

Enigma, Donatus' third subspecies of allegory, occurs when an obscure thought is concealed within an expression because of certain resemblances. For example, *Mater me genuit, edem mox gignitur me* (a mother begat me, and now the same is begat from me). Does *eodem* refer to *me* (meaning perhaps a son) or to *mater* (meaning a mother)? The answer is uncertain. Hence, the expression is termed an enigma.

Charientismos is a trope through which a harsh statement is expressed graciously. For example, rather than saying that someone has died, people often say that a person has "passed away."

Paronomia is a proverb used for appropriate circumstances. This trope involves the use of such stock expressions as *adversum stimulum calces* (scratch where it itches) and *lupus in fabula* (the wolf in the story—the ancient world's version of "speak of the devil").

Sarcasmos is mockery filled with hostility. It is essentially an irony or *antiphrasis* with an edge.

Astismos is an expression that lacks rustic simplicity and substitutes for it with urbane wit. Donatus' example comes from Virgil's *Ecologues*: "Let him who hates not Bavius love your songs, Maevius; and let him also yoke foxes and milk billy goats."

Homoeosis is a trope that identifies something unknown through its resemblance to something better known.

Its first species, icon involves the comparison of one person to another through the characteristics of the better-known person.

Parabole is the comparison of different kinds of things as in the passage from the *Aeneid* where Laocoön's screaming is likened to the "bellowing of a wounded bull that has fled from the altar."

Paradigma features the use of an example to encourage or discourage a person from taking a particular action.

Notes

Rhetoric and Grammar

Introduction

1. Marshall McLuhan, *The Gutenberg Galaxy: The Making of Typographic Man* (Toronto: University of Toronto Press, 1962). My particular framework for the orality / literacy tension is based primarily on Walter J. Ong, *Orality and Literacy: The Technologizing of the World* (New York: Methuen, 1982) and Eric A. Havelock, *The Literate Revolution in Greece and Its Cultural Consequences* (Princeton: Princeton University Press, 1982). See also Jacqueline de Romilly, *Magic and Rhetoric in Ancient Greece* (Cambridge, Mass.: Harvard University Press, 1975); John O. Ward, "Magic and Rhetoric from Antiquity to the Renaissance: Some Ruminations," *Rhetorica* 6 (1988): 57–118.

2. Ong, *Orality and Literacy,* 12.

3. See Richard Leo Enos' comments on Cicero's conversion of his own speeches into texts in *The Literate Mode of Cicero's Legal Rhetoric* (Carbondale: Southern Illinois University Press, 1988).

4. Charles Sears Baldwin, *Medieval Rhetoric and Poetic (to 1400): Interpreted from Representative Works* (New York: MacMillan, 1928); J. W. H. Atkins, *English Literary Criticism: The Medieval Phase* (1943; reprint, Gloucester, Mass.: Peter Smith, 1961); George A. Kennedy, *Classical Rhetoric in its Christian and Secular Tradition from Ancient to Modern Times* (Chapel Hill: University of North Carolina Press, 1980); Brian Vickers, *In Defence of Rhetoric* (Oxford: Clarendon Press, 1988). See also James J. Murphy's comments on this phenomena in "The Middle Ages" in *The Present State of Scholarship in Historical and Contemporary Rhetoric,* ed. Winifred Bryan Horner (Columbia: University of Missouri Press, 1983), 54–58.

5. See Vickers, 214–93.

6. Marjorie Curry Woods, "The Teaching of Writing in Medieval Europe," in *A Short History of Writing Instruction From Ancient Greece to Twentieth-Century America,* ed. James J. Murphy (Davis, Calif.: Hermagoras Press, 1990), 78–80; see also Marjorie Curry Woods, "Among Men—Not Boys: Histories of Rhetoric and the Exclusion of Pedagogy," *Rhetoric Society Quarterly* 22 (1992): 18–26.

7. The section in which this hierarchy is developed spans pages 3–9.

8. Woods, "Teaching," 93.

9. Atkins 200–203; James J. Murphy, *Rhetoric in the Middle Ages: A History of Rhetorical Theory from St. Augustine to the Renaissance* (Berkeley: University of California Press, 1974), 170–73.

10. See Murphy, *Rhetoric in the Middle Ages,* 56–57.

11. Murphy, *Rhetoric in the Middle Ages,* 135; Alex Preminger, O. B. Hardison, and Kevin Kerrane, eds. *Classical and Medieval Literary Criticism: Translations and Interpretations* (New York: Frederick Ungar, 1974), 385, 388; Jane Baltzell Kopp, "Geoffrey of Vinsauf: The New Poetics (Poetria nova)," in *Three Medieval Rhetorical Arts,* ed. James J. Murphy (Berkeley: University of California Press, 1971), 31; Atkins, 96–97.

12. See Ernst Robert Curtius, *European Literature and the Latin Middle Ages,* trans. Willard R. Trask (1953; reprint, Princeton University Press, 1973), esp. 62–105, 128–66; F. J. E. Raby, *A History of Christian Latin Poetry from the Beginning to the Close of the Middle Ages* (Oxford: Clarendon Press, 1927), esp. 4–5; Baldwin, 184–205; Atkins, 1–35.

13. O. B. Hardison, Jr., "Medieval Literary Criticism: General Introduction," in *Classical and Medieval Literary Criticism: Translations and Interpretations,* eds. Alex Preminger, O. B. Hardison, and Kevin Kerrane (New York: Frederick Ungar, 1974), 263–98.

14. Hardison, 263–64.

15. Hardison, 264.

16. Aldo Scaglione, *The Classical Theory of Composition From Its Origins to the Present: A Historical Survey* (Chapel Hill: University of North Carolina Press, 1972).

17. Scaglione, 97.

18. Richard McKeon, "Rhetoric in the Middle Ages," *Speculum* 17 (1942): 1–32. The text referenced here is reprinted in Joseph Schwartz and John A. Rycenga, eds., *The Province of Rhetoric* (New York: Ronald Press, 1965), 172–212.

19. McKeon, 174.

20. McKeon, 175.

21. Geoffrey of Vinsauf's *Poetria nova* and *Documentum de modo et arte dictandi et versificandi;* Matthew of Vendôme's *Ars versificatoria;* and Eberhard the German's *Laborintus.*

22. Hans-Jürgen Gräbener, ed., *Ars poetica: Kritische Ausgabe* (Münster Westfallen: Aschendorf, 1965); Traugott Lawler, ed. and trans., *The Parisiana Poetria of John of Garland* (New Haven: Yale University Press, 1974).

23. See Margaret F. Nims, trans., *The Poetria nova of Geoffrey of Vinsauf* (Toronto: Pontifical Institute of Mediaeval Studies, 1967); Ernest Gallo, trans., *The Poetria nova and Its Sources in Early Rhetorical Doctrine* (The Hague: Mouton, 1971); Kopp, 32–108; Ernest Gallo, "Matthew of Vendôme: Introductory Treatise on the Art of Poetry," *American Philosophical Society Proceedings* 118 (1974): 51–92; Aubrey E. Galyon, trans., *The Art of Versification* (Ames: Iowa State University Press, 1980);

Roger P. Parr, trans., *Ars versificatoria (The Art of the Versemaker)* (Milwaukee: Marquette University Press, 1981); Roger P. Parr, *Documentum de modo et arte dictandi et versificandi (Instruction in the Art and Method of Speaking and Versifying)* (Milwaukee: Marquette University Press, 1968); Lawler; Catherine Yodice Giles, "Gervais of Melkley's Treatise on the Art of Versifying and the Method of Composing on Prose: A Translation and Commentary," Ph.D. diss., Rutgers University, 1973; Evelyn Carlson, "Laborintus of Eberhard Rendered into English with Introduction and Notes," M.A. thesis, Cornell University, 1930.

24. Marjorie Curry Woods, *An Early Commentary on the Poetria nova of Geoffrey of Vinsauf* (New York: Garland, 1985).

24. Walter B. Sedgewick, "The Style and Vocabulary of the Latin Arts of Poetry of the Twelfth and Thirteenth Centuries," *Speculum* 3 (1928): 349–65; Douglas Kelly, "The Scope of the Treatment of Composition in the Twelfth and Thirteenth Century Arts of Poetry," *Speculum* 41 (1966): 261–78; Douglas Kelly, "Theory and Composition in Medieval Narrative Poetry and Geoffrey of Vinsauf's *Poetria nova*," *Medieval Studies* 31 (1969): 117–48; Ernest Gallo, "The Poetria nova of Geoffrey of Vinsauf," in *Medieval Eloquence: Studies in the Theory and Practice of Medieval Rhetoric*, ed. James J. Murphy (Berkeley: University California Press, 1971), 68–84; Margaret F. Nims, "Translatio: 'Difficult Statement' in Medieval Poetic Theory," *University of Toronto Quarterly* 43 (1974): 215–30; Marjorie Curry Woods, "An Unfashionable Rhetoric in the Fifteenth Century," *Quarterly Journal of Speech* 75 (1989): 312–20; Martin Camargo, "Toward a Comprehensive Art of Written Discourse: Geoffrey of Vinsauf and the *Ars Dictaminis*," *Rhetorica* 6 (1988): 167–94; Marjorie Curry Woods, "A Medieval Rhetoric Goes to School—and to the University: The Commentaries on the *Poetria nova*," *Rhetorica* 9 (1991): 55–65.

26. Interestingly, Kelly introduces a new author to the corpus—Matthias of Linköping. Matthias' *Poetria*, a Swedish work written in the fourteenth century, is not generally included in the genre. Kelly himself indicates the work is "geographically, chronologically and conceptually unique" and perhaps more a commentary than *poetria*. Douglas Kelly, *The Arts of Poetry and Prose* (Turnhout-Belgium: Brepols, 1991), 12.

Chapter 1—Ancient Rhetoric and Grammar: Orality versus Literacy

1. Gorgias, "Gorgias' On The Nonexistent or On Nature," trans. George Kennedy, in *The Older Sophists*, ed. Rosamond Kent Sprague (Columbia: University of South Carolina Press, 1972), 42.

2. Gorgias, 46.

3. De Romilly, *Magic and Rhetoric in Ancient Greece*, 16.

4. *Plato's Phaedrus, Translated with an Introduction and Commentary*, trans. R. Hackforth (1952; reprint, Cambridge: Cambridge University Press, 1979), 158.

5. *Plato's Phaedrus*, 158.

6. *Rhetoric*, 1355b, 25–30; this is a paraphrase based on Aristotle, *Rhetoric*, in *The Rhetoric and Poetics of Aristotle*, trans. W. Rhys Roberts (1954; reprint, New York: Modern Library, 1984), 24; Aristotle, *The "Art" of Rhetoric*, trans. John Henry Freese (1926; reprint Cambridge: Harvard University Press, 1975), 15; and Aristotle, *Aristotle on Rhetoric: A Theory of Civic Discourse*, trans. George A. Kennedy (New York: Oxford University Press, 1991), 36–37.

7. John Poulakos, "Rhetoric, the Sophists, and the Impossible," *Communication Monographs* 51 (1984): 223–24.

8. For a discussion of the ramifications naming had in early Greek rhetorical theory, see Edward Schiappa, "Rhêtorikê: What's in a Name? Toward a Revised History of Early Greek Rhetorical History," *Quarterly Journal of Speech* 78 (1992): 1–15, especially 8–11.

9. See Otto Alvin Loeb Dieter, "Stasis," *Speech Monographs* 17 (1950): 369; Michael Carter, "*Stasis* and *Kairos:* Principles of Social Construction in Classical Rhetoric," *Rhetoric Review* 7 (1988): 99–101.

10. See *De inventione*, 2.4.31, in Cicero, *De inventione, De optimo genere oratorium, Topica*, trans. H. M. Hubbard (1949; reprint, Cambridge, Mass.: Harvard University Press, 1976).

11. Michael C. Leff, "The Topics of Argumentative Invention in Latin Rhetorical Theory from Cicero to Boethius," *Rhetorica* 1 (1983): 24.

12. Donald Lemen Clark, *Rhetoric in Greco-Roman Education* (New York: Columbia University Press, 1957), 76. For a description of writing instruction in the Greco-Roman system, see James J. Murphy, "Roman Writing Instruction as Described by Quintilian," in *A Short History of Writing Instruction From Ancient Greece to Twentieth-Century America*, ed. James J. Murphy (Davis, Calif.: Hermagoras Press, 1990), 19–76.

13. Quotations from *Rhetorica ad Herennium* are taken from [Cicero], *Ad C. Herennium: De ratione dicendi (Rhetorica ad Herennium)*, trans. Harry Caplan (1954; reprint, Cambridge: Harvard University Press, 1981).

14. Quintilian, *Institutio oratoria*, trans. H. E. Butler (1920, 1921, 1922; reprint, Cambridge: Harvard University Press, 1976), 8.6.

15. Cf. [Cicero], *Ad C. Herennium*, 4.8–55 and Quintilian, *Institutio oratoria*, 8–9.

16. George Kennedy, *The Art of Rhetoric in the Roman World 300 B.C.–A.D. 300* (Princeton: Princeton University Press, 1972), 121.

17. R. H. Robins, *Ancient and Medieval Grammatical Theory in Europe, with Particular Reference to Modern Linguistic Doctrine* (1951; reprint, Port Washington, N.Y.: Kennikat Press, 1971), 1–36; Scaglione, 8–11; R. H. Kennedy, *The Art of Persuasion in Greece* (Princeton: Princeton University Press, 1963), 295–99; Jeffrey Huntsman, "Grammar," in *The Seven Liberal Arts in the Middle Ages*, ed. David L. Wagner (Bloomington: Indiana University Press, 1983), 63–64; Dionysius Thrax, "The TEKHNÉ GRAMMATIKÉ of Dionysius Thrax Translated into English," trans. Alan Kemp, *Historiographica Linguistica* 13 (1986): 343–46.

18. Huntsman, 62.

19. Scaglione, 1–74; Louis Holtz, *Donat et la tradition de L'enseignement grammatical: Étude sur L'Ars Donati et sa diffusion (IVe–IXe siècle) et Édition Critique* (Paris: Centre National De la Recherche Scientifique, 1981).

20. The treatise has traditionally been attributed to the first century, B.C., but some scholars argue that it may date as late as the fifth century, A.D. See Dionysius Thrax, 343–45.

21. Dionysius Thrax, 346.

22. Dionysius Thrax, 346–59.

23. Robins, 47–48.

24. Robins, 57.

25. The Latin text may be found in Heinrich Keil, ed., *Grammatici Latini*, 4 vols. (1863; rpt. Hildesheim, Germany: Georg Olms, 1961), vol. 4: 355–402. A newer edition was published by Holtz, 585–674. Subsequent references will be to the page numbers in the Keil edition. Paraphrases and translations are mine unless otherwise indicated.

26. See the introduction to Wayland Johnson Chase, *The Ars Minor of Donatus: For One Thousand Years the Leading Textbook of Grammar Translated from the Latin, With Introductory Sketch* (Madison: University of Wisconsin Press, 1926), 3–26. Chase's introduction is an excellent survey of the treatise's influence.

27. Robins, 63.

28. Chase, 28–29.

29. Chase, 38–39.

30. Chase, 12–13.

31. *Laborintus*, lines 69–70.

32. See Murphy, "Roman Writing," 32–35.

33. Holtz, 148.

34. *Virgil, With an English Translation* by H. Rushton Fairclough, 2 vols. (1918; Cambridge, Mass.: Harvard University Press, 1969), vol. 2: 308–11.

35. Murphy, "Roman Writing," 35.

36. Murphy, "Roman Writing," 34.

37. Latin text in Keil, vol. 2: 1–597 and vol. 3: 1–377. Subsequent references are to chapter numbers.

38. Latin text is in Keil, vol. 3: 430–40; an English paraphrase is found in Donald Lemen Clark, "Rhetoric and the Literature of the English Middle Ages," *Quarterly Journal of Speech* 45 (1959): 19–28.

39. Clark, "Rhetoric," 19–28.

40. G. J. Engelhardt, "Beowulf: A Study in Dilation," *PMLA* 70 (1955): 825–52.

41. Clark, "Rhetoric," 181.

42. Clark, "Rhetoric," 186.

43. Clark, "Rhetoric," 181–208; see also Baldwin's translation of Hermogenes 23–38; Ray Nadeau, "The *Progymnasmata* of Apthonius in Translation," *Speech Monographs* 19 (1952): 264–86; and Murphy, "Roman Writing," 56–65.

44. Robert A. Kaster, *Guardians of Language: The Grammarian and Society in Late Antiquity* (Berkeley: University of California Press, 1988), 175.

45. Kaster, 183.

Chapter 2—Grammar and Rhetoric: Absorption and Inversion

1. Rita Copeland, *Rhetoric, Hermeneutics, and Translation in the Middle Ages: Academic Traditions and Vernacular Texts* (Cambridge: Cambridge University Press, 1991), 20.

2. Michael C. Leff, "The Material of the Art in the Latin Handbooks of the Fourth Century A.D.," in *Rhetoric Revalued: Papers from the International Society for the History of Rhetoric,* ed. Brian Vickers (Binghampton: Center for Medieval and Early Renaissance Studies, State University of New York at Binghampton, 1982), 71–78.

3. Leff, "Material," 73–74.

4. Leff, "Material," 74.

5. Leff, "Material," 75; see also Michael C. Leff, "The Latin Stylistic Rhetorics of Antiquity," *Communication Monographs* 40 (1973): 273–79.

6. Baldwin, 94.

7. Murphy, *Rhetoric in the Middle Ages,* 45.

8. Baldwin, 25.

9. Murphy, *Rhetoric in the Middle Ages,* 66; Kennedy, *Classical Rhetoric,* 178.

10. Murphy, *Rhetoric in the Middle Ages,* 74.

11. Murphy, *Rhetoric in the Middle Ages,* 70.

12. Paul E. Prill, "Rhetoric and Poetics in the Early Middle Ages," *Rhetorica* 5 (1987): 133; see also Curtius, 62–105, 128–66; Raby, 4–5; Hardison, 263–98.

13. Prill, 133.

14. Prill, 135–36.

15. Clark, "Rhetoric," 24; Curtius, 158–59.

16. Prill, 138–40.

17. Copeland, 20.

18. Copeland, 35.

19. Copeland, 42.

20. Copeland, 62.

21. Copeland, 64.

22. Copeland, 65.

23. Samuel Jaffe, "Antiquity and Innovation in Notker's *Nova rhetorica:* The Doctrine of Invention," *Rhetorica* 3 (1985): 173–76; Beth S. Bennett, "The Function of Adaptation in Notker's *Rhetorica,*" *Rhetorica* 7 (1989): 171–84.

24. Jaffe, 173–76.

25. Bennett, "Function," 184.

26. Beth S. Bennett, "The Significance of the *Rhetorimachia* of Anselm de Besate to the History of Rhetoric," *Rhetorica* 5 (1987): 247–48.

27. Beth S. Bennett, "The Rhetoric of Martianus Capella and Anselm de Besate in the Tradition of Menippean Satire," *Philosophy and Rhetoric* 24 (1991): 128–42.

28. Murphy, *Rhetoric in the Middle Ages*, 276–311; Kennedy, *Classical Rhetoric*, 190–91; Camargo, "Rhetoric," 111–13.

29. Matthew 22.37: 39–40; 1 Timothy 1: 5; Romans 13: 9–10.

30. Copeland, 154.

31. St. Augustine, *On Christian Doctrine*, trans. D. W. Robertson, Jr. (Indianapolis: Library of the Liberal Arts, 1958).

32. *De inventione* 1.1.1.

33. Cicero's words are "Erit igitur eloquens—hunc enim auctore Antonio quaerimus—is qui in foro causisque civilibus ita dicet, ut probet, ut delectet, ut flectet. Probare necessitatis est, delectare suavitatis, flectere victoriae" (*Orator*, 20.69–70). I read *probare* more in the sense of to demonstrate or instruct than as to prove.

34. Augustine seems to be adding some words to *Orator*, 29.101. Nonetheless, the connection of each of the styles to particular duties of the orator is found earlier at 21.69–70.

35. Ĉelica Milovanović-Barham, "Three Levels of Style in Augustine of Hippo and Gregory of Nazianzus," *Rhetorica* 11 (1993): 1–25.

36. Baldwin, 51.

37. Murphy, *Rhetoric in the Middle Ages*, 289.

38. Kennedy, *Classical Rhetoric*, 158.

39. Guibert de Nogent, "*A Book on the Way a Sermon Ought to Be Given*," trans. Joseph M. Miller, in *Readings in Medieval Rhetoric*, ed. Joseph M. Miller, Michael H. Prosser, and Thomas W. Benson (Bloomington: Indiana University Press, 1973), 170–71; See also Murphy, *Rhetoric in the Middle Ages* 302; Hardison attributes the four levels of interpretation to John Cassian (360–435), 266.

40. Murphy, *Rhetoric in the Middle Ages*, 303.

41. Murphy, *Rhetoric in the Middle Ages*, 310–31.

42. Camargo, "Rhetoric," 113.

43. Murphy, *Rhetoric in the Middle Ages*, 310–55.

44. Robert of Basevorn, "The Form of Preaching (*Forma Praedicandi*)," trans. Leopold Krul, in *Three Medieval Rhetorical Arts*, ed. James J. Murphy (Berkeley: University of California Press, 1971), 128–31.

45. Otto A. L. Dieter, "*Arbor Picta:* The Medieval Tree of Preaching," *Quarterly Journal of Speech* 51 (1965): 123–44; Harry Caplan, "A Late Medieval Tractate on Preaching," in *Studies in Rhetoric and Public Speaking in Honor of James Albert Winans by His Pupils and Colleagues*, ed. A. M. Drummond (New York: Century, 1925), 61–90.

46. Murphy, *Rhetoric in the Middle Ages*, 242–43.

47. Murphy, *Rhetoric in the Middle Ages*, 196.

48. Murphy, *Rhetoric in the Middle Ages,* 210; Kennedy, *Classical Rhetoric,* 186; Camargo, "Rhetoric," 108.

49. Murphy, *Rhetoric in the Middle Ages,* 204–207.

50. Murphy, *Rhetoric in the Middle Ages,* 207.

51. Murphy, *Rhetoric in the Middle Ages,* 210; Kennedy, *Classical Rhetoric,* 186; Camargo, "Rhetoric," 109.

52. Camargo, "Rhetoric," 109.

53. Anonymous of Bologna, "The Principles of Letter-writing (*Rationes dictandi*)," trans. James J. Murphy, in *Three Medieval Rhetorical Arts,* ed. James J. Murphy (Berkeley: University of California Press, 1971), 1–25.

54. Anonymous, 7.

55. Anonymous, 10–19.

56. Anonymous, 21–25.

57. Murphy, *Rhetoric in the Middle Ages,* 266.

58. Murphy, *Rhetoric in the Middle Ages,* 266.

59. Murphy, *Rhetoric in the Middle Ages,* 135.

60. The Latin text is found in Dietrich Reichling, ed., *Das Doctrinale des Alexander de Villa-Dei: Kritsche-Exegetische Ausgabe, mit einleitung verzeichniss der handschriften und drucke nebst registern,* in *Monumenta germaniae paedagogica,* 12 (Berlin: A. Hofmann, 1893). Paraphrases and translations are mine unless otherwise noted.

61. Murphy, *Rhetoric in the Middle Ages,* 147; Nicholas Orme, *English Schools in the Middle Ages* (London: Methuen, 1973), 88.

62. Orme, 88; Paul Abelson, *The Seven Liberal Arts* (New York: Teachers' College, Columbia University Press, 1906) reported 250 manuscripts and 295 printed editions, 43.

63. Murphy, *Rhetoric in the Middle Ages,* 146.

64. Abelson, 43.

65. Orme, 89–90; also see Abelson, 44n.

66. Orme, 90.

67. Murphy, *Rhetoric in the Middle Ages,* 150.

68. The Latin text is found in Evrard of Bethune, *Eberhardi Bethuniensis Graecismus,* Johannes Wrobel, ed. (Bratislava, 1887). Subsequent references are to chapter and line numbers in this edition. Translations and paraphrases are my own.

69. Murphy, *Rhetoric in the Middle Ages,* 151.

70. The category appears in the title of an earlier treatise, Onulf of Speyer's *Colores rhetorici* (ca. 1050). Murphy, *Rhetoric in the Middle Ages,* suggests the title may not necessarily have originated with Onulf, 183n.

71. See Caroline Walker Bynum, *Docere Verbo et Exemplo: An Aspect of Twelfth-Century Spirituality* (Missoula, Mont.: Scholars Press, 1979). Bynum studied a

number of treatises offering spiritual advice written by regular Canons (teaching priests) in the twelfth century. Without exception the Canons subscribed to a pedagogy that required one to exemplify the very principles they were teaching. This pedagogy seems quite prevalent in the twelfth- and thirteenth-century grammars as well as the *ars poetriae.*

Ars poetriae

Auctores poetriarum

1. See biographical details in Edmond Faral, ed., *Les arts poétiques du XIIe et du XIIIe siècle* (Paris: Librarie Ancienne Honore Champion, 1924), 1–3; Gallo, "Matthew of Vendôme," 51; Galyon, 19–20; Parr, *Documentum,* 8–9.

2. Faral, 321–27. Geoffrey's colors of rhetoric are: *repetitio, conversio, complexio, traductio, contentio, ratiocinatio, contrarium, articulus, similitudo cadens, similitudo desinens, gradatio, correctio, annominatio, exclamatio, conduplicatio, disjunctum, conjunctum, adjunctum, dissolutum, dubitatio, subjectio, interpretatio, circuito, translatio, et significatio.* The list is slightly idiosyncratic, but it repeats fifteen of Evrard's twenty-two colors of rhetoric and seems to capture the spirit of other accounts of rhetorical colors.

3. See Max Manitius, *Geschichte Der Latenischen Literatur Des Mittelalters,* 3 vols. (Munich: C. H. Beck'sche, 1931), 751–52; Faral, 34–37; Atkins, 96–97; Murphy, *Rhetoric in the Middle Ages,* 169, 230; Gallo, "The Poetria nova," 68–84; Kopp, 27–31; Hardison, 383–88.

4. For more on John's various contributions, see Rebecca A. Baltzer, "Johannes de Garlandia," in *The New Grove Dictionary of Music and Musicians,* ed. Stanley Sadie, vol. 9 (London: Macmillan, 1980), 662–64; Louis John Paetow, *Morale Scolarium of John of Garland,* in *Two Medieval Satires on the University of Paris,* Memoirs of the University of California 4, part 2 (Berkeley: University of California Press, 1927); Rudolf A. Rasch, *Johannes de Garlandia* (Brooklyn, N.Y.: Institute of Medieval Music, 1969); William G. Waite, "Johannes de Garlandia, Poet and Musician," *Speculum* 35 (1960): 179–95.

5. Lawler, xi–xv; Murphy, *Rhetoric in the Middle Ages,* 115–20.

6. Murphy, *Rhetoric in the Middle Ages,* 32; see also Murphy's abstract of the work, 29–31.

7. Horace, *The Art of Poetry,* trans. D. A. Russell, in *Classical Literary Criticism,* ed. D. A. Russell and M. Winterbottom (New York: Oxford University Press, 1989), 98.

8. Horace, 99.

9. Horace, 100.

10. Karsten Friis-Jensen, "The *Ars poetica* in Twelfth-Century France: The Horace of Matthew of Vendôme, Geoffrey of Vinsauf, and John of Garland," *Universite de Copenhague Cahiers de l'institute du moyen-âge grec et latin* 60 (1990): 319–388.

Chapter 3—Matthew of Vendôme's *Ars versificatoria*

1. Subsequent quotations from *Ars versificatoria* will be to the Galyon translation unless otherwise noted. Galyon follows the section and paragraph numbers in Faral. Therefore, the references refer to both the Latin text and the translation.

2. See biographical details in Faral, 1–3; Gallo, "Matthew of Vendôme," 51; Galyon, 19–20;, and Parr, *Documentum*, 8–9.

3. See Bennett, "The Rhetoric of Martianus Capella," 128–42.

4. My translation.

5. Kelly, "Scope," 261.

6. Kelly, "Scope," 261.

7. Gallo, "The Poetria nova," 56–57; see also Galyon, 6.

8. Prill, 133.

9. I differ here from Galyon who renders the phrase as "figurative expression."

10. See Karl P. Harrington, *The Roman Elegiac Poets* (New York: American Book Company, 1914).

11. I have provided my own translation of the last two examples to demonstrate the use of the various devices.

Chapter 4—Geoffrey of Vinsauf's *Poetria nova* and *Documentum de modo et arte dictandi et versificandi*

1. Kelly, "Scope," 278n.

2. Woods, *An Early Commentary*, 7.

3. Alex Preminger, O. B. Hardison, and Kevin Kerrane, eds. *Classical and Medieval Literary Criticism: Translations and Interpretations* (New York: Frederick Ungar, 1974), 383; Gallo, "The Poetria nova," 68. The passage from Chaucer remarks on one of Geoffrey's examples, a lament on the death of Richard the Lionhearted, and illustrates the familiarity schoolchildren had with the work:

> O Geoffrey, thou my dear and sovereign master
> Who, when they brought King Richard to disaster
> And shot him dead, lamented so his death,
> Would that I had thy skill, thy gracious breath
> To chide a Friday half so well as you.
>
> (Geoffrey Chaucer, *The Canterbury Tales*, trans. Neville Coghill [1951; reprint, New York: Penguin Books, 1980], 246

This passage has incited much speculation among English scholars concerning Chaucer's rhetorical background. In particular, see John M. Manly,

"Chaucer and the Rhetoricians," *Proceedings of the British Academy* 12 (1926): 95–113. For a summary and counterargument, see James J. Murphy, "A New Look at Chaucer and the Rhetoricians," *Review for English Studies* NS 15 (1964): 1–20.

As Preminger et al. note, it also shows a little contempt for the poem that schoolchildren no doubt committed to memory (383).

4. Kopp, 32. The Latin text reads as follows:

> Papa stupor mundi, si dixero Papa Nocenti,
> Acephatum nomen tribuam; sed sit caput addam,
> Hostis erit metri. Nomen tibi vult similari:
> Nec nomen metro, nec vult tua maxima virtus
> Claudi mensura. Nihil est quo metiar illam:
> Transit mensuras hominum. Sed divide nomen,
> Divide sic nomen: "In" praefer, et adde "nocenti,"
> Efficiturque comes metri. (Faral, 197)

5. Alexandre Leupin, "Absolute Reflexivity: Geoffroi de Vinsauf," in *Medieval Texts & Contemporary Readers*, eds. Laurie A. Finke and Martin B. Shictman (Ithaca, N.Y.: Cornell University Press, 1987), 135.

6. Leupin, 122.

7. Leupin, 123.

8. Woods, *An Early Commentary*, 3, 5.

9. Kopp, 36. Translations are from Kopp unless otherwise indicated.

10. Kopp, 36–41. See also Kelly's comments on natural and artificial order in Kelly, *Arts*, 68–71.

11. See also Camargo, "Toward a Comprehensive Art," 177–78.

12. Gallo, *The Poetria nova and Its Sources*, 140–50.

13. Kopp, 41.

14. Woods, "A Medieval Rhetoric," 56.

15. Kopp, 60.

16. Faral, 48–54.

17. Faral, 48–54.

18. Gallo, *The Poetria nova and Its Sources*, 134.

19. The following excerpt demonstrates the disparity between the three translations and the Latin text:

> Quando tuum proprium transsumis, plus sopit istud quod venit exproprio. Talis transsumptio verbi est tibi pro speculo: quia te specularis in illo et proprias cognoscis oves in rure alieno. (Faral, 222)

> When you transpose a word whose literal meaning is proper to man, it affords greater pleasure, since it comes from what is your own. Such a metaphor serves you as mirror, for you see yourself in it, and recognize your own sheep in another's field. (Margaret F. Nims, *The Poetria Nova*, 14)

> It is more pleasing to apply human characteristics in such a way. Such a metaphorical use of words serves you like a mirror, for you can see yourself in it, and recognize your own sheep in a strange countryside. (Gallo, *The Poetria nova and Its Sources,* 57)

Nims wavered between transpose and metaphor. Gallo ignored *transsumis* and equated *transsumptio* to metaphor. Only Kopp translated *transsumptio* as a meaningful term.

20. Kopp, 67.

21. A similar analysis is featured in Boethius, *De topicis differentiis,* trans. Eleonore Stump (Ithaca, N.Y.: Cornell University Press, 1978), 61.

22. My translation of: "In metalepsin quoque cadit ratio dictorum, ut Fabius Maximus incusans Augusti congiarium, quae amicis dabantur, exquitatem, heminaria esse dixit; nam congiarium commune liberalitatis atque mensurae, a mensura ducta imminuto rerum."

23. Quintilian, 323.

24. My translation of: "Nam id eius frequentissimum exemplum est cano canto, canto dico; it cano dico. Interest medium illud canto."

25. Quintilian, 323.

26. *Ars grammatica,* 400.

27. *Liber de schematibus et tropis,* in Karl Halm, ed., *Rhetores Latini minores* (Leipzig: B. G. Teubneri, 1863), 612.

28. *Doctrinale,* 168

29. Parr, *Ars versificatoria,* 3.42.

30. For further explication of *transsumptio,* see William M. Purcell, "*Transsumptio:* A Rhetorical Doctrine of the Thirteenth Century," *Rhetorica* 5 (1987): 369–410.

31. See also Woods, *An Early Commentary,* 67–85.

32. Kopp, 61.

33. Kopp, 62; Faral, lines 779–95.

34. Kopp, 65; Faral, lines 862–67.

35. Faral, lines 921–22. My translation.

36. Kopp, 66; Faral, lines 924–26.

37. Kopp, 66; Faral, lines 930–35.

38. Kopp, 67. My emphasis on *transsumptio.*

39. Kopp, 67; Faral, lines 957–60.

40. See also Leupin's insightful comments, 127–32.

41. Gallo, *The Poetria nova and Its Sources,* 199.

42. Kopp, 72.

43. Kopp, 63.

44. See also Kelly, *Arts,* 79–81.

45. Gallo, *The Poetria nova and Its Sources,* 207.

46. See Kelly, *Arts,* 81–82.

47. Gallo, *The Poetria nova and Its Sources,* 212.
48. Kopp, 90.
49. Gallo, *The Poetria nova and Its Sources,* 209.
50. Kopp, 91.
51. Kopp, 96.
52. Kopp, 100.
53. Kopp, 103.
54. Kopp, 104.
55. Parr, *Documentum,* 43.
56. Geoffrey refers to *sententiae* in *Poetria nova,* but to *proverba* in the *Documentum.*
57. Parr, *Documentum,* 43.
58. Excerpted in Lawler, 328–32.
59. Excerpted in Camargo, "Toward a Comprehensive Art," 186–92.
60. Camargo, "Toward a Comprehensive Art," 177–78.
61. Gallo, *The Poetria nova and Its Sources,* 224.
62. Copeland, 174.
63. Woods, "An Unfashionable Rhetoric," 312–20.
64. Leupin, 141.

Chapter 5—John of Garland's *De arte prosayca, metrica, et rithmica*

1. John is also thought to have written a revision of Alexander's *Doctrinale,* see Marvin L. Colker, "New Evidence that John of Garland Revised the *Doctrinale* of Alexander de Villa Dei," *Scriptorium* 28 (1974): 68–71; Geoffrey L. Bursill-Hall, "Johannes de Garlandia: Forgotten Grammarian and the Manuscript Tradition," *Historiographia Linguistica* 3 (1976): 155–77.
2. Lawler, 2–3. I have substituted "transsumptively" where Lawler has rendered *transumptive* as "metaphorically."
3. See Lawler's comments on xviii.
4. Lawler, xviii.
5. Murphy, *Rhetoric in the Middle Ages,* 180.
6. Copeland, 163.
7. Copeland, 164–65.
8. Copeland, 16.
9. Copeland, 164.
10. Lawler, 116–19.
11. Lawler, 146–55.
12. Lawler, 194–219.
13. Lawler, 264–65.

Chapter 6—Gervasius of Melkley's *Ars poetica*

1. For a somewhat uneven summary of the treatise, see Giles, vi–lxxxii.
2. Gräbener, 1–2; Giles, 1–2.
3. Gräbener, 2–3; Giles, 2–3. Giles has rendered *consilium* as "advice."
4. Gräbener, 2–3; Giles, 3.
5. Gräbener, 6; Giles, 7. The late medieval commentaries on Geoffrey of Vinsauf's *Poetria nova* speak of *similitudo* in regard to the section on tropes. See Woods, *An Early Commentary*, 77.
6. Gräbener, 6; Giles, 7.
7. Gräbener, 6–7; Giles, 7–9.
8. Gräbener, 7–9; Giles, 9–10. For Gervasius, a color is a particular type of figure that is aesthetically pleasing. Arguments, on the other hand, go beyond the aesthetic to appeal to one's capacities for reasoning. Gervasius does not further distinguish between the two terms. They are ultimately subsumed, however, by the three *loci* and their divisions.
9. Gräbener, 9; Giles, 10–11.
10. Gräbener, 10; Giles, 11.
11. Gräbener, 10; Giles, 12.
12. Gräbener, 10–20; Giles, 12–18.
13. Gräbener, 20–22; Giles, 18–19.
14. Gräbener, 23–24; Giles, 19–20.
15. Gräbener, 24–26; Giles, 20–21.
16. Gräbener, 26–27; Giles, 21–22.
17. Gräbener, 33–34; Giles, 26.
18. Gräbener, 34–35; Giles, 27–28.
19. Gräbener, 35–38; Giles, 28–30.
20. Gräbener, 38–40; Giles, 30–32.
21. Gräbener, 40–55; Giles, 32–45.
22. Gräbener, 55–59; Giles, 45–48.
23. Gräbener, 59–65; Giles, 48–54.
24. Gräbener, 65–79; Giles, 54–66.
25. Giles has rendered *Sinthesis est hyperbaton ex omni parte confusum* as "Synthesis is hyperbaton joined together from each part [of the statement]." I read this passage as referring to disordered parts. Cf. Gräbener, 82, and Giles, 68.
26. Gräbener, 79–88; Giles, 66–72.
27. Gräbener, 89; Giles, 93.
28. Gräbener, 89; Giles, 93.
29. Gräbener, 89; Giles, 93.
30. Gräbener, 90; Giles, 94.
31. Gräbener, 89–90; Giles, 104–105.
32. Gräbener, 89; Giles, 105.

33. See Giles, xli.
34. Gräbener, 108; Giles, 107.
35. Gräbener, 108; Giles, 107.
36. Gräbener, 109–10; Giles, 107–109.
37. Gräbener, 111; Giles, 110.
38. Gräbener, 111–12; Giles, 110, 146.
39. Gräbener, 114–15; Giles, 114–15.
40. Gräbener, 123; Giles, 119.
41. Gräbener, 141; Giles, 133.
42. Gräbener, 141; Giles, 133, 152.
43. Gräbener, 141; Giles, 133.
44. Gräbener, 143; Giles, 133, 152.
45. Gräbener, 144; Giles, 134–35.
46. Gräbener, 149; Giles, 139.
47. Gräbener, 126; Giles, 120.
48. Gräbener, 132; Giles, 126.
49. Gräbener, 134; Giles, 127.
50. Gräbener, 135; Giles, 128.
51. Giles, 151.
52. Giles 128.
53. Gervasius includes allegory as a category of *contrarietas*. However, his discussion of *transsumptio* features a discussion of *antismos* and enigma, tropes conventionally subsumed by allegory (see Donatus, *Ars grammatica,* in *Grammatici Latini,* ed. Heinrich Keil (1863; reprint, Hildesheim: Georg Olms, 1961), 401–2. Moreover his examples of *antismo* and enigma are of the type usually associated with allegory.
54. Gräbener, 150; Giles, 139.
55. Gräbener, 150; Giles, 139, 154.
56. Gräbener, 150; Giles, 140, 154.
57. Gräbener, 151–52; Giles, 140, 155. The example from Aristotle is lost. However, cf. [Cicero], *Ad C. Herennium,* 4.34.46.
58. Gräbener, 152–53; Giles, 141, 153.
59. See Giles, 107 (metaphor), 137 (hyperbole), and 138 (allegory).
60. Gräbener, 150–54; Giles, 139–42.
61. Gräbener, 155; Giles, 156.
62. Gräbener, 155–56; Giles, 156–57.
63. Cicero, *Topica,* in *De inventione, De optimo genere oratorium, Topica,* trans. H. M. Hubbell (1949; reprint, Cambridge, Mass.: Harvard University Press, 1976), 422–25; cf. Gräbener, 157, and Cicero, *Topica,* 13.55–19.56.
64. Gräbener, 158; Giles, 157–58.
65. Gräbener, 158–59; Giles, 158.
66. Giles, 174, n8.
67. Gräbener, 159–61; Giles, 158–60.

68. Gräbener, 161–62; Giles, 160. The quotation is from Giles, 175, n18.
69. Gräbener, 162–66; Giles, 160–63. The quotation is from Giles, 175, n21.
70. Gräbener, 166–67; Giles, 163–64.
71. Gräbener, 167–69; Giles, 164–65.
72. Gräbener, 169–70; Giles, 165–66.
73. Gräbener, 169; Giles, 165. The quotation is from Giles, 177, n50 and n51.
74. Gräbener, 169–72; Giles, 166–67. Giles reads *determinatum aliud indeterminatum* as "modified or unmodified."
75. Gräbener, 182–84; Giles, 182–83.
76. Gräbener, 185; Giles, 185.
77. Gräbener, 185–87; Giles, 185–89.
78. Gräbener, 189–200; Giles, 189–96.
79. Gräbener, 201–204; Giles, 202–205.
80. Gräbener, 205–15; Giles, 207–14.
81. Gräbener, 216–22; Giles, 216–21.
82. Gräbener, 224–29; Giles, 222–27.

Chapter 7—Eberhard the German's *Laborintus*

1. James J. Murphy, "Rhetoric in the Earliest Years of Printing, 1465–1500," *Quarterly Journal of Speech* 70 (1984): 7.
2. Woods, "An Unfashionable Rhetoric," 316.
3. Woods, "An Unfashionable Rhetoric," 314–17.
4. Baldwin, 189–91; Murphy, *Rhetoric in the Middle Ages*, 180–82.
5. Kelly, "Scope," 261–78.
6. Kelly, "Scope," 278n.
7. Murphy, *Rhetoric in the Middle Ages*, 180–82.
8. Both Carlson (1–2) and Murphy (*Rhetoric in the Middle Ages*, 181) render the title as "having misery in it." The connotations of work and struggle are much more constructive and more in keeping with the pedagogical nature of the treatise.
9. Carlson, 2.
10. *The Compact Edition of the Oxford English Dictionary: Complete Text Reproduced Micrographically*, 1971.
11. I disagree here with Baldwin. See 189–91.
12. Subsequent parenthetical references are to line numbers in Faral. Translations are from Carlson unless otherwise indicated.
13. Carlson, 10.
14. Carlson, 11.
15. Cf. Martianus Capella, *Martianus Capella and the Seven Liberal Arts*, William Harris Stahl and Richard Johnson with E. L. Burge, trans., vol. 2: *The Marriage of Philology and Mercury* (New York: Columbia University Press, 1977), 64–66.

16. Carlson, 12.
17. Carlson, 13.
18. Carlson, 14. The wax metaphor is found in Geoffrey of Vinsauf's *Poetria nova,* lines 213–17.
19. Carlson, 15.
20. Carlson, 15.
21. This particular piece of advice is expressed with a delightful play on whippings (*verbere*) and words (*verbis*): "Corrige delicta verbis et verbere, verbis asperius, virgis conveniente modo" (231–32). The passage is an example of *traductio* (see note 40).
22. Carlson, 16.
23. See chapter 3 for a discussion of Matthew of Vendôme's work.
24. Eberhard only uses some of this traditional terminology. In the cases of *interpretatio, digressio,* and *oppositio,* he has described the device but not given it a name. I concur, however, with Faral's identification of these figures in the margins of his edition of the Latin text. What Eberhard identifies as *collatio* is generally known as *comparatio.* See Faral, 347–48, lines 305–36.
25. Cf. *Laborintus,* 369–72 with *Poetria nova,* 924–27, *Ars poetria* (Gräbener, 109; Giles, 108), *Laborintus,* 383–84 with *Poetria nova,* 943, *Ars poetria* (Gräbener, 108; Giles, 107).
26. Baldwin, 189.
27. A particularly elegant form of *traductio* involves repetition of the word with different meaning. The second type is what is used in this example. *Parentes minime* is used to render "disobedience." *Parentes* in its second usage refers to parents.
28. Carlson, 32.
29. Carlson, 33.
30. Carlson, 34.
31. Carlson, 34–35. *Conpar, similiter cadens,* and *similiter desinens* are virtually impossible to render into English.
32. Carlson, 39.
33. *The Holy Bible, containing the Old and New Testaments with the Apocryphal/ Deuterocanonical Books, New Revised Standard Version* (New York: Oxford University Press, 1989).
34. Carlson, 40.
35. Carlson, 42–43.
36. Carlson, 43.
37. Carlson, 44.
38. Carlson, 44–45.
39. In *Ad Herennium* the *Commoratio* "occurs when one remains rather long upon, and often returns to the strongest topic on which the whole case rests. . . . I have been unable to subjoin a quite appropriate example of the figure, because the topic is not isolated from the whole cause like some limb, but like blood is spread through the whole body of the discourse." ([Cicero], *Ad C. Herennium,*

375). Eberhard then provides no single example, rather the figure pervades all of his examples.

40. The duel mnemonic nature of the homily and figures is reminiscent of the acrostics found in Psalms 9, 10, 25, 34, 37, 111, 112 119, and 145 in which verses begin with consecutive letters of the Hebrew alphabet.

41. See Murphy, *Rhetoric in the Middle Ages*, 302, 320.

42. Carlson, 47.

43. Carlson, 50–51.

44. Carlson, 52.

45. Carlson, 61.

46. Carlson, 61.

47. Carlson, 62.

48. Carlson, 65.

49. Carlson, 65–66.

Conclusion—The Margins of Literacy

1. Walter J. Ong, *Ramus: Method, and the Decay of Dialogue from the Art of Discourse to the Art of Reason* (Cambridge: Harvard University Press, 1957), 53–91.

2. See Frank Pierrepont Graves, *Peter Ramus and the Educational Reformation of the Sixteenth Century* (New York: MacMillan, 1912), 110–15; Pierre Albert Duhamel, "The Logic and Rhetoric of Peter Ramus," *Modern Philology* 46 (1948–1949): 165; Wilbur Samuel Howell, *Logic and Rhetoric in England, 1500–1700* (1956; reprint, New York: Russell and Russell, 1961), 150–53.

3. Walter Ong, *Interface of the Word: Studies in the Evolution of Consciousness and Culture* (Ithaca, N.Y.: Cornell University Press, 1977), 162–63.

4. I. A. Richards, *The Philosophy of Rhetoric* (New York: Oxford University Press, 1936).

5. M. M. Bakhtin, "The Problem of Speech Genres," in *Speech Genres and Other Essays*, trans. Vern W. McGee, ed. Caryl Emerson and Michael Holquist (Austin: University of Texas Press, 1986); V. N. Voloshinov, *Marxism and the Philosophy of Language*, trans. Ladislav Matejka and I. R. Titunik (New York: Academic Press, 1973). There is an ongoing dispute among scholars as to whether these works are the product of one author (Bakhtin).

6. The theme is present in all of Kenneth Burke's works, though *A Grammar of Motives* (1945; reprint, Berkeley: University of California Press, 1969) might prove to be the best synecdochic representation of his project.

7. Michel Foucault, *The Order of Things: An Archaeology of the Human Sciences*, trans. Alan M. Sheridan-Smith (1970; reprint, New York: Vintage Books, 1973); Michel Foucault, *The Archaeology of Knowledge and Discourse on Language*, trans. A. M. Sheridan Smith (New York: Pantheon Books, 1972).

8. Jacques Derrida, "Signature Event Context," in *The Rhetorical Tradition:*

Readings from Classical Times to the Present, ed. Patricia Bizzell and Bruce Herzberg (Boston: Bedford Books of St. Martin's Press, 1990), 1168–84.

9. Hélène Cixous, "Sorties," in *New French Feminisms: An Anthology,* ed. Elaine Marks and Isabelle de Courtivron (1980; reprint, New York: Schocken Books, 1981), 90–98; Hélène Cixous, "The Laugh of the Medusa," in *New French Feminisms: An Anthology,* ed. Elaine Marks and Isabelle de Courtivron (1980; reprint, New York: Schocken Books, 1981), 245–64.

10. Julia Kristeva, "Women's Time," trans. Alice Jardine and Harry Blake, *Signs* 7 (1981): 13–35.

11. Henry Louis Gates, Jr., *The Signifying Monkey: A Theory of Afro-American Literary Criticism* (Cambridge: Oxford University Press, 1988).

12. Stephen Toulmin, *The Uses of Argument* (Cambridge: Cambridge University Press, 1958); Chaim Perelman and Lucie Olbrechts-Tyteca, *The New Rhetoric: A Treatise on Argumentation,* trans. Purcell Weaver (Notre Dame, Ind.: University of Notre Dame Press, 1969).

13. Herbert August Wichelns, "The Literary Criticism of Oratory," in *Studies in Rhetoric and Public Speaking in Honor of James Albert Winans by Pupils and Colleagues* (New York: Century and Company, 1925), 181–216.

14. Raymie E. McKerrow, "Critical Rhetoric: Theory and Praxis," *Communication Monographs* 56 (1989): 91–111; Michael Calvin McGee, "Text, Context, and the Fragmentation of Contemporary Culture," *Western Journal of Speech Communication* 54 (1990): 276.

15. Paul Ricoeur, "Toward," *Pretext* 5 (1984): 12.

16. Ricoeur, "Toward," 13.

17. Paul Ricoeur, *The Rule of Metaphor: Multi-disciplinary Studies of the Creation of Meaning in Language,* trans. Robert Czerny with Kathleen McLaughlin and John Costello (Toronto: University of Toronto Press, 1977), 106–108, 204; *metalepsis* or *transsumptio* is also a central component of Harold Bloom's map of misprison, see *A Map of Misreading* (New York: Oxford University Press, 1975), 85–105, 125–43.

18. Alexandre Leupin, "Absolute Reflexivity: Geoffroi de Vinsauf," in *Medieval Texts & Contemporary Readers,* eds. Laurie A. Finke and Martin B. Shictman (Ithaca, N.Y.: Cornell University Press, 1987), 121–22.

19. Leupin, 125.

20. Leupin, 127–28.

21. Leupin, 129.

22. Leupin, 139.

23. See Purcell, "*Transsumptio:* A Rhetorical Doctrine," 397–404.

Select Bibliography

Primary Sources

Alan of the Isles. "*A Compendium on the Art of Preaching,* Preface and Selected Chapters." Trans. Joseph M. Miller. In *Readings in Medieval Rhetoric,* ed. Joseph M. Miller, Michael H. Prosser, and Thomas H. Benson, 228–39. Bloomington, Ind.: Indiana University Press, 1973.

Alcuin. *The Rhetoric of Alcuin and Charlemagne,* trans. Wilbur Samuel Howell. Princeton: Princeton University Press, 1941.

Alexander of Villedieu. *Das Doctrinale des Alexander de Villa-Dei: Kritisch-Exegetische Ausgabe,* ed. Dietrich Reichung. In *Monumenta germaniae paedagogica,* 12. Berlin: A. Hoffmann, 1893.

Anonymous of Bologna. "The Principles of Letter-Writing (*Rationes dictandi*)." Trans. James J. Murphy. In *Three Medieval Rhetorical Arts,* ed. James J. Murphy, 1–25. Berkeley: University California Press, 1971.

Aristotle. *The "Art" of Rhetoric.* Trans. John Henry Freese. 1926. Reprint, Cambridge: Harvard University Press, 1975

———. *Rhetoric.* In *The Rhetoric and Poetics of Aristotle,* trans. W. Rhys Roberts. 1954. Reprint, New York: Modern Library, 1984.

———. *Aristotle on Rhetoric: A Theory of Civic Discourse.* Trans. George A. Kennedy. New York: Oxford University Press, 1991.

Augustine, St. *On Christian Doctrine.* Trans. D. W. Robertson, Jr. Indianapolis, Ind.: Library of the Liberal Arts, 1958.

Boethius. *De topicis differentiis.* Trans. Eleonore Stump. Ithaca, N.Y.: Cornell University Press, 1978.

Caplan, Harry. "A Late Medieval Tractate on Preaching." In *Studies in Rhetoric and Public Speaking in Honor of James Albert Winans by His Pupils and Colleagues,* ed. A. M. Drummond, 61–90. New York: Century, 1925.

Carlson, Evelyn. "The *Laborintus* of Eberhard Rendered into English with Introduction and Notes." M.A. thesis, Cornell University, 1930.

Chase, Wayland Johnson. *The Ars Minor of Donatus: For One Thousand Years the Leading Textbook of Grammar Translated from the Latin, with Introductory Sketch.* Madison: University Wisconsin Press, 1926.

Chaucer, Geoffrey. *The Canterbury Tales.* Trans. Neville Coghill. 1951. Reprint, New York: Penguin Books, 1980.

[Cicero]. *Ad C. Herennium: De ratione dicendi (Rhetorica ad Herennium).* Trans. Harry Caplan. 1954. Reprint, Cambridge: Harvard University Press, 1981.

———. *Brutus, Orator.* Trans. G. L. Hendrickson and H. M. Hubbell. Cambridge: Harvard University Press, 1971.

———. *De inventione, De optimo genere oratorium, Topica.* Trans. H. M. Hubbard. 1949. Reprint, Cambridge, Mass.: Harvard University Press, 1976.

Dieter, Otto A. L. "*Arbor Picta:* The Medieval Tree of Preaching." *Quarterly Journal of Speech* 51 (1965): 123–44.

Dionysius Thrax. "The TEKHNÉ GRAMMATIKÉ of Dionysius Thrax Translated into English." Trans. Alan Kemp. *Historiographica Linguistica* 13 (1986): 343–63.

Donatus. *Ars grammatica.* In *Grammatici Latini,* ed. Heinrich Keil, vol. 4: 355–402. 1863. Reprint, Hildesheim: Georg Olms, 1961.

Evrard of Bethune. *Eberhardi Bethuniensis Graecismus.* Ed. Johannes Wrobel. Bratislava, 1887.

Faral, Edmond, ed. *Les arts poétiques du XIIe et du XIIIe siècle.* Paris: Librarie Ancienne Honore Champion, 1924.

Gallo, Ernest, ed. and trans. *The Poetria nova and Its Sources in Early Rhetorical Doctrine,* by Geoffrey of Vinsauf. The Hague: Mouton, 1971.

Galyon, Aubrey E., trans. *The Art of Versification,* by Matthew of Vendôme. Ames: Iowa State University Press, 1981.

Giles, Catherine Yodice. "Gervais of Melkley's Treatise on the Art of Versifying and the Method of Composing in Prose: A Translation and Commentary." Ph.D. diss., Rutgers University, 1973.

Gräbener, Hans-Jürgen, ed. *Ars poetica: Kritische Ausgabe,* by Gervais of Melkley. Münster Westfallen: Aschendorf, 1965.

Guibert de Nogent. "*A Book on the Way a Sermon Ought to Be Given.*" Trans. Joseph M. Miller. In *Readings in Medieval Rhetoric,* ed. Joseph M. Miller, Michael H. Prosser, and Thomas H. Benson, 162–81. Bloomington, Ind.: Indiana University Press, 1973.

Halm, Karl, ed. *Rhetores Latini minores.* Leipzig: B. G. Teubneri, 1863.

Holtz, Louis. *Donat et la tradition de L'enseignement grammatical: Étude sur L'Ars Donati et sa diffusion (IVe–IXe siècle) et Édition Critique.* Paris: Centre National De la Recherche Scientifique, 1981.

Horace. *The Art of Poetry.* Trans. D. A. Russell. In *Classical Literary Criticism,* ed. D. A. Russell and M. Winterbottom. New York: Oxford University Press, 1989.

Keil, Heinrich. *Grammatici Latini.* 4 vols. 1863. Reprint, Hildesheim, Germany: Georg Olms, 1961.

Kopp, Jane Baltzell, trans. "Geoffrey of Vinsauf: The New Poetics (Poetria nova)," by Geoffrey of Vinsauf. In *Three Medieval Rhetorical Arts,* ed. James J. Murphy, 32–108. Berkeley: University California Press, 1971.

Lawler, Traugott, ed. and trans. *The Parisiana Poetria of John of Garland,* by John of Garland. New Haven: Yale University Press, 1974.

Martianus Capella. *Martianus Capella and the Seven Liberal Arts.* Trans. William Harris Stahl and Richard Johnson with E. L. Burge. 2 vols. New York: Columbia University Press, 1977.

Matthew of Vendôme. "Matthew of Vendôme: Introductory Treatise on the Art of Poetry." *American Philosophical Society Proceedings* 118 (1974): 51–92.

Nadeau, Ray. "The *Progymnasmata* of Apthonius in Translation." *Speech Monographs* 19 (1952): 264–86.

Nims, Margaret F., trans. *The Poetria nova of Geoffrey of Vinsauf,* by Geoffrey of Vinsauf. Toronto: Pontifical Institute of Mediaeval Studies, 1967.

Parr, Roger P., trans. *Ars versificatoria (The Art of the Versemaker),* by Matthew of Vendôme. Milwaukee: Marquette University Press, 1981.

———. trans. *Documentum de modo et arte dictandi et versificandi (Instruction in the Art and Method of Speaking and Versifying).* Milwaukee: Marquette University Press, 1968.

Plato's Phaedrus Translated With an Introduction and Commentary. Trans. R. Hackforth. 1952. Reprint, Cambridge: Cambridge University Press, 1979.

Priscian. *Institutiones grammaticae.* In *Grammatici Latini,* ed. Heinrich Keil, vol. 2: 1–597, and vol. 3: 1–377. 1863. Reprint, Hildesheim: Georg Olms, 1961.

———. *Praeexercitamina.* In *Grammatici Latini,* ed. Heinrich Keil, vol. 3: 430–40. 1863. Reprint, Hildesheim: Georg Olms, 1961.

Quintilian. *Institutio oratoria.* Trans. H. E. Butler. 4 vols. 1920, 1921, 1922. Reprint, Cambridge: Harvard University Press, 1976.

Robert of Basevorn. "The Form of Preaching (*Forma Praedicandi*)." Trans. Leopold Krul. In *Three Medieval Rhetorical Arts,* ed. James J. Murphy, 109–215. Berkeley: University California Press, 1971.

Sprague, Rosamond Kent, ed. *The Older Sophists.* Columbia: University of South Carolina Press, 1972.

Virgil. *Virgil, With an English Translation by H. Rushton Fairclough.* 2 vols. 1918. Reprint, Cambridge, Mass.: Harvard University Press, 1969.

Woods, Marjorie Curry. *An Early Commentary on the Poetria nova of Geoffrey of Vinsauf.* New York: Garland, 1985.

Secondary Sources

Abelson, Paul. *The Seven Liberal Arts.* New York: Teachers' College, Columbia University Press, 1906.

Atkins, J. W. H. *English Literary Criticism: The Medieval Phase.* 1943. Reprint, Gloucester, Mass.: Peter Smith, 1961.

Baldwin, Charles Sears. *Medieval Rhetoric and Poetic (to 1400): Interpreted From Representative Works.* New York: MacMillan, 1928.

Baltzer, Rebecca A. "Johannes de Garlandia." In *The New Grove Dictionary of Music and Musicians,* ed. Stanley Sadie. Vol. 9: 662–64. London: Macmillan, 1980.

Bakhtin, M. M. "The Problem of Speech Genres." In *Speech Genres and Other Essays,* trans. Vern W. McGee; ed. Caryl Emerson and Michael Holquist, 60–102. Austin: University of Texas Press, 1986.

Bennett, Beth S. "The Significance of the *Rhetorimachia* of Anselm de Besate to the History of Rhetoric." *Rhetorica* 5 (1987): 231–50.

———. "The Function of Adaptation in Notker's *Rhetorica.*" *Rhetorica* 7 (1989): 171–84.

———. "The Rhetoric of Martianus Capella and Anselm De Besate in the Tradition of Menippean Satire." *Philosophy and Rhetoric* 24 (1991): 128–42.

Bloom, Harold. *A Map of Misreading.* New York: Oxford University Press, 1975.

Brown, Peter. *Augustine of Hippo: A Biography.* 1967. Reprint, New York: Dorset Press, 1986.

Burke, Kenneth. *A Grammar of Motives.* 1945. Reprint, Berkeley: University of California Press, 1969.

Bursill-Hall, Geoffrey L. "Johannes de Garlandia: Forgotten Grammarian and the Manuscript Tradition." *Historiographia Linguistica* 3 (1976): 155–77.

Bynum, Caroline Walker. *Docere Verbo et Exemplo: An Aspect of Twelfth Century Spirituality.* Missoula, Mont.: Scholars Press, 1979.

Camargo, Martin. "Rhetoric." In *The Seven Liberal Arts in the Middle Ages,* ed. David L. Wagner, 96–124. Bloomington: Indiana University Press, 1983.

———. "Toward a Comprehensive Art of Written Discourse: Geoffrey of Vinsauf and the *Ars Dictaminis.*" *Rhetorica* 6 (1988): 167–94.

Carter, Michael. "*Stasis* and *Kairos:* Principles of Social Construction in Classical Rhetoric." *Rhetoric Review* 7 (1988): 97–112.

Cixous, Hélène. "Sorties." In *New French Feminisms: An Anthology,* ed. Elaine Marks and Isabelle de Courtivron, 90–98. 1980. Reprint, New York: Schocken Books, 1981.

———. "The Laugh of the Medusa." In *New French Feminisms, An Anthology,* ed. Elaine Marks and Isabelle de Courtivron, 245–64. 1980. Reprint, New York: Schocken Books, 1981.

Clark, Donald Lemen. *Rhetoric in Greco-Roman Education.* New York: Columbia University Press, 1957.

———. "Rhetoric and the Literature of the English Middle Ages." *Quarterly Journal of Speech* 45 (1959): 19–28.

Colker, Marvin L. "New Evidence that John of Garland Revised the *Doctrinale* of Alexander de Villa Dei." *Scriptorium* 28 (1974): 64–71.

Copeland, Rita. *Rhetoric, Hermeneutics, and Translation in the Middle Ages: Academic Traditions and Vernacular Texts.* Cambridge: Cambridge University Press, 1991.

Curtius, Ernst Robert. *European Literature and the Latin Middle Ages.* Trans. Willard R. Trask. 1953. Reprint, Princeton University Press, 1973.

de Romilly, Jacqueline. *Magic and Rhetoric in Ancient Greece.* Cambridge, Mass.: Harvard University Press, 1975.

Derrida, Jacques. "Signature Event Context." In *The Rhetorical Tradition: Readings from Classical Times to the Present,* ed. Patricia Bizzell and Bruce Herzberg, 1168–84. Boston: Bedford Books of St. Martin's Press, 1990.

Dictionary of the Middle Ages. Ed. Joseph R. Strayer. 13 vols. New York: Charles Scribner's Sons, 1982–1989.

Dieter, Otto Alvin Loeb. "Stasis." *Speech Monographs* 17 (1950): 345–69.

Duhamel, Pierre Albert. "The Logic and Rhetoric of Peter Ramus." *Modern Philology* 46 (1948–1949): 163–71.

Englehardt, G. J. "Beowulf: A Study in Dilation." *PMLA* 70 (1955): 825–52.

Enos, Richard Leo. *The Literate Mode of Cicero's Legal Rhetoric.* Carbondale: Southern Illinois University Press, 1988.

Foucault, Michel. *The Order of Things: An Archaeology of the Human Sciences.* Trans. Alan M. Sheridan-Smith. 1970. Reprint, New York: Vintage Books, 1973.

———. *The Archaeology of Knowledge and Discourse on Language.* Trans. A. M. Sheridan Smith. New York: Pantheon Books, 1972.

Fraker, Charles F. "Oppositio in Geoffrey of Vinsauf and Its Background." *Rhetorica* 11 (1993): 63–85.

Friis-Jensen, Karsten. "The *Ars poetica* in Twelfth-Century France: The Horace of Matthew of Vendôme, Geoffrey of Vinsauf, and John of Garland." *Universite de Copenhague Cahiers de l'institute du moyen-âge grec et latin* 60 (1990): 319–88.

Gallo, Ernest. "Matthew of Vendôme: Introductory Treatise on the Art of Poetry," *American Philosophical Society Proceedings* 118 (1974): 59–92.

———. "The Poetria nova of Geoffrey of Vinsauf." In *Medieval Eloquence: Studies in the Theory and Practice of Medieval Rhetoric,* ed. James J. Murphy, 68–84. Berkeley: University California Press, 1971.

Gates, Henry Louis, Jr. *The Signifying Monkey: A Theory of Afro-American Literary Criticism.* Cambridge: Oxford University Press, 1988.

Graves, Frank Pierrepont. *Peter Ramus and the Educational Reformation of the Sixteenth Century.* New York: MacMillan, 1912.

Harrington, Karl P. *The Roman Elegiac Poets.* New York: American Book Company, 1914.

Havelock, Eric A. *The Literate Revolution in Greece and Its Cultural Consequences.* Princeton: Princeton University Press, 1982.

Howell, Wilbur Samuel. *Logic and Rhetoric in England, 1500–1700.* 1956. Reprint, New York: Russell and Russell, 1961.

Huntsman, Jeffrey. "Grammar." In *The Seven Liberal Arts in the Middle Ages,* ed. David L. Wagner, 58–95. Bloomington: Indiana University Press, 1983.

Jaffe, Samuel. "Antiquity and Innovation in Notker's *Nova rhetorica:* The Doctrine of Invention." *Rhetorica* 3 (1985): 165–81.

Kaster, Robert A. *Guardians of Language: The Grammarian and Society in Late Antiquity.* Berkeley: University California Press, 1988.

Kelly, Douglas. "The Scope of the Treatment of Composition in the Twelfth and Thirteenth Century Arts of Poetry." *Speculum* 41 (1966): 261–78.

———. "Theory and Composition in Medieval Narrative Poetry and Geoffrey of Vinsauf's *Poetria nova.*" *Medieval Studies* 31 (1969): 117–48.
———. *The Arts of Poetry and Prose.* Turnhout-Belgium: Brepols, 1991.
Kennedy, George. *The Art of Rhetoric in the Roman World 300* B.C.–*a.d. 300.* Princeton: Princeton University Press, 1972.
———. *Classical Rhetoric in its Christian and Secular Tradition from Ancient to Modern Times.* Chapel Hill: University of North Carolina Press, 1980.
Kristeva, Julia. "Women's Time." Trans. Alice Jardine and Harry Blake. *Signs* 7 (1981): 13–35.
Leff, Michael C. "The Latin Stylistic Rhetorics of Antiquity." *Communications Monographs* 40 (1973): 273–79.
———. "The Material of the Art in the Latin Handbooks of the Fourth Century A.D." In *Rhetoric Revalued: Papers from the International Society for the History of Rhetoric,* ed. Brian Vickers, 71–78. Binghampton: Center for Medieval and Early Renaissance Studies, State University of New York at Binghampton, 1982.
———. "The Topics of Argumentative Invention in Latin Rhetorical Theory from Cicero to Boethius." *Rhetorica* 1 (1983): 23–44.
Leupin, Alexandre. "Absolute Reflexivity: Geoffroi de Vinsauf." In *Medieval Texts and Contemporary Readers,* ed. Laurie A. Finke and Martin B. Shictman, 120–41. Ithaca, N.Y.: Cornell University Press, 1987.
Manitius, Max. *Geschichte Der Latenischen Literatur Des Mittelalters.* 3 vols. Munich: C. H. Beck'sche, 1931.
Manly, John M. "Chaucer and the Rhetoricians." *Proceedings of the British Academy* 12 (1926): 95–113.
McGee, Michael Calvin. "Text, Context, and the Fragmentation of Contemporary Culture." *Western Journal of Speech Communication* 54 (1990): 274–89.
McKeon, Richard. "Rhetoric in the Middle Ages." *Speculum* 17 (1942): 1–32.
McKerrow, Raymie E. "Critical Rhetoric: Theory and Praxis." *Communication Monographs* 56 (1989): 91–111.
McLuhan, Marshall. *The Gutenberg Galaxy: The Making of Typographic Man.* Toronto: University of Toronto Press, 1962.
Milovanović-Barham, Ĉelica. "Three Levels of Style in Augustine of Hippo and Gregory of Nazianzus." *Rhetorica* 11 (1993): 1–25.
Murphy, James. J. "A New Look at Chaucer and the Rhetoricians." *Review for English Studies* NS 15 (1964): 1–20.
———. *Rhetoric in the Middle Ages: A History of Rhetorical Theory from St. Augustine to the Renaissance.* Berkeley: University of California Press, 1974.
———. "The Middle Ages." In *The Present State of Scholarship in Historical and Contemporary Rhetoric,* ed. Winifred Bryan Horner, 54–58. Columbia: University of Missouri Press, 1983.
———. "Rhetoric in the Earliest Years of Printing, 1465–1500." *Quarterly Journal of Speech* 70 (1984): 1–11.

———. "Roman Writing Instruction as Described by Quintilian." In *A Short History of Writing Instruction From Ancient Greece to Twentieth-Century America*, ed. James J. Murphy, 19–76. Davis, Calif.: Hermagoras Press, 1990.

Nims, Margaret F. "Translatio: 'Difficult Statement' in Medieval Poetic Theory." *University of Toronto Quarterly* 43 (1974): 215–30.

Ong, Walter J. *Ramus: Method, and the Decay of Dialogue from the Art of Discourse to the Art of Reason.* Cambridge: Harvard University Press, 1957.

———. *Interface of the Word: Studies in the Evolution of Consciousness and Culture.* Ithaca, N.Y.: Cornell University Press, 1977.

———. *Orality and Literacy: The Technologizing of the World.* New York: Methuen, 1982.

———. "Writing is a Technology that Restructures Thought." In *The Written Word: Literacy in Transition*, ed. Gerd Baumann, 23–50. Oxford: Clarendon Press, 1986.

Orme, Nicholas. *English Schools in the Middle Ages.* London: Methuen, 1973.

Paetow, Louis John. *Morale Scolarium of John of Garland.* In *Two Medieval Satires on the University of Paris.* Memoirs of the University of California 4, Part 2. Berkeley: University of California Press, 1927.

Perelman, Chaim, and Lucie Olbrechts-Tyteca. *The New Rhetoric: A Treatise on Argumentation.* Trans. Purcell Weaver. Notre Dame, Ind.: University of Notre Dame Press, 1969.

Poulakos, John. "Rhetoric, the Sophists, and the Impossible." *Communication Monographs* 51 (1984): 215–26.

Preminger, Alex, O. B. Hardison, and Kevin Kerrane, eds. *Classical and Medieval Literary Criticism: Translations and Interpretations.* New York: Frederick Ungar, 1974.

Prill, Paul E. "Rhetoric and Poetics in the Early Middle Ages." *Rhetorica* 5 (1987): 129–47.

Purcell, William M. "*Transsumptio:* A Rhetorical Doctrine of the Thirteenth Century." *Rhetorica* 5 (1987): 369–410.

Raby, F. J. E. *A History of Christian Latin Poetry from the Beginning to the Close of the Middle Ages.* Oxford: Clarendon Press, 1927.

Rasch, Rudolf A. *Johannes de Garlandia.* Brooklyn, N.Y.: Institute of Medieval Music, 1969.

Richards, I. A. *The Philosophy of Rhetoric.* New York: Oxford University Press, 1936.

Riché, Pierre. *Education and Culture in the Barbarian West.* Trans. John J. Contreni. Columbia: University of South Carolina Press, 1976.

Ricoeur, Paul. *The Rule of Metaphor: Multi-disciplinary Studies in the Creation of Meaning in Language.* Trans. Robert Czerny with Kathleen McLaughlin and John Costello. Toronto: University of Toronto Press, 1977.

———. "Toward a 'Post-Critical Rhetoric'?" *Pretext* 5 (1984): 9–16.

Robins, R. H. *Ancient and Medieval Grammatical Theory in Europe, with Particular Reference to Modern Linguistic Doctrine.* 1951., Reprint, Port Washington, N.Y.: Kennikat Press, 1971.

Scaglione, Aldo. *The Classical Theory of Composition From Its Origins to the Present: A Historical Survey.* Chapel Hill: University of North Carolina Press, 1972.

Schiappa, Edward. "Rhêtorikê: What's in a Name? Toward a Revised History of Early Greek Rhetorical Theory." *Quarterly Journal of Speech* 78 (1992): 1–15.

Sedgewick, Walter B. "The Style and Vocabulary of the Latin Arts of Poetry of the Twelfth and Thirteenth Centuries." *Speculum* 3 (1928): 349–65.

Toulmin, Stephen. *The Use of Argument.* Cambridge: Cambridge University Press, 1958.

Vickers, Brian. *In Defence of Rhetoric.* Oxford: Clarendon Press, 1988.

Voloshinov, V. N. *Marxism and the Philosophy of Language.* Trans. Ladislav Matejka and I. R. Titunik. New York: Academic Press, 1973.

Waite, William G. "Johannes de Garlandia, Poet and Musician." *Speculum* 35 (1960): 179–95.

Ward, John O. "Magic and Rhetoric from Antiquity to the Renaissance: Some Ruminations." *Rhetorica* 6 (1988): 57–118.

Wichelns, Herbert August. "The Literary Criticism of Oratory." In *Studies in Rhetoric and Public Speaking in Honor of James Albert Winans by Pupils and Colleagues,* 181–216. New York: Century and Co., 1925.

Woods, Marjorie Curry. "An Unfashionable Rhetoric in the Fifteenth Century." *Quarterly Journal of Speech* 75 (1989): 312–20.

———. "The Teaching of Writing in Medieval Europe." In *A Short History of Writing Instruction From Ancient Greece to Twentieth-Century America,* ed. James J. Murphy. Davis, Calif.: Hermagoras Press, 1990.

———. "A Medieval Rhetoric Goes to School—and to the University: The Commentaries on the *Poetria nova.*" *Rhetorica* 9 (1991): 55–65.

———. "Among Men—Not Boys: Histories of Rhetoric and the Exclusion of Pedagogy." *Rhetoric Society Quarterly* 22 (1992): 18–26.

Index